50 MOST POPULAR

CUT YOUR UTILITY BILLS COLUMNS AND UPDATES

Published by
Starcott Media Services
6906 Royalgreen Drive
Cincinnati, Ohio 45244

Printed in the United States of America
Copyright © 1990 by James T. Dulley
All rights reserved
9 8 7 6 5 4 3
ISBN 0-9625583-0-3

We recommend care and adherence to standard construction safety procedures. Wear adequate protective clothing and safety gear (approved safety eyeglasses, work gloves, breathing filter mask) when working with power and hand tools, and with building and insulation materials. If you have questions about proper safety procedures or protective clothing to wear, contact your local health department, Occupational Safety and Health Administration, or Environmental Protectiion Agency. Neither the author nor the publisher takes responsibility for accidents that may occur during the building or use of any of the projects or products described in this book.

TABLE OF CONTENTS

INTRODUCTION

Many of my readers have asked me to compile the most useful and popular Utility Bills Updates and columns into a book. I have selected 50 Utility Bills Updates and related columns which I feel are the most helpful and interesting to readers.

This book is divided into fifteen general topic sections with several Utility Bills Updates and columns in each. The topic section refers to the subject of the first primary question of each column and to the subject of the Utility Bills Update.

Since some of the columns and Utility Bills Updates were written several years ago, I have recently updated the names and addresses of manufacturers and model numbers of products to provide the most current and state-of-the-art product information. If some of the model numbers have changed very recently, a retail dealer or the manufacturer can provide you with the new model numbers based on the old one.

Before attempting any of the do-it-yourself projects, read the Update completely. Always wear adequate protective clothing and glasses. When these projects effect any mechanical systems in your house (furnace, air conditioner, water heater, etc.), contact a contractor or technician familiar with your specific model. Some models are unique and require specific clearances and adjustments when making improvements. Check your local building and fire codes.

The acutal savings that you realize from making some of these improvements or by installing various products depend on the efficiency of your current systems and your local utility rates. Always do a payback analysis before investing your time and money in a project or product.

Several of the Utility Bills Updates show lists of manufacturers and model numbers of various types of products. Also, product information and specifications are sometimes provided. These lists of manufacturers and product information are for your information only and are NOT AN ENDORSEMENT of these types of products or a specific manufacturer or model.

By following the advice and tips in this book, you should be able to reduce your utility bills. This not only saves money, but it stretches our limited energy supplies and reduces the environmental hazards of energy production and consumption.

This book is dedicated to my mother and father who provided much support and many hours of hard work toward the development of my column. Without their help, it would not have grown to weekly syndication in more than 300 newspapers nationwide.

Q - I need to install a new heating and air-conditioning system and I was considering one of the new special super-high-efficiency heat pumps. Will one really save much on my utility bills and how does it work?

A - A new "ground-source" heat pump is extremely energy-efficient in all types of climates. It can pump more than three dollars worth of heat into your home for each dollar you spend for the electricity to run it. In the summer, it switches to become a very efficient central air conditioner.

If you currently have an electric furnace, it can cut your heating bills by two-thirds and can be less expensive to operate than an oil or bottled gas furnace. It can also cool more efficiently than a standard air conditioner, especially in a hot climate.

It is possible to set up a ground-source heat pump to heat your domestic hot water too. With annual water heating cost reaching several hundred dollars for many families, the savings are significant.

A heat pump is a simple device that basically works like a refrigerator. It draws heat from a cold area and "pumps" it, by means of a standard refrigeration cycle, to a warmer area. In the summer, valves inside the heat pump reverse direction so it becomes an air conditioner.

Common air-source heat pumps lose efficiency and heat output as it gets colder outdoors. It is harder to draw heat from the colder outdoor air. When it gets colder outside and the heat pump can't supply enough heat to keep your house warm, the energy-guzzling backup furnace comes on instead.

In contrast, a ground-source heat pump draws its heat from a water solution circulating in pipes buried in the ground. Since the ground temperature stays fairly constant (warmer in the winter and cooler in the summer than outdoor air), its energy efficiency remains extremely high year-round.

With a ground-source heat pump, the heated air coming from the registers is warmer than with a standard heat pump. That reduces the "cool" feeling that some people experience with a standard unit.

The pipes for the heat pump can either be laid horizontally or vertically in the ground. Horizontal pipes are buried about five feet deep in a narrow trench. The vertical pipes are put in a drilled hole. Once they are installed and covered, the system is unnoticeable and quiet. The special polymer piping is very durable.

Q - We have an exterior storm door over the sliding glass patio door. It faces west. On cold overcast days last winter, it fogged up. What can we do to stop the fogging?

A - The fog on your storm door is probably by moisture getting in past your sliding glass door. It leaks around the doors seals, and passes directly through the wall itself. On overcast days without the sun shining on the storm door, the glass can cold enough for the moisture to fog.

You can reduce the problem somewhat, but you will not be able to totally eliminate it. Try to lower the indoor humidity level in your home on the coldest days. You can run your kitchen and bathroom vent fans a little longer when you use those rooms.

UTILITY BILLS UPDATE

Dear Reader,

Thank you for your interest in writing to me about ground-source heat pumps. They provide efficient heating and cooling.

The chart at the bottom of this page shows the relative costs of various fuels to heat your home. These costs are based on the fuel cost shown below the chart. You can adjust these costs up or down depending on the actual fuel costs in your area. The cost to operate a typical ground-source heat pump is used as a reference of 1. To determine the cost to use a ground-source heat pump, multiply your current heating bills by the factor (or your adjusted factor) for the type of fuel you are using now.

This literature and list of manufacturers are for your information only and are not an endorsement of this type of product or a specific manufacturer or brand.

Sincerely,

Jim Dulley

MANUFACTURERS

BARD MFG. CO., Bryan, OH 43506

CANTHERM INC., 1475 Shelburne Rd., S. Burlington, VT 05401

COMMAND-AIRE CORP., P.O. Box 7916, Waco, TX 76714

GEO SYSTEMS, INC., 3623 N. Park Dr., Stillwater, OK 74075

JNJNRG (TEMPMASTER), 1775 Central Florida Pky.,Orlando, FL 32809

TETCO, 1290 U.S. 42 N., Delaware, OH 43015

WATERFURNACE, 4307 Arden Dr., Fort Wayne, IN 46804

RELATIVE COST TO OPERATE A GROUND-SOURCE HEAT PUMP

IF YOUR CURRENT HEATING SYSTEM IS:	COST TO OPERATE GROUND-SOURCE HEAT PUMP FOR EACH $1.00 YOU NOW SPEND
ELECTRIC RESISTANCE	$ .33
STD.-EFFICIENCY GAS 70%	.82
HIGH-EFFICIENCY GAS 95%	1.11
STD.-EFFICIENCY PROPANE 70%	.53
HIGH-EFFICIENCY PROPANE 95%	.73
STD.-EFFICIENCY OIL 65%	.74
HIGH-EFFICIENCY OIL 90%	.90

Based on $.07/KWH of electricity, $6.00/1,000 cubic ft. of natural gas $.83/gallon of heating oil, $.81/gallon of propane

WaterFurnace™

Engineering Guide Specs

GENERAL — The liquid source heat pumps shall be either suspended type with horizontal air inlet and discharge, or floor mounted type with horizontal air inlet and vertical air discharge reverse cycle heating/cooling units. Units shall be A.R.I. performance certified, and listed by a nationally recognized safety testing laboratory, or agency, such as Electrical Testing Laboratory (E.T.L.), or Canadian Standards Association (C.S.A.). Each unit shall be computer run-tested at the factory. Each unit shall be shipped in a corrugated box.

The units shall be warranted by the manufacturer against defects in materials and workmanship for a period of one year. An optional four year extended warranty on the motor compressor unit and major refrigerant circuit components shall be available.

The liquid source heat pump units shall be designed to operate with entering liquid temperature between 20°F and 110°F as manufactured by WaterFurnace International of Fort Wayne, Indiana.

CASING AND CABINET — The cabinet shall be fabricated from heavy-gauge steel and finished with corrosion resistant textured epoxy coating. The interior shall be insulated with 1/2" thick, multi-density, coated glass fiber with edges sealed or tucked under flanges to prevent the introduction of glass fibers into the discharge air. One blower and two compressor compartment access panels shall be removable with supply and return ductwork in place. A duct collar shall be provided on the supply air opening. A 1" thick throwaway glass fiber filter shall be provided with each unit. Insulated galvanized steel condensate drain pans shall be provided and extend beyond the coil to catch blow off. The units shall have an insulated divider panel between the air handling section and the compressor-control section to minimize the transmission of compressor noise, and to permit operational service testing through either compressor access panel without having air by-pass the refrigerant to air coil.

Vertical units can be supplied in left-hand return air or front (can be used right) return air configurations (as viewed from the water and electrical connection side).

All units shall have 7/8" knockouts for entrance of low and line voltage wiring.

REFRIGERANT CIRCUIT — All units shall contain a sealed refrigerant circuit including a hermetic motor-compressor, bi-directional capillary tube/thermal expansion valve assembly, finned-tube air-to-refrigerant heat exchanger, reversing valve, coaxial tube water-to-refrigerant heat exchanger, factory installed high and low pressure safety switches and service ports for connection of high and low pressure gauges.

Compressors shall be designed for heat pump duty with internal isolation and mounted on vibration isolators. Compressor motors shall have overload protection and will be three-phase or single-phase PSC type. The finned-tube coil shall be constructed of rippled and corrugated aluminum fins bonded to seamless copper tubes in a staggered pattern.

The water-to-refrigerant heat exchanger shall be a coaxial type constructed of a convoluted copper (optional cupronickel) inner tube and a steel outer tube capable of withstanding 450 PSIG working pressure on the refrigerant side. The parallel capillary tube/thermal expansion valve assembly shall provide proper superheat over the 20°F-110°F liquid temperature range with minimal "hunting". The assembly shall operate bi-directionally without the use of check valves.

The water-to-refrigerant heat exchanger, optional desuperheater coil, and refrigerant suction lines shall be insulated to prevent condensation at low liquid temperatures.

FAN AND MOTOR ASSEMBLY — The fan shall be a direct drive centrifugal type. The fan wheel shall be dynamically balanced. On unit sizes 009 and 012, the fan housing shall have a removable end ring for ease of fan wheel removal. On unit sizes 019 through 059, the fan housing shall be disconnectable from the unit without removing the supply air ductwork for servicing of the fan motor. The fan motor shall be a multi-speed, PSC type. The fan motor shall be isolated from the housing by rubber grommets. The motor shall be permanently lubricated and have thermal overload protection. On horizontal units, the fan discharge shall be supplied as end discharge or straight discharge with the capability of field conversion from one to the other.

ELECTRICAL — Controls and safety devices will be factory wired and mounted within the unit. Controls shall include fan relay, compressor contactor, 24V transformer, reversing valve coil and reset relay. A terminal block with screw terminals shall be provided for field control wiring. On all vertical units and on horizontal unit sizes 019 through 033, the control box can be rotated for access through the adjacent access panel. To prevent short cycling, the reset relay shall provide a lockout circuit when the safety controls are activated which requires resetting at the thermostat or main circuit breaker. A lockout indicating signal shall be provided on the low voltage terminal block.

PIPING — Condensate, supply, and return water connections (and optional desuperheater connections) shall be copper threaded fittings mechanically fastened to the unit cabinet, eliminating the need for backup wrenches when making field piping connections. All water piping shall be insulated to prevent condensation at low liquid temperatures.

HANGER KIT (Field Installed — Horizontal Units Only) — The hanger kit shall consist of four (4) galvanized steel brackets, bolts, lockwashers, and isolators and shall be designed to fasten to the unit bottom panel for suspension from 3/8" threaded rods.

ACCESSORIES AND OPTIONS

THERMOSTAT (Field Installed) — One of the following room thermostats shall be provided: (1) A standard manual changeover room thermostat with a subbase for manual selection of "HEAT-OFF-COOL" system operation and "ON-AUTO" blower operation; or (2) A standard automatic changeover room thermostat with a subbase for manual selection of "AUTO-OFF" system operation and "ON-AUTO" blower operation. Thermostat shall have separate levers for heating and cooling set points. (3) A deluxe manual changeover room thermostat with a built-in 8°F night heating temperature setback initiated by the setback relay (timeclock). Subbase switching is similar to the standard MCO thermostat with the addition of a "normal-override" mode switch. (4) A deluxe automatic changeover room thermostat with built-in 8°F night heating temperature setback initiated by the setback relay (timeclock). Set point levers and subbase switching are similar to the standard ACO thermostat with the addition of a "normal-override" mode switch. (5) A manual changeover auxiliary heat thermostat with two stages of heating, "HEAT-OFF-COOL" system operation, "ON-AUTO" blower operation and "HP-NORM-EM" mode switches. "AUX HEAT and EM HEAT" indicating LED's are provided.

DESUPERHEATER — An optional heat reclaiming desuperheater coil of vented double wall copper construction suitable for potable water shall be provided.

RETURN AIR DUCT COLLAR (Field Installed) — A specially designed duct collar kit shall provide for a return air duct connection. The kit shall include 1" standard size filters.

ELECTROSTATIC FILTER — A permanent cleanable 93% efficient electrostatic filter may be provided in lieu of the standard throwaway type.

RANDOM START RELAY (Field Installed) — A time delay relay shall provide random delayed start-up from 1 to 60 seconds. The relay may be factory wired.

NIGHT SET BACK RELAY (Field Installed) — A relay shall shut down the unit from a separate 24V signal. The relay may be factory wired.

THERMOSTAT GUARD (Field Installed) — A replacement thermostat cover with keylock and external thermometer provides a tamperproof feature.

EARTH LOOP PUMP KIT (Field Installed) — A specially designed module shall provide all liquid flow, fill, and connection requirements for independent single unit systems.

DESUPERHEATER PUMP KIT (Field Installed) — A pump kit provides for connecting desuperheater coil in heat pump with water storage tank.

AUXILIARY ELECTRIC HEATER — A duct mounted electric heater shall provide supplemental and/or emergency heating capability when used with the optional auxiliary heat thermostat.

ACCESSORY POWER RELAY (Field Installed) — A 120 volt power supply relay (energized with compressor) with in line fusing shall be provided. The relay may be factory wired. (Only available on 208/230 volt single phase units and requires neutral line at unit.)

FREE COOLING COIL MODULE (Field Installed) — A chilled water finned-tube coil shall provide "free" cooling when liquid temperatures allow. The coil module shall contain an adjustable temperature control and flow switching valves for fully automatic operation.

SPECIFICATIONS (CONT'D)

EB SERIES VERTICAL & HORIZONTAL FAN COIL DATA

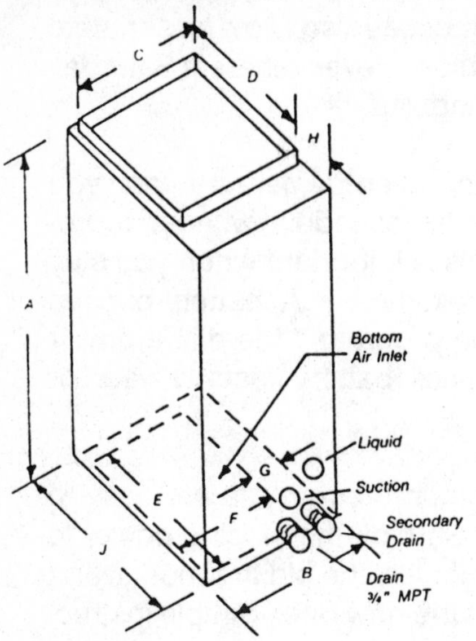
C
D
H
A
Bottom
Air Inlet
Liquid
G
Suction
E
F
Secondary
Drain
J
B
Drain
¾" MPT

PHYSICAL DIMENSIONS

UNIT MODEL	A	B	C	D	E	F	G	H	J	LIQ.	SUC.
BC28-10	40	14	12½	15¾	18¾	8⅜	4¾	3⅝	20	⅜	⅝
BC40-10	42	20	18	16	18	14½	4½	3	20	⅜	⅝
BC52-10	48	21¼	19⅞	18½	26⅛	15⅜	5	8⅞	28	½	⅞

BC64-15 DATA TO FOLLOW, CONSULT TETCO FOR DETAILS.

BLOWER DATA

UNIT MODEL	FAN SPEED	DUTY	VOLTS	CFM VS. STATIC PRESSURE 0.05	0.10	0.15	0.20	0.25	0.30
BC28-10	HIGH	COOL	240	845	830	820	805	785	760
			208	740	735	730	720	705	680
	LOW	HEAT	240	730	725	720	705	685	660
			208	620	615	610	600	585	550
BC40-10	HIGH	COOL	240	1250	1230	1210	1190	1165	1140
			208	1150	1130	1110	1090	1065	1040
	LOW	HEAT	240	1010	1100	1085	1070	1055	1035
			208	1015	1000	985	970	955	935
BC52-10	HIGH	COOL	240	1850	1825	1795	1750	1690	1620
			208	1630	1620	1600	1570	1540	1480
	LOW	HEAT	240	1100	1090	1085	1080	1060	1030
			208	880	860	850	830	810	790

NOTE: BC64-15 DATA TO FOLLOW.

PERFORMANCE DATA

UNIT MODEL	NOM. CFM	(1) NOM. TONS	ELECTRIC RESISTANCE HEATING CAPACITY KW 240V	KW 208V	BTUH 240V	BTUH 208V	TOTAL AMPS 240V	208V	MIN. CIR. AMPACITY SEE (3) 240V	208V	MAX. FUSE 240V	208V
BC28-10	800	2	10	7.5	34,100	25,600	45	39	56	49	60	50
BC40-10	1200	3	10	7.5	34,100	25,600	44.2	38.5	56	49	60	50
BC52-10	1600	4	10	7.5	34,100	25,600	46	40	57	50	60	50

BC64-15 DATA TO FOLLOW.

EA SERIES VERTICAL & HORIZONTAL CASED COILS —

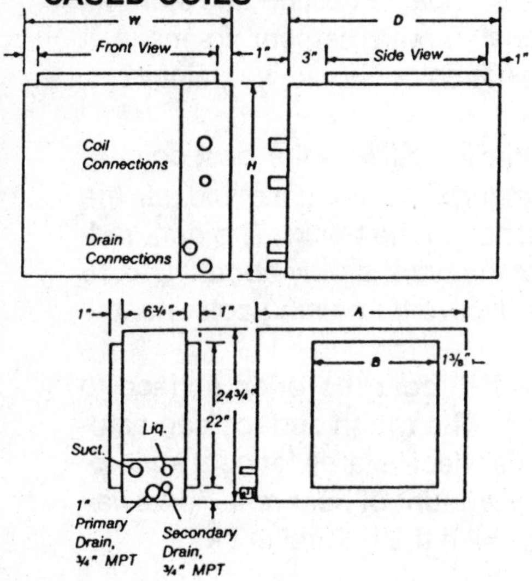
W
D
Front View
1"
3"
Side View
1"
Coil
Connections
H
Drain
Connections
1"
6¾"
1"
A
B
1⅜"
24¾"
22"
Liq.
Suct.
1"
Primary
Drain,
¾" MPT
Secondary
Drain,
¾" MPT

PHYSICAL DIMENSIONS

MODEL	NOMINAL TONS*	W	D	H	OUTLET W	OUTLET D	SUCTION O.D.	LIQUID O.D.
DX28A	2	16½	21	13	14½	17	⅝	⅜
DX40A	3	21	21	17	19	17	¾	⅜
DX52A	4	24½	21	21½	22½	17	⅞	½
DX64A	5	25½	21	22½	23½	17	⅞	½

*Nominal Capacities are based on 80DB/67WB at approximately 45°F suction with 400cfm/ton.

MODEL	NOMINAL TONS*	A	B	SUCTION O.D.	LIQUID O.D.
DX28H	2	22½	18	⅝	⅜
DX40H	3			⅞	
DX52H	4	30½	26	⅞	½
DX64H	5				

*Nominal Capacities are based on 80DB/67WB at approximately 45°F suction with 400cfm/ton.

TETCO®
Corporate Headquarters
1290 U.S. Rte. 42 N.
Delaware, OH 43015
1-800-GO-TETCO
1-800-468-3826
IN OHIO —
1-614-363-5002

Q - I try to set my furnace thermostat back at night to lower my heating bills, but I often forget. It's also cold in the morning. How should I select a programmable automatic thermostat and will it save much?

A - Setting your furnace thermostat lower is the best and least expensive method to significantly lower your heating bills. You can save from one to two percent for each degree you lower it for an eight-hour period. Since the furnace or heat pump runs less, it may require fewer repairs.

A programmable thermostat can also cut your summer air-conditioning costs even more. Some thermostats automatically switch to a summer time/temperature schedule when cooling is needed. A year-round savings of more than $100 is not uncommon. The cost of many programmable thermostats ranges from $50 to $100.

With a programmable thermostat, you won't have to sacrifice comfort. By programming the proper time/temperature schedule, you hardly notice the cooler temperatures. For example, with a nighttime temperature setback, it heats up your house in the morning 30 minutes before you get out of bed.

If there are other times during the day when the temperature can be lower, the savings will be greater. For example, if everyone is gone for several hours during the day, program the thermostat to lower the temperature.

An important selection consideration is the number of daily time/temperature schedules the thermostat will accommodate. Some thermostats allow you to program a different schedule for each day of the week. This is convenient if you work just several days a week or have other regularly-scheduled activities away from your home.

Other thermostats allow you to program only one schedule for weekdays. Most programmable thermostats also allow for separate weekend schedules or even different Saturday and Sunday schedules.

A temporary override feature lets you bypass the regular schedule without reprogramming it. This is important when you stay home sick, for example. A battery-backup feature saves the program if there is a power outage. The small battery lasts a year or longer.

Most automatic thermostats are easy to install yourself. Shut off the electric power to your furnace. Unscrew the old thermostat and wires and attach the new one. Simple instructions show how to hook up the wires on the thermostat and to program the time/temperature schedules you desire.

Q - We are attaching a kit solar greenhouse to our house and we want or use the brick wall for solar heat collection and storage. Should we coat it with cement to make it smooth and what color should we paint it?

A - Flat black is always the best color to use for solar absorption, but that could ruin the rustic appearance of the brick. The dark red-brown color of the brick is only about 10 to 15 percent less effective for gaining solar heat.

You shouldn't coat the brick surface to make it smooth. The rough surface can actually increase the effective area for heat absorption. Also, the amount of heat reflected away and lost is less with the natural brick.

Dear Reader,

    Thank you for your interest in writing to me about
programmable thermostats. Setting your thermostat lower in the
winter and higher in the summer is the easiest and least
expensive method to significantly lower your utility bills.

    The charts on the following pages show the savings by
setting your thermostat back by ten degrees for
one or two eight-hour periods each day. With your schedule, if
you are able to set your thermostat back for only 12 hours a day,
then average the one- and the two-eight-hour-period figures.
These savings figures are only estimated savings for the typical
house. The actual savings that you realize may vary from these.

    It may seem a little confusing that the milder climates show
greater percentage savings. This is because in a mild climate,
and 10-degree setback is a greater percentage of the indoor-to-
outdoor-temperature difference. In mild climates, the indoor-to-
outdoor-temperature differences are smaller. Heat loss is
dependent on that temperature difference. Even though the
percentage savings is smaller for cold climates, the total dollar
savings is greater. That is because the total heating bills are
so much greater.

    These savings charts are based on Annual Heating Degree
Days, a measure of the severity of the weather. Find the Heating
Degree Days for your city or the nearest city. Use that number
to find the approximate percentage savings in the savings charts.

    This list of manufacturers and product information are for
your information only and are not an endorsement of this type of
product of a specific manufacturer or model.

                                              Sincerely,

                                              Jim Dulley

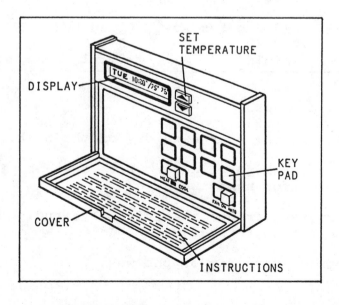

SET
TEMPERATURE

DISPLAY

TUE 10:30 75 75

KEY
PAD

HEAT COOL

FAN ON AUTO

COVER

INSTRUCTIONS

MANUFACTURERS OF PROGRAMMABLE THERMOSTATS

```
 1)  DAYTON ELECTRIC, 5959 W. Howard St., Chicago, IL 60648
           Model    #2E745     Cycles  5+1+1
                    #2E824             7

 2)  EMERSON ELECTRIC, 9797 Reavis Rd., St. Louis, MO 63123
                    #1F90-17           5+1+1
                    #1F97-17           7

 3)  HONEYWELL, 1985 Douglas Dr. N., Golden Valley, MN 55422
                    MAGIC STAT 300     7
                    #CT2601            5+2
                    #CT2550            7
                    #T8600D            7
                    #T8611F7           7

 4)  HUNTER ENERGY MONITOR, 2500 Frisco Ave., Memphis, TN 38114
                    #42203             5+1+1

 5)  JADE CONTROLS, P.O. Box 271, Montclair, CA 91763
                    #H/C-CL2           5+2

 6)  JOHNSON CONTROLS, 1250 E. Diehl Rd., Naperville, IL 60540
                    #T100              7

 7)  PITTWAY CORP., 480 McClure Ave., Aurora, IL 60504
                    #AS550             5+2

 8)  PSG INDUSTRIES, 1225 Tunnel Rd., Perkasie, PA 18944
                    #CAH-22A           1

 9)  ROBERTSHAW, 100 W. Victoria St., Long Beach, CA 90805
                    #T60-1044          7
                    #T70               7

10)  THE STANLEY WORKS, 5740 E. Nevada Ave., Detroit, MI 48234
                    #400               7
                    #500               7

11)  VALERA CORP., 812 Proctor Ave., Ogdensburg, NY 13669
                    #K3-WN             5+1+1
                    #HP-1N             5+1+1
```

The cycle notation means -

    7 - different programs for each day of the week

    5+1+1 - same program for 5 consecutive days and individual
            programs for next two days.

    5+2 - same program for 5 consecutive days and one different
          program for next two days.

    1 - same program every day of the week.

UTILITY BILLS UPDATE

SAVINGS FROM ONE AND TWO EIGHT-HOUR-SETBACK PERIODS

HEATING DEGREE DAYS	ONE 8-HOUR SETBACK %	TWO 8-HOUR SETBACKS %
500	18	29
1,000	17	28
2,000	16	27
3,000	15	25
4,000	13	23
5,000	12	21
6,000	11	19
7,000	10	18
8,000	9	17
9,000	8	16

ANNUAL HEATING DEGREE DAYS FOR VARIOUS CITIES

ALABAMA
- Birmingham 2,551
- Huntsville 3,070
- Mobile 1,560

ALASKA
- Anchorage 10,864
- Barrow 20,174
- Fairbanks 14,279

ARIZONA
- Flagstaff 7,152
- Phoenix 1,442
- Tucson 1,800

ARKANSAS
- Fort Smith 3,292
- Little Rock 3,219

CALIFORNIA
- Fresno 2,492
- Los Angeles 1,204
- San Diego 1,439
- Sacramento 2,843
- San Francisco 3,015

COLORADO
- Alamosa 8,529
- Denver 6,283
- Pueblo 5,462

CONNECTICUT
- Bridgeport 5,617
- Hartford 6,172
- New Haven 5,897

DELAWARE
- Wilmington 4,930

FLORIDA
- Jacksonville 1,239
- Miami 199
- Orlando 656
- Tampa 683

GEORGIA
- Atlanta 2,983
- Augusta 2,568
- Columbus 2,383
- Savannah 1,819

IDAHO
- Boise 5,809
- Idaho Falls 8,475

ILLINOIS
- Cairo 3,821
- Chicago 6,155
- Springfield 5,429

INDIANA
- Evansville 4,435
- Indianapolis 5,699
- South Bend 6,439

IOWA
- Des Moines 6,808
- Dubuque 7,376

KANSAS
- Dodge City 4,986
- Topeka 5,319
- Wichita 4,787

KENTUCKY
- Lexington 4,814
- Louisville 4,660

LOUISIANA
- Baton Rouge 1,560
- New Orleans 1,385
- Shreveport 2,184

MAINE
- Caribou 9,767
- Portland 7,511

MARYLAND
- Baltimore 4,654
- Frederick 5,087

MASSACHUSETTS
- Boston 5,634
- Nantucket 5,891
- Worcester 6,950

MICHIGAN
- Detroit 6,232
- Grand Rapids 6,894
- Marquette 8,393

MINNESOTA
- Duluth 10,000
- Minneapolis 8,382
- Rochester 8,295

MISSISSIPPI
- Jackson 2,239
- Vicksburg 2,041

MISSOURI
- Kansas City 4,711
- St. Joseph 5,484
- Springfield 4,561
- St. Louis 4,980

MONTANA
- Great Falls 7,750
- Billings 7,212
- Missoula 8,125

NEBRASKA
- Lincoln 5,864
- Omaha 6,612
- Valentine 7,425

NEVADA
- Ely 7,733
- Las Vegas 2,709
- Reno 6,332

NEW HAMPSHIRE
- Concord 7,383

NEW JERSEY
- Atlant. City 4,812
- Newark 4,972
- Trenton 4,980

NEW MEXICO
- Albuquerque 4,348
- Silver City 3,705

NEW YORK
- Albany 6,875
- Buffalo 7,062
- NYC 4,871
- Syracuse 6,756

NORTH CAROLINA
- Charlotte 3,342
- Raleigh 3,393
- Wilmington 2,347

NORTH DAKOTA
- Bismarck 8,851
- Fargo 9,226

OHIO
- Cincinnati 4,806
- Columbus 5,281
- Cleveland 6,351

OKLAHOMA
- OKC 3,725
- Tulsa 3,860

OREGON
- Medford 5,008
- Portland 4,635

PENNSYLVANIA
- Erie 6,451
- Philadelphia 5,101
- Pittsburgh 5,278
- Scranton 6,254

RHODE ISLAND
- Providence 5,954

SOUTH CAROLINA
- Charleston 2,003
- Spartanburg 3,074

SOUTH DAKOTA
- Huron 8,223
- Rapid City 7,345

TENNESSEE
- Chattanooga 3,254
- Memphis 3,207
- Nashville 3,756

TEXAS
- Amarillo 3,985
- Austin 1,711
- Dallas 2,405
- El Paso 645
- Houston 1,396

UTAH
- Salt L. C. 5,802
- Milford 6,497

VERMONT
- Burlington 8,269

VIRGINIA
- Lynchburg 4,166
- Norfolk 3,421
- Richmond 3,960
- Roanoke 4,315

WASHINGTON
- Seattle 4,424
- Spokane 6,655

WASHINGTON DC 4,122

WEST VIRGINIA
- Charleston 4,476
- Huntington 4,676
- Parkersburg 4,754

WISCONSIN
- Green Bay 8,029
- La Crosse 7,589
- Madison 7,863
- Milwaukee 7,635

WYOMING
- Landers 7,870
- Sheridan 7,683

Q - I need a new gas or LPG-fired furnace and I was considering a super-high-efficiency one. What are the highest-efficiency gas furnaces made and will one reduce my heating costs very much?

A - The highest-efficiency gas or LPG (propane) furnaces utilize what is called a condensing heat exchanger design. This reduces the wasted heat up the chimney to less than five percent. For comparison, your present old furnace may waste as much as 40 percent of your gas bill.

A condensing furnace cools the exhaust gases so that the water vapor in the gases condenses. This releases extra heat for your home. It is not unusual to reduce your annual heating costs by one-third or more.

Over the life of the furnace, the savings from installing a super-high-efficiency condensing furnace can often pay back it higher initial cost several times over.

There is a new "smart" super-high-efficiency condensing furnace available. It is called smart because it utilizes a microprocessor to constantly monitor and adjust its operation for maximum fuel savings and comfort.

This smart condensing furnace uses a two-stage gas burner and special variable-speed DC motors. This allows the microprocessor to control the speed of the combustion air fan and the blower to circulate the warm air throughout your home. At a slower speed, less electricity is used.

Each time your thermostat calls for heat and the furnace burner comes on, the microprocessor measures and readjusts the furnace settings. So it may operate in a slightly different mode each time depending on the heating needs of your home at that specific time.

The burner first comes on at the high setting so you immediately get hot air. Then, if the heating needs are low, like on mild or average days, it switches to the lower burner-setting. During extremely cold weather, when your heating needs are great, it stays on the high-burner setting.

With the variable speed-blower and two-stage burner, the burner cycles on and off less often so you get more even heat and greater comfort. Another advantage is that with the condensing design, you don't need a chimney. The cool flue gases are exhausted outdoors through a plastic pipe. Also, combustion air is drawn from outdoors, so indoor drafts are minimized.

Q - I am planning to caulk my windows to make them airtight. However, I can't use an entire tube of caulk at one time. Is there any good way to store a half-used tube for future use?

A - In order to store a half-used tube of caulk, you must tightly seal the tube. One way I have found that works is to insert a nail into the nozzle on the tube. Insert the nail with the head first.

It should extend into the caulk inside of the nozzle. Then twist the nail around in the caulk and pull the nail back out just a little. That leaves a small gap between the caulk in the tube and the glob around the nail head. Then when you use it again, the hardened glob will pull out easily with the nail and you will have soft caulk ready for use.

UTILITY BILLS UPDATE

Dear Reader,

Thank you for your interest in writing to me about super-high-efficiency condensing furnaces. The list of furnaces below shows the efficiency (AFUE) for furnaces in the 75,000 to 80,000 BtuH size range. The "smart" two-stage burner furnaces are made by Carrier and Bryant (called Payne, and Day & Night). The Model No. for Carrier is 58SXB and for Bryant is 398B. There standard none-two-stage condensing units are 58SX and 398A respectively.

This literature and list of manufacturers are for your information only and are not an endorsement of these types of products or a specific manufacturer or model.

Sincerely,

Jim Dulley

MANUFACTURERS

MANUFACTURER	MODEL NO.	AFUE - %
BRYANT	398A	93
BRYANT	398B	95
CARRIER	58SX	93
CARRIER	58SXB	95
COLEMAN	2900	93
LENNOX	G14	93
RHEEM	RGEB	93
RUDD	UGEB	93
TEMPSTAR	NUGK	93
TRANE	TUO	93
WILLIAMSON	WU47	93
YORK	P1UDD	93

SAVINGS BY INSTALLING A NEW HIGH-EFFICIENCY FURNACE

The savings shown are the dollar amounts per $500 you now spend for heating costs. It is based on an existing furnace with an efficiency (AFUE) of 60%. Check with your furnace contractor to estimate the efficiency of your existing furnace.

AFUE OF NEW FURNACE - %	SAVINGS PER $500 NOW SPENT - $
70	70
75	100
80	125
85	145
90	165
95	185

chamber. This cuts cold air infiltration into the structure and reduces heat loss. As an added benefit, the sealed combustion (direct vent) system protects the furnace from corrosive chloride fumes given off by laundry products and other household chemicals inside the structure.

MONOPORT INSHOT BURNERS—produce precise air-to-gas mixture which gives a clean burn.

The large monoport on the inshot (or injection-type) burners seldom, if ever, needs cleaning.

FOUR-PASS HEAT EXCHANGERS—This design accelerates heat transfer and extracts heat that conventional heat exchangers waste up the flue. The heat exchanger is aluminized steel for corrosion resistance. 20-year Limited Warranty.

The condensing heat exchanger is also a four-pass design. It is positioned in the furnace to extract additional Btu's of heat from the combustion products as they move through its four passes. This heat exchanger is high-grade stainless steel for corrosion resistance. 20-year Limited Warranty.

COMBUSTION AIR AND VENTILATION—The 398A design is so advanced that Schedule 40 PVC, PVC-DWV, SDR-21 PVC, SDR-26 PCV, or ABS-DWV pipe can be used to bring outdoor air into the furnace for combustion. The heat extracted lowers the temperature of the combustion products (typically below 115°F) to a point that PVC pipe can also be used for venting combustion products outside the structure. The combustion air and vent pipes can terminate through a side wall or through the roof when using our approved vent termination kit.

SAFETY—The 398A has two exclusive safety control features: (1) a self-checking draft control circuit that must reset before another burner cycle can begin, (2) a negative pressure condensate trap system that prevents combustion products from entering the drain system when the trap is not primed.

SOLID-STATE BLOWER CONTROL OFF-TIMING ADJUST-ABLE—Timed blower operation stops annoying recycling thermally activated blower controls. The off timing can be adjusted by turning a knob.

PRINTED-CIRCUIT CONTROL CENTER—The printed-circuit board and all internal wiring are factory installed. Low-voltage terminals permit quick-connecting a humidifier, an air cleaner, and air conditioning control circuits.

FULLY INSULATED CASING—Foil-faced insulation in the heat exchanger section cuts the heat loss and double-density insulation in the blower section reduces noise levels. The casing also has the required openings for left- or right-side connection of gas, electric, drain, and vent connections.

OLD FURNACE REPLACEMENT—The 46-3/16-inch casing height makes the Model 398A Furnace ideal for replacement applications.

CERTIFICATIONS—The 398A units are A.G.A. design certified for use with natural and LP (propane) gases. The efficiency is GAMA efficiency rating certified. The Model 398A exceeds California minimum seasonal efficiency requirements by a wide margin, and meets the oxides of nitrogen (NO_x) emission levels set by South Coast and Bay Area Air Quality Management Districts in California.

Form No. PDS 398A.40.4B

Using advanced technology and craftsmanship, BDP Company has reached its goal of developing a gas-fired condensing furnace second to none in the market place.

The Model 398A Deluxe Gas-Fired Condensing Furnace is the result of an extensive, systematic, research and development project to build an affordable condensing furnace that exceeds a rating of 90% AFUE (Annual Fuel Utilization Efficiency). The 398A is designed for reliability, high efficiency, and quiet operation. Its unique arrangement of gas controls, sealed combustion system, and direct venting, make this furnace an industry pacesetter.

FEATURES
SEALED COMBUSTION (DIRECT VENT) SYSTEM—Enclosed burner assembly isolates operating noise without the expense of sound deadening devices. With the sealed combustion (direct vent) system, outdoor air is brought directly into the combustion

Bryant
Air Conditioning

Indianapolis, IN
City of Industry, CA

DELUXE GAS-FIRED ELECTRONIC CONDENSING FURNACE

Model 398B
Sizes 060 and 080
Series A

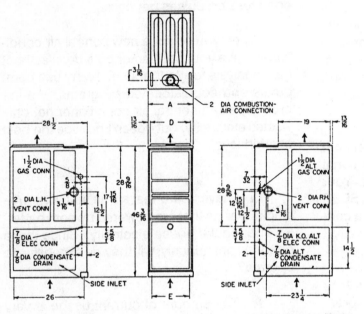

TABLE I—DIMENSIONS (In Inches)

Size	A	D	E
036060	17-1/2	15-7/8	15
036080	17-1/2	15-7/8	15

TABLE II—CLEARANCES (In Inches)

SIZE	060 & 080
Sides	0
Back	0
Top of Plenum	1
Vent Connector	0
Front—Casing Ventilation	3
Service	30

SPECIFICATIONS

SIZE		060	080
RATINGS AND PERFORMANCE			
Input, Btuh* (Low/High)		43,5000/63,000	58,000/84,000
Output Capacity† Btuh		41,000/60,000‡	55,000/80,000‡
AFUE%		94‡	94‡
California Seasonal Efficiencies (CSE)†%		90.5‡	90.5‡
Certified Temperature Rise Range °F**		60—90/45—75	60—90/45—75
Certified External Static Pressure	Heating	0.12	0.15
Inches Water	Cooling	0.5	0.5
Airflow, Cfm	Heating	500—925	667—1234
	Cooling	1200	1200
ELECTRICAL			
Unit Volts—Hertz—Phase		115—60—1	
Minimum Wire Size, AWG		14	
Maximum Fuse Size, Amps		15	
Transformer (24-V)		60VA	
External Control	Heating	14VA	
Power Available	Cooling	24VA	
Accessory Relay		Standard	
CONTROLS			
Limit Control		SPST	
Heating Blower Control		Microprocessor Time Operation 60—240 Seconds @ 20 Second Intervals	
Burners (Monoport)		3	4
Gas Connection Size		1/2-inch NPT	
GAS CONTROLS			
Gas Valve (Redundant 2-Stage)		Model SX345NSRX-14	
	Minimum Inlet Pressure	4.5 Inches Water	
	Maximum Inlet Pressure	13.6 Inches Water	
Pilot Safety (Non-100% Shutoff)		Model 740A	
BLOWER DATA			
Direct-Drive Motor HP—Type		1/3—ECM	1/3—ECM
Motor Full Load Amps		3.3	3.3
RPM (Nominal)—Speeds		Variable 300—1300	Variable 300—1300
Blower Wheel Diameter x Width, Inches		10 x 7	10 x 7
Filter Size—Permanent Washable, Inches		15-7/8 x 27-3/4 x 1	
DEALER-INSTALLED OPTIONS			
Side Filter Rack (Less Filter)		306040-101 (Filter Size 16 x 25 x 1)	
Return Filter Cabinet (Less Filters)		301728-101 (Filter Size 2—20 x 25 x 1)	

Q - My old central air conditioner required several service calls and I need a new one. Are there any new designs that are very efficient and more reliable?

A - The most recent major design innovation for central air conditioners is a high-efficiency scroll compressor in place of a standard piston-type compressor. A new scroll compressor air conditioner can cut your cooling costs by as much as half and minimize maintenance costs.

Several air conditioner manufacturers are now using scroll compressors with seasonal energy efficiency ratios (SEER) up to 12. Your old unit may have a SEER as low as 6. SEER relates the amount of cooling output of a central air conditioner to the amount of electricity it uses.

By its design, the scroll compressor is very reliable. Unlike conventional compressors with many moving parts - pistons, valves, seals, etc., a scroll compressor has only four moving parts.

As it gets older, the few moving parts of a scroll compressor actually wear in and operate better. It is also more tolerant of foreign matter and fluids in the system.

Without the pistons and valves used in a standard compressor, a scroll compressor operates quieter and more vibration-free. This is an advantage both for you and your neighbors.

The operating principle of a scroll compressor is simple. Two spiral-shaped members fit together. One remains stationary, while the other orbits relative to it. This creates gas pockets which gradually decrease in size to compress the freon.

Since several pockets of freon are compressed simultaneously in the scroll members, it produces a smooth and nearly-continuous compression cycle. In contrast, a standard piston compressor produces fewer and larger compression pulses per cycle.

When you select a new central air conditioner, have your contractor do a detailed heat gain analysis for your house. Many use computers and sophistocated programs. An improperly-sized central air conditioner not only wastes electricity, but doesn't provide the best comfort level.

Q - I have heard that some states require smoke alarms that are powered by both batteries and regular house electricity. Since these operate continuously, will they be expensive to operate?

A - The amount of current usage is very low and the operating cost is negligible. The reason for requiring two power sources, batteries and house current, is that people often let the batteries run down. They plan to replace them, but never get around to doing it and then they forget. Without power, the smoke alarm provides no protection.

To keep people from removing the batteries to avoid annoying false alarms when cooking, some new smoke alarms offer a hush control. This allows you to press a button to temporarily decrease the sensitivity of the alarm. It resets to normal sensitivity automatically.

Dear Reader,

Thank you for your interest in writing to me about central air conditioners using scroll compressors. These compressors have very few moving parts, are very energy efficient, and should require little maintenance. The chart on the following page lists the air conditioner manufacturers using the scroll compressor and the model numbers and efficiencies (SEER).

Currently, Copeland produces the scroll compressors for these air conditioners manufacturers. The technology for scroll compressors is not new, but Copeland has developed a proprietary and economically feasible method to produce them for the residential-sized air conditioner market.

The chart below shows the costs to operate air conditioners of various SEER's relative to your current system. You should contact your heating and air conditioning contractor for an estimate of the SEER of your present system. Then you can use the chart below to determine how much less it would cost to operate a new high-efficiency model.

These numbers are based on $100 of your current operating costs. For example, if your current annual operating costs are $300., and your current system is estimated at an SEER of 7, then installing a new unit with an SEER of 10 would reduce your annual operating costs to $210.

This list of manufacuters and product information are for your information only and are not an endorsement of these types of products or a specific manufacturer or model.

Sincerely,

Jim Dulley

NEW OPERATING COSTS PER $100 OF CURRENT OPERATING COSTS								
	NEW SEER							
CURRENT SEER	7	8	9	10	11	12	13	14
6	$ 86	75	67	60	55	50	46	43
7	100	88	78	70	64	58	54	50
8	114	100	89	80	73	67	62	57

CENTRAL AIR CONDITIONERS USING SCROLL COMPRESSORS		
MANUFACTURER	MODEL#	SEER
HEIL-QUAKER	712AC	12.0
LENNOX	HP20 (Heat Pump)	10.0
RHEEM	RAJA	12.0

HOW A SCROLL COMPRESSOR WORKS

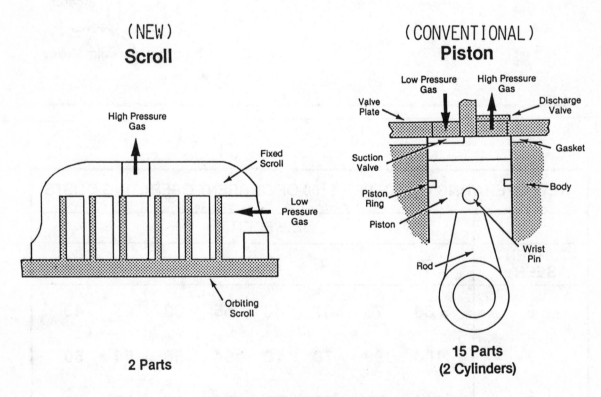

(NEW)
Scroll

High Pressure Gas

Fixed Scroll

Low Pressure Gas

Orbiting Scroll

2 Parts

(CONVENTIONAL)
Piston

Low Pressure Gas   High Pressure Gas

Valve Plate

Discharge Valve

Suction Valve

Gasket

Piston Ring

Body

Piston

Wrist Pin

Rod

15 Parts
(2 Cylinders)

Scroll and Reciprocating Compressors

SCROLL COMPRESSOR TECHNOLOGY

Overview

During the past 30 years, piston compressors have been the workhorses of the residential air conditioning market. Piston compressors have offered good efficiency levels and, through proper design and application, have become very reliable for both air conditioning and heat pump applications. In addition, the design and operating parameters of piston compressors are well developed and understood, and the technology presents no particular manufacturing problems.

Industry requirements placed on systems are changing, however, with requirements for compressors changing accordingly. Competition, high energy costs, and increased federal regulations are compeling manufacturers to develop even more efficient systems. To do this cost-effectively (e.g. without inordinate heat exchanger size) will require compressor efficiencies higher than piston technology can achieve. At the same time, end users are beginning to demand improved comfort characteristics from air conditioning and heat pump systems. System noise is becoming a greater concern, with local regulations on system sound levels now becoming more common. Japanese manufacturers, compelled by a long-standing precedent in Japan for quiet systems, have developed residential split systems with noise levels that are typically below those of comparable U.S. models.

In the future, market demands will move the industry to expand its product lines into modulated systems (two speed, variable speed, etc.) in order to further improve efficiency and comfort levels. These requirements will pose even greater challenges for compressor technology.

Scroll Gas Flow

Compression in the scroll is created by the interaction of an orbiting spiral and a stationary spiral. Gas enters an outer opening as one of the spirals orbits.

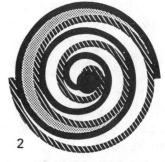

1

2

The open passage is sealed off as gas is drawn into the spiral.

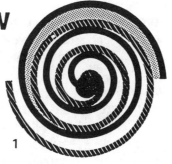

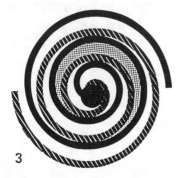

3

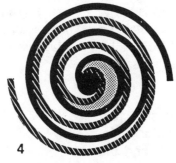

4

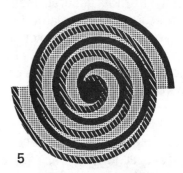

5

As the spiral continues to orbit, the gas is compressed into an increasingly smaller pocket.

By the time the gas arrives at the center port, discharge pressure has been reached.

Actually, during operation, all six gas passages are in various stages of compression at all times, resulting in nearly continuous suction and discharge.

Scroll Gas Flow

Q - I have made energy improvements to my house and my furnace doesn't come on as often or for as long as before. How can I tell if my furnace is over-sized for my house now and is that inefficient?

A - When you make your house more energy efficient by insulating, caulking, etc., its heating needs are reduced. This is why your furnace runs less often and for a shorter time.

Your furnace may no longer be an energy-efficient match with your house and may be losing too many of your energy dollars up the chimney. In fact, if your furnace is more than ten years old, it probably was too big initially. Contractors often determined the proper heating capacity and then sized the furnace several percent larger for good measure.

A furnace loses a substantial amount of energy when the burners are off, called off-time losses. Since the flue and chimney are still hot, an upward draft continues after the burners go off. This draws already-heated air out of your house and may create chilly drafts.

These can make you feel colder, so you often turn up the thermostat wasting even more energy. A properly-sized furnace that runs more frequently also provides more comfortable and even heat and better air-cleaning.

The most accurate method to determine if your furnace is too large for your house is to have a furnace contractor do a computerized heat loss analysis on your house. Contractor sometimes charge for this analysis unless you purchase a new furnace.

He may use a simple "on-off-cycle" chart first. He will have you record how many minutes your furnace runs for an hour and the outside temperature. You should make several readings at several outside temperatures. If this indicates an oversized furnace, he will do the computerized analysis.

If you find that your furnace is too large now, you may be able to have it down-sized. Your furnace technician may be able to change the nozzle or orifice sizes or block off portions of burners.

Even though your present furnace is working properly, you are sometimes better off by replacing your furnace now with a new and smaller capacity high-efficiency model. It can save money in the long-run and greatly increase your family's comfort.

Q - I have to do some caulking around a damaged window frame outdoors. The caulk cartridge instructions say not to use it below 40 degrees. Is there any trick to using it at colder temperatures?

A - If you must caulk in cold weather, your best chance for a good job is to try to raise the temperature of the area around the gaps and of the caulk itself. You will need a helper for this.

First, store the cartridge indoors to make sure it's warm. Run an electric extension cord outdoors to the damaged area. Wrap the caulking gun, with the cartridge in it, with a regular heating pad to keep it warm. Have your helper direct the air flow from a hair dryer on the crack to warm it. He should direct it a couple of inches ahead of the tip of the caulking gun as you move it.

Dear Reader,

Thank you for your interest in writing to me about how to estimate if your furnace output is in the proper range for your house and climate. As you tighten and make your house more energy efficient, its heating needs are lower. Therefore, the heating output of your existing furnace may be too great for your house's needs. This can result in inefficiencies and wasted energy.

The chart on page 2 shows the Heating Degree Days (HDD) for many cities. This is one reference figure to determine the proper size of a furnace. A greater number of heating degree days means you need a larger-output furnace to keep your house warm during the coldest weather.

The On-Off Cycle Chart on page 3 shows how many minutes a properly-sized furnace should run for a particular outdoor temperature. Check the Heating Degree Days Chart for the number of HDD for your area. Set your furnace thermostat to attain an indoor temperature of 70 degrees and let it stabilize for several hours at that temperature.

Check the outdoor temperature with a good thermometer. Then check the number of minutes the furnace is running in an hour. Make several readings at several outdoor temperatures.

Compare your readings to the projected ones in the On-Off Cycle Chart for those outdoor temperatures. If you furnace has run for significantly fewer minutes than the chart indicates, it may be oversized.

You should contact your furnace contractor and have him do an analysis of your house. He may be able to downsize your existing furnace. If not, have him do a payback analysis of replacing it with a new smaller, high-efficiency one.

The Payback Chart on page 3 shows estimated savings from replacing an existing furnace with new ones of various efficiencies. The existing furnace efficiency is estimated to be 60%.

Sincerely,

Jim

Jim Dulley

UTILITY BILLS UPDATE

NORMAL TOTAL HEATING DEGREE DAYS (Base 65°)

STATE AND STATION	JUL	AUG	SEP	OCT	NOV	DEC	JAN	FEB	MAR	APR	MAY	JUN	ANNUAL
ALA. Birmingham	0	0	6	93	363	555	592	462	363	108	9	0	2551
Huntsville	0	0	12	127	426	663	694	557	434	138	19	0	3070
Mobile	0	0	0	22	213	357	415	300	211	42	0	0	1560
ALASKA Anchorage	245	291	516	930	1284	1572	1631	1316	1293	879	592	315	10864
Barrow	803	840	1035	1500	1971	2362	2517	2332	2468	1944	1445	957	20174
Fairbanks	171	332	642	1203	1833	2254	2359	1901	1739	1068	555	222	14279
Juneau	301	338	483	725	921	1135	1237	1070	1073	810	601	381	9075
Nome	481	496	693	1094	1455	1820	1879	1666	1770	1314	930	573	14171
ARIZ. Flagstaff	46	68	201	558	867	1073	1169	991	911	651	437	180	7152
Prescott	0	0	27	245	579	797	865	711	605	360	158	15	4362
Tucson	0	0	0	25	231	406	471	344	242	75	6	0	1800
ARK. Fort Smith	0	0	12	127	450	704	781	596	456	144	22	0	3292
Little Rock	0	0	9	127	465	716	756	577	434	126	9	0	3219
Texarkana	0	0	0	78	345	561	626	468	350	105	0	0	2533
CALIF. Eureka	270	257	258	329	414	499	546	470	505	438	372	285	4643
Fresno	0	0	0	78	339	558	586	406	319	150	56	0	2492
Mt. Shasta	25	34	123	406	696	902	983	784	738	525	347	159	5722
San Diego	6	0	15	37	123	251	313	249	202	123	84	36	1439
San Francisco	81	78	60	143	306	462	508	395	363	279	214	126	3015
COLO. Alamosa	65	99	279	639	1065	1420	1476	1162	1020	696	440	168	8529
Denver	6	9	117	428	819	1035	1132	938	887	558	288	66	6283
Pueblo	0	0	54	326	750	986	1085	871	772	429	174	15	5462
CONN. Bridgeport	0	0	66	307	615	986	1079	966	853	510	208	27	5617
Hartford	0	6	99	372	711	1119	1209	1061	899	495	177	24	6172
New Haven	0	12	87	347	648	1011	1097	991	871	543	245	45	5897
DEL. Wilmington	0	0	51	270	588	927	980	874	735	387	112	6	4930
FLA. Jacksonville	0	0	0	12	144	310	332	246	174	21	0	0	1239
Miami Beach	0	0	0	0	0	40	56	36	9	0	0	0	141
Tallahassee	0	0	0	28	198	360	375	286	202	36	0	0	1485
Tampa	0	0	0	0	60	171	202	148	102	0	0	0	683
GA Atlanta	0	0	18	127	414	626	639	529	437	168	25	0	2983
Columbus	0	0	0	87	333	543	552	434	338	96	0	0	2383
Savannah	0	0	0	47	246	437	437	353	254	45	0	0	1819
IDAHO Boise	0	0	132	415	792	1017	1113	854	722	438	245	81	5809
Idaho Falls 46W	16	34	270	623	1056	1370	1538	1249	1085	651	391	192	8475
ILL. Cairo	0	0	36	164	513	791	856	680	539	195	47	0	3821
Chicago	0	0	81	326	753	1113	1209	1044	890	480	211	48	6155
Springfield	0	0	72	291	696	1023	1135	935	769	354	136	18	5429
IND. Evansville	0	0	66	220	606	896	955	767	620	237	68	0	4435
Indianapolis	0	0	90	316	723	1051	1113	949	809	432	177	39	5699
South Bend	0	6	111	372	777	1125	1221	1070	933	525	239	60	6439
IOWA Des Moines	0	9	99	363	837	1231	1398	1165	967	489	211	39	6808
Dubuque	12	31	156	450	906	1287	1420	1204	1026	546	260	78	7376
KANS. Dodge City	0	0	33	251	666	939	1051	840	719	354	124	9	4986
Goodland	0	6	81	381	810	1073	1166	955	884	507	236	42	6141
KY. Covington	0	0	75	291	669	983	1035	893	756	390	149	24	5265
Louisville	0	0	54	248	609	890	930	818	682	315	105	9	4660
LA. Baton Rouge	0	0	0	31	216	369	409	294	208	33	0	0	1560
New Orleans	0	0	0	19	192	322	363	258	192	39	0	0	1385
Shreveport	0	0	0	47	297	477	552	426	304	81	0	0	2184
MAINE Caribou	78	115	336	682	1044	1535	1690	1470	1308	858	468	183	9767
Portland	12	53	195	508	807	1215	1339	1182	1042	675	372	111	7511
MD. Baltimore	0	0	48	264	585	905	936	820	679	327	90	0	4654
Frederick	0	0	66	307	624	955	995	876	741	384	127	12	5087
MASS. Blue Hill Obsy	0	22	108	381	690	1085	1178	1053	936	579	267	69	6368
Boston	0	9	60	316	603	893	1088	972	846	513	208	36	5634
Nantucket	12	22	93	332	573	896	992	941	896	621	384	129	5891
MICH. Detroit (City)	0	0	87	360	738	1088	1181	1058	936	522	220	42	6232

NORMAL TOTAL HEATING DEGREE DAYS (Base 65°)

STATE AND STATION	JUL	AUG	SEP	OCT	NOV	DEC	JAN	FEB	MAR	APR	MAY	JUN	ANNUAL
Grand Rapids	9	28	135	434	804	1147	1259	1134	1011	579	279	75	6894
Marquette	59	81	240	527	936	1268	1411	1268	1187	771	468	177	8393
Sault Ste. Marie	96	105	279	580	951	1367	1525	1380	1277	810	477	201	9048
MINN. Duluth	71	109	330	632	1131	1581	1745	1518	1355	840	490	198	10000
International Falls	71	112	363	701	1236	1724	1919	1621	1414	828	443	174	10606
Minneapolis	22	31	189	505	1014	1454	1631	1380	1166	621	288	81	8382
Rochester	25	34	186	474	1005	1438	1593	1366	1150	630	301	93	8295
MISS. Jackson	0	0	0	65	315	502	546	414	310	87	0	0	2239
Vicksburg	0	0	0	53	279	462	512	384	282	69	0	0	2041
MO. Columbia	0	0	54	251	651	967	1076	874	716	324	121	12	5046
Kansas	0	0	39	220	612	905	1032	818	682	294	109	0	4711
St. Joseph	0	6	60	285	708	1039	1172	949	769	348	133	15	5484
Springfield	0	0	45	223	600	877	973	781	660	291	105	6	4561
MONT. Great Falls	28	53	258	543	921	1169	1349	1154	1063	642	384	186	7750
Havre	28	53	306	595	1065	1367	1584	1364	1181	657	338	162	8700
Missoula	34	74	303	651	1035	1287	1420	1120	970	621	391	219	8125
NEBR. Lincoln	0	6	75	301	726	1066	1237	1016	834	402	171	30	5864
Omaha	0	12	105	357	828	1175	1355	1126	939	465	208	42	6612
Valentine	9	12	165	493	942	1237	1395	1176	1045	579	288	84	7425
NEV. Ely	28	43	234	592	939	1184	1308	1075	977	672	456	225	7733
Las Vegas	0	0	0	78	387	617	688	487	335	111	6	0	2709
Reno	43	87	204	490	801	1026	1073	823	729	510	357	189	6332
N. H. Concord	6	50	177	505	822	1240	1358	1184	1032	636	298	75	7383
Mt. Wash. Obsy.	493	536	720	1057	1341	1742	1820	1663	1652	1260	930	603	13817
N. J. Atlantic City	0	0	39	251	549	880	936	848	741	420	133	15	4812
Trenton	0	0	57	264	576	924	989	885	753	399	121	12	4980
N. MEX. Albuquerque	0	0	12	229	642	868	930	703	595	288	81	0	4348
Silver City	0	0	6	183	525	729	791	605	518	261	87	0	3705
N. Y. Albany	0	19	138	440	777	1194	1311	1156	992	564	239	45	6875
Buffalo	19	37	141	440	777	1156	1256	1145	1039	645	329	78	7062
Central Park	0	0	30	233	540	902	986	885	760	408	118	9	4871
Syracuse	6	28	132	415	744	1153	1271	1140	1004	570	248	45	6756
N. C. Nasheville	0	0	48	245	555	775	784	683	592	273	87	0	4042
Cape Hatteras	0	0	0	78	273	521	580	518	440	177	25	0	2612
Raleigh	0	0	21	164	450	716	725	616	487	180	34	0	3393
Wilmington	0	0	0	74	291	521	546	462	357	96	0	0	2347
N. DAK. Bismarck	34	28	222	577	1083	1463	1708	1442	1203	645	329	117	8851
Devils Lake	40	53	273	642	1191	1634	1872	1579	1345	753	381	138	9901
Fargo	28	37	219	574	1107	1569	1789	1520	1260	690	332	99	9226
OHIO Akron	0	9	96	381	726	1070	1138	1016	871	489	202	39	6037
Cincinnati	0	0	54	248	612	921	970	837	701	336	118	9	4806
Cleveland	9	25	105	384	738	1088	1159	1047	918	552	260	66	6351
OKLA. Oklahoma City	0	0	15	164	498	766	868	664	527	189	34	0	3725
Tulsa	0	0	18	158	522	787	893	683	539	213	47	0	3860
OREG. Eugene	34	34	129	366	585	719	803	627	589	426	279	135	4726
Medford	0	0	78	372	678	871	918	697	642	432	242	78	5008
Portland	25	28	114	335	597	735	825	644	586	396	245	105	4635
PA. Erie	0	25	102	391	714	1063	1169	1081	973	585	288	60	6451
Philadelphia	0	0	60	291	621	964	1014	890	744	390	115	12	5101
Scranton	0	19	132	434	762	1104	1156	1028	893	498	195	33	6254
R. I. Block Is.	0	16	78	307	594	902	1020	955	877	612	344	99	5804
Providence	0	16	96	372	660	1023	1110	988	868	534	236	51	5954
S. C. Charleston	0	0	0	59	282	471	487	389	291	54	0	0	2033
Spartanburg	0	0	15	130	417	667	663	560	453	144	25	0	3074
S. DAK. Huron	9	12	165	508	1014	1432	1628	1355	1125	600	288	87	8223
Rapid City	22	12	165	481	897	1172	1333	1145	1051	615	326	126	7345
TENN. Bristol	0	0	51	236	573	828	828	700	598	261	68	0	4143
Chattanooga	0	0	18	143	468	698	722	577	453	150	25	0	3254
TEX. Amarillo	0	0	18	205	570	797	877	664	546	252	56	0	3985
Austin	0	0	0	31	225	388	468	325	223	51	0	0	1711
Corpus Christi	0	0	0	0	120	220	291	174	109	0	0	0	914
Fort Worth	0	0	0	65	324	536	614	448	319	99	0	0	2405
Houston	0	0	0	6	183	307	384	288	192	36	0	0	1396
UTAH Milford	0	0	99	443	867	1141	1252	988	822	519	279	87	6497
Wendover	0	0	48	372	822	1091	1178	902	729	408	177	51	5778
VT. Burlington	28	65	207	539	891	1349	1513	1333	1187	714	353	90	8269
VA. Cape Henry	0	0	0	112	360	645	694	633	536	246	53	0	3279
Lynchburg	0	0	51	223	540	822	849	731	605	267	78	0	4166
Norfolk	0	0	0	136	408	698	738	655	533	216	37	0	3421
WASH. Olympia	68	71	198	422	636	753	834	675	645	450	307	177	5236
Seattle	50	47	129	329	543	657	738	599	577	396	242	117	4424
Spokane	9	25	168	493	879	1082	1231	980	834	531	288	135	6655
Stampede Pass	273	291	393	701	1008	1178	1287	1075	1085	855	654	483	9283
W. VA. Charleston	0	0	63	254	591	865	880	770	648	300	96	9	4476
Elkins	9	25	135	400	729	992	1008	896	791	444	198	48	5675
Parkersburg	0	0	60	264	606	905	942	826	691	339	115	6	4754
WIS. Green Bay	28	50	174	484	924	1333	1494	1313	1141	654	335	99	8029
La Crosse	12	19	153	437	924	1339	1504	1277	1070	540	245	69	7589
Madison	25	40	174	474	930	1330	1473	1274	1113	618	310	102	7863
Milwaukee	43	47	174	471	876	1252	1376	1193	1054	642	372	135	7635
WYO. Cheyenne	19	31	210	543	924	1101	1228	1056	1011	672	381	102	7278
Lander	6	19	204	555	1020	1299	1417	1145	1017	654	381	153	7870
Sherian	25	31	219	539	948	1200	1355	1154	1054	642	366	150	7683

FURNACE ON-OFF CYCLE CHART

MINUTES ON PER HOUR AT 70° INDOOR TEMP. AND OUTDOOR TEMP. LISTED

OUTDOOR TEMP. (°F)	HEATING DEGREE DAYS (base 65°)									
	500	1000	2000	3000	4000	5000	6000	7000	8000	9000
-30										60
-20									60	54
-10								60	54	48
0							60	53	47	42
10					60	55	51	45	40	36
20			60	55	50	46	43	38	34	30
30		52	48	44	40	37	34	30	27	24
40	60	39	36	33	30	28	26	23	20	17
50	40	26	24	22	20	19	17	15	13	11
60	15	13	12	11	10	10	9	8	7	6

SAVINGS BY INSTALLING A NEW HIGH-EFFICIENCY FURNACE

The savings shown are the dollar amounts per $500 you now spend for heating costs. It is based on an existing furnace with an efficiency (AFUE) of 60%. Check with your furnace contractor to estimate the efficiency of your existing furnace.

AFUE OF NEW FURNACE - %	SAVINGS PER $500 NOW SPENT - $
70	70
75	100
80	125
85	145
90	165
95	185

Q - Would you explain what a vent damper is for a furnace and can it save much on our heating bills? I have also heard that one can reduce cold drafts in a home.

A - Installing a vent damper in your furnace flue can reduce your heating bills and chilly drafts in your home. The actual savings varies from home to home, but 10 to 15 percent lower heating bills are not unreasonable.

A furnace can waste a substantial amount of energy when the burner shuts off, called off-time losses. Since warm air naturally rises, as long as the furnace heat exchanger and flue pipe are warm, a wasteful upward draft is created.

If your furnace is located in a utility room or partially heated basement, it continuously draws heated room air up the flue. This not only wastes energy and increases your heating bills, but it creates a chilly draft in your home. You often set the thermostat higher to get more comfortable, so your heating bills grow even larger.

A vent damper is designed to close off the furnace or water heater flue opening when the burner shuts off. This blocks the flow of warm room air up the flue. When the burner comes on again, the vent damper opens to allow the hot exhaust gases to flow up and out the flue.

This can save additional energy. With the air flow blocked, the furnace heat exchanger doesn't cool down as fast as when the burner shuts off. This leaves more energy to heat your home.

There are several types of vent dampers. The simplest and least expensive type uses temperature-sensitive metal shutter blades. When the burner comes on and the blades get hot, they flex to an open position. When the burner goes off, the blades cool down and flex closed again.

Electrically-operated vent dampers use a motor to open and close a damper baffle. Although the wiring can be somewhat complicated, it basically opens when the burner lights, and closes when the burner shuts off. There are safety switches so the gas or oil won't start flowing to the burner until the damper baffle is in the open position.

The simple metal shutter blade vent damper can only be used on gas furnaces and water heaters. The electrically-operated type can be used on either gas or oil systems.

Q - We have been washing our clothes in cold water to save energy, but they just don't get as clean as in hot water. Do you have any hints to help us get better results with cold water washing?

A - The majority of clothes washing energy, about 90 percent, is used to heat the water. Many detergents don't dissolve well in cool water. First dissolve the detergent in a small quantity of hot water to make a paste. You can also use some of this paste to pretreat badly soiled spots.

Generally, you'll have to use a little more detergent with cold water. If you can control the cycle on your washer, let it agitate a little longer. As a last resort, use a hot water wash every other wash day. At least you'll save half of the energy to heat the water.

Dear Reader,

Thank you for your interest in writing to me about vent dampers for furnaces and water heaters. You should always have a vent damper installed by a qualified professional. He will make many checks on your furnace before installing a vent damper. The charts on the following page shows how to estimate the savings. Have your professional installer do a detailed savings analysis for you.

This literature and list of manufacturers are for your information only and are not an endorsement of this type of product or a specific manufacturer or model.

Sincerely,

Jim Dulley

MANUFACTURERS

AMERICAN METAL PRODUCTS, P.O. Box 22050, Los Angeles, CA 90040

ENERGY VENT, 915 Valley St., Dayton, OH 45404

HONEYWELL, INC., 1885 Douglas Dr. N., Golden Valley, MN 55422

LAUVENT, 4509 Springfield St., Dayton, OH 45401

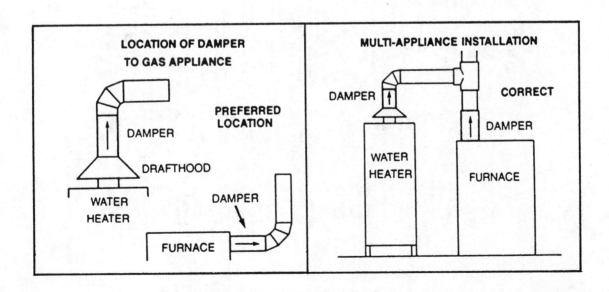

UTILITY BILLS UPDATE

AMERI-THERM® VENT DAMPER SAVINGS CHART (3" to 6" Sizes)

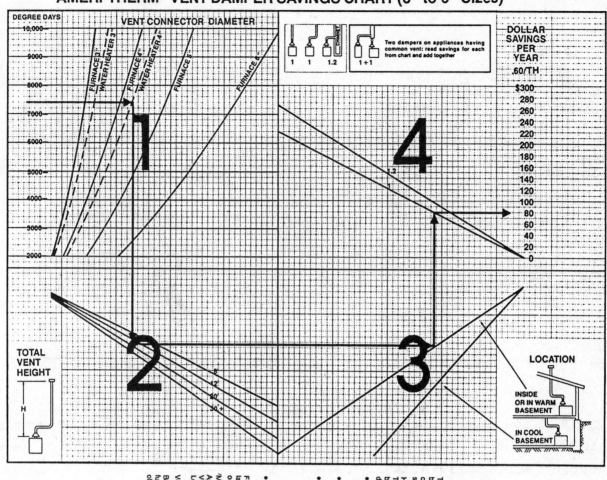

Energy Vent®'s Energy-Saving Electro Mechanical Vent Dampers

a unique line of Gas & Oil models from 4″ to 12″ vent sizes in Aluminized Steel and Stainless Steel

Benefits:
- Higher efficiency for your heating and cooling systems.
- Fewer on/off cycles prolong furnace life and reduce fuel costs.
- Reduces drafts.
- Reduces air conditioning costs.
- Pilot light blowout is eliminated.
- Saves energy and energy costs all year long.
- Improves interior humidity level.

Special Features:
- If a power loss occurs, the vent damper springs open.
- Contains flue temp safety switch which opens unit in the event of gas valve failure.
- First solenoid operated vent damper approved by the American Gas Association (A.G.A.).
- A.G.A. tested and design certified to A.N.S.I. Standard Z21.66. (Gas). Current Edition.
- Tube constructed of corrosion resistant materials.
- UL tested and listed to meet or exceed UL17 (Oil).
- Can be installed vertically or horizontally.

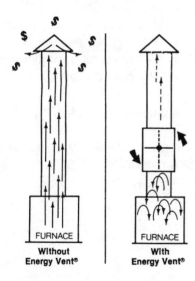

Without Energy Vent®   **With Energy Vent®**

Products are protected by one or more of the following U.S. or Canadian patents with others pending. US4,108,369; US4,139,541; US4,236,668; US3,542,018; C906,687; C47,276; US4,290,552; US264,376; US264,375; C48,016; C1,113,329; US4,193,541; US4,361,272; C1,129,742.

Applications:
Gas models recommended for use on gas-fired appliances with standing or intermittent ignition, atmospheric or power burner. All GAS installations MUST have a draft hood and/or barometric damper. Oil model recommended for use on oil-fired furnaces, boilers, or water heaters. All OIL installations MUST have a barometric damper.

Models:

Single Gas Valve Systems - Gas
EVS-GCS	—24 VAC only
EVS-GCCS	—24 VAC, 110 VAC or millivolt

Duel Gas Valve Systems - Gas
EVS-GCD	—24 VAC only
EVS-GCCD	—24 VAC, 110 VAC or millivolt

Oil Systems
EVO	—24 VAC

Vent dampers MUST be installed between the draft hood and/or barometric damper and vent pipe leading to chimney. Installation of Energy Vent® dampers must be done by a qualified installer even though this product has been engineered with installation simplicity in mind. Energy Vent® use in all cases is subject to the approval of local code authorities.

LIMITED WARRANTY:

The Energy Vent® vent damper is warranted against defects in workmanship and materials for a period of three (3) years from date of purchase when installed by a qualified installer. Upon return of the defective unit, transportation charges prepaid to the factory or designated repair station, and provided inspection reveals no evidence of misuse or abuse, Energy Vent® will repair or replace, at its option, the defective unit without charge.

The responsibility and liability of Energy Vent® under this warranty or for any reason is limited to repair or replacement and Energy Vent® shall not be responsible for consequential damages. Any implied warranties of merchantibility and fitness for purpose are limited to the duration of the applicable express warranty. This warranty is intended to comply with the requirements of the Magnuson-Moss Warranty Act, regulations of the Federal Trade Commission issued thereunder, and any applicable State or local laws, rules, or regulations. Any part of this warranty in conflict with any such law, rule or regulation shall be ineffective to the extent required thereby.

Should it become necessary to use the above-stated Limited Warranty, send the Warranty Record Card (enclosed) and return to the factory with the defective part. (Fill in the requested information and attach a copy of your sales slip, showing date of purchase.)

Energy Vent® will not be responsible for:

1. Normal maintenance such as yearly inspection to verify safe operation.
2. Damage or repairs required as a consequence of faulty installation or application by others.
3. Failure to start due to voltage conditions, blown fuses, open circuit breakers, or other damages due to the inadequacy or interruption of electrical service.
4. Damage or repairs needed as a consequence of any misapplication, abuse, improper servicing, unauthorized alteration, or improper operation.
5. Damage as a result of floods, winds, fires, lightning accidents, corrosive atmosphere or other conditions beyond the control of ENERGY VENT®.

Q - I have seen some very attractive circular-looking houses. I was wondering if they are very energy-efficient and expensive to have built or build myself?

A - You are referring to a panelized-type of house that appears to be circular. Actually, it is a series of eight-foot long, heavily-insulated wall panels connected together.

These types of houses are extremely energy efficient and easy to build yourself. If you do much of the construction work yourself, the cost can be substantially reduced.

The panels can be custom-made to your plans and delivered to your site. The most common insulation package includes fiberglass batts covered with insulated sheathing for an insulating value of R-19. You can order the panels with high-efficiency windows and doors already assembled in them.

What is particularly unique about these houses is that the roof is self-supporting. It is supported by a special truss system design, so there are no interior supporting walls required.

That allows you to locate the interior walls wherever you desire. Therefore, you have the option of making a very open floor plan to effectively utilized solar, space, or wood-burning heating.

The circular shape improves energy efficiency for several reasons. With a circular shape, there is 15 percent less wall area for a given interior floor space size. That reduces heat loss in the winter and heat gain in the summer.

Winds tend to flow smoothly around the circular shape reducing the pressure differences on the sides of the house. That minimizes air leakage into it and indoor drafts. The circular shape provides wall space for large windows in each room for effective passive solar heating.

You can order a basic house plan kit or have one designed for your floor plans. The sizes can range from 600 square feet to more than 3,000 square feet. For additional space and unique designs, you can add rectangular rooms to the sides or combine several circular sections.

With the circular shape and no tight corners on outside walls, you get more actual usable floor space than with a rectangular house. Therefore, you may be able to get by with less floor area than you had thought. That reduces your building costs and further reduces your utility bills.

Q - You have written about high-efficiency central air conditioners. I was wondering which is more energy efficient for cooling a house, a central air conditioner or a heat pump?

A - There is no clear-cut answer to your question. There are great ranges of energy efficiency for both central air conditioners and heat pumps in the cooling mode.

You should compare the energy efficiency rating (SEER) for each unit. If you are comparing the very-highest-efficiency units, then the best central air conditioner SEER is slightly higher than the best heat pump SEER.

Dear Reader,

　　Thank you for your interest in writing to me about circular-looking houses. There are several manufacturers listed below. The diagrams, floorplans, specifications are for Deltec houses. You should contact each of the manufacturers for detailed information about its products.

　　This literature and list of manufacturers are for your information only and are not an endorsement of this type of product or a specific manufacturer or model.

Sincerely,

Jim Dulley

MANUFACTURERS

DELTEC HOMES, P.O. Box 6279, Asheville, NC 28816
(704) 253-0483   (800) 642-2508

HELICON DESIGN CORP., Rt. 66 N., Cavetown, MD 21720
(301) 824-2254

OCTA-STRUCTURE of FL, 2516 W. 23th St. Panama City, FL 32405
(904) 763-6553

POLY-RAMA SPECIFICATIONS (Basic Package)

FACTORY ASSEMBLED EXTERIOR WALL PANELS
SIDING: 5/8" x 4' x 8' Rough Sawn Reverse Board and Batten Douglas Fir Applied with Aluminum Nails
STUDS: 2" x 4" on 16" Centers
HEADERS: All Panels, 2" x 10" Southern Yellow Pine (SYP)
SILL: 2" x 4" (Treated for Slab Construction)
INSULATION: 3½" Fiberglass, Kraft paper Back (R-11)
WINDOWS: Kinco Aluminum Sliders (Meets AAMA Specs), Insulated Glass, Bronzed Finish
DOORS: 3'0" x 6'8" x 1¾ Steel Door, Foam Insulated, w/Magnetic Weatherseal
CORNER BATTENS: 1" x 3" Pine or fir, Factory Shaped, Field Applied
EXTERIOR DOOR LOCK: Antiqued Bronze Finish, Field Applied
PRECUT ROOF FRAMING AND MATERIAL
TRUSSES: 2" x 6" #1 Kiln Dried SYP (See Plans for Special Conditions) 2" x 4" #2 Kiln Dried SYP, KD Galvanized Truss Plates, Factory Assembled Framing Anchors
SHEATHING: 5/8" CD Exterior Grade Plywood, Precut
OVERHANG: 5/8" CD Exterior Grade Plywood Top, 2" x 6" Sub-fascia; 3/8" Plywood, Pine or Fir Soffit with Screened Vents, Factory Assembled
FASCIA: 1" x 8" Pine or Fir, Field Installed
ASSEMBLED HARDWARE: Steel Compression Ring, per plan; Tension Collars with Bolts, Nuts and Washers, per plan
FELT: #15

SHINGLES: Fiberglass
ROOF INSULATION: 6" Fiberglass Battens, Field Installed (R-19)
ROOF VENT: 2" x 6" SYP, Precut; 5/8" CD Exterior Grade Plywood; Aluminum Screening and 1" x 3" Pine Fascia
FACTORY ASSEMBLED FLOOR PANELS AND BEAMS
TOP SKIN: 5/8" CD Exterior Grade Plywood, Sub-Floor
BOTTOM SKIN: 3/8" Exterior Grade Plywood
FRAMING: 2" x 4" Framing (Spruce or SYP)
INSULATION: 3½" R-11 Fiberglass
BEAMS: 3 - 2" x 10" SYP, Assembled and Precut
NAILS: 8" Gutter Spikes, Cadmium Coated
ANCHOR ROD: ¾" Steel Threaded Rod
ANCHOR ROD PLATE: ½" x 12" diameter Steel and 5/8" x 12" Plywood Disc
EXTERIOR DECKS
BEAMS: 3 - 2" x 10" Assembled and Precut Pressure Treated Pine
FRAMING: 2" x 8" SYP Pressure Treated, Field Cut
DECKING: 2" x 4" or 2" x 6" Treated SYP
RAILING: 2" x 4" and 2" x 6" Treated Pine, Field Cut
DECK POSTS: 2" x 4", Precut and Drilled
COLUMNS: Optional - 5" Min. Treated Wood Posts
NAILS: 16-d and 10-d Galvanized
EXTERIOR STAIRS OR RAMPS (Optional Feature)
STRINGERS: 2" x 12" Treated SYP
POST: 2" x 4" Treated SYP, Precut
RAILS: 2" x 4" and 2" x 6" Treated Pine, Field Cut

DELTEC HOMES

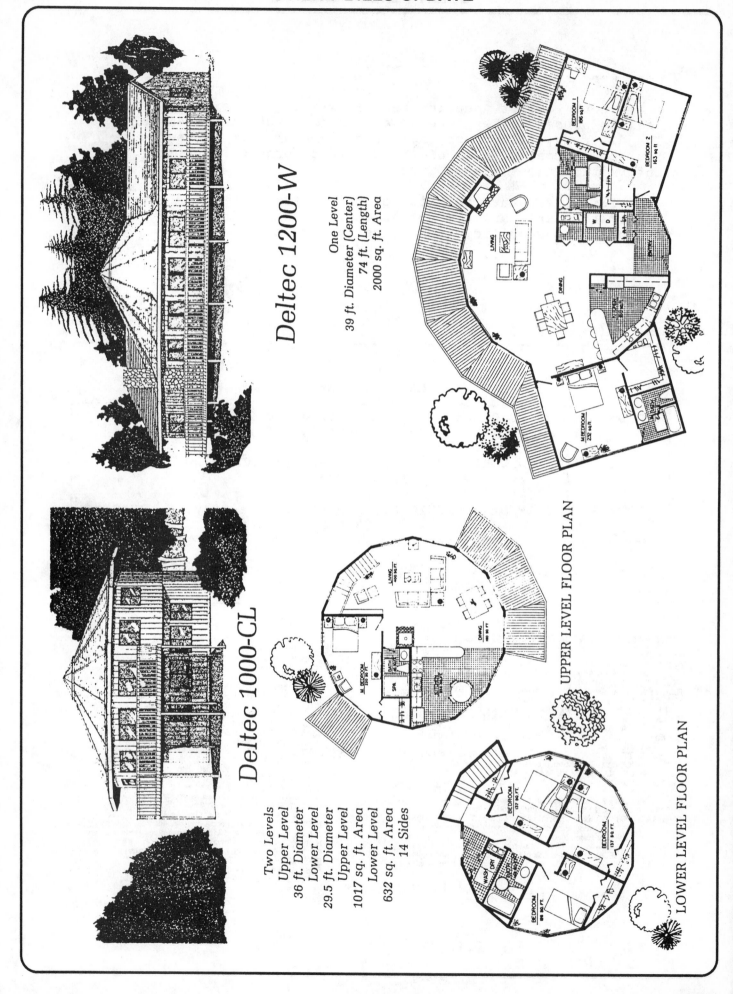

Deltec 1200-W

One Level
39 ft. Diameter (Center)
74 ft. (Length)
2000 sq. ft. Area

Deltec 1000-CL

Two Levels
Upper Level
36 ft. Diameter
Lower Level
29.5 ft. Diameter
Upper Level
1017 sq. ft. Area
Lower Level
632 sq. ft. Area
14 Sides

UPPER LEVEL FLOOR PLAN

LOWER LEVEL FLOOR PLAN

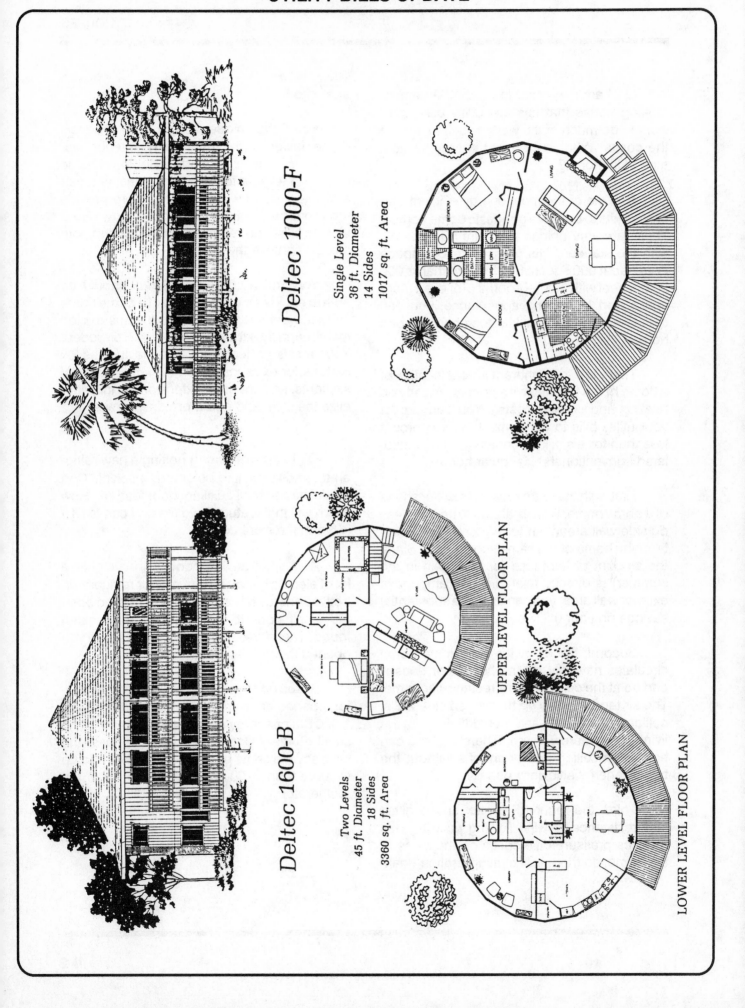

Deltec 1000-F

Single Level
36 ft. Diameter
14 Sides
1017 sq. ft. Area

Deltec 1600-B

Two Levels
45 ft. Diameter
18 Sides
3360 sq. ft. Area

UPPER LEVEL FLOOR PLAN

LOWER LEVEL FLOOR PLAN

Q - I am interested in building a unique-looking house that has low utility bills and I want to do much of the work myself to reduce the costs. What is the most energy efficient type of kit home?

A - One of the most energy efficient and easiest kits to build are geodesic dome homes. These are very unique and attractive homes, with the standard kits ranging in floor space from about 900 square feet to more than 3,000 square feet with five bedrooms. For even more space and interesting appearance, you can cluster several smaller kits together into one home.

There are four inherent characteristics of a dome home that make it extremely miserly on heating and cooling costs. You can expect your utility bills to be as much as 40 percent less than for a similarly-constructed and insulated conventional rectangular home.

First, with the basic rounded exterior shape of a dome home, there is about 30 percent less outside wall area than for a conventional rectangular home of the same floor space. Since the amount of heat loss (or heat gain in the summer) is directly related to the amount of exterior wall area, you can expect a substantial savings on your utility bills.

Second, the air inside of a dome home circulates naturally, so the heated air doesn't end up at the ceiling as in a rectangular home. The air tends to flow up the sloped side walls, collide in the center, and then drift down to the living area where you are. Therefore, you can have high ceiling and open lofts without the typical energy efficiency penalty.

Third, the rounded exterior shape gives less resistance to wind flowing past it. This reduces pressure differences on the sides of the home, so there is less air infiltration (leak-age) into it.

Fourth, a unique feature of a geodesic dome design is that there are no interior support walls needed. With the sloping outside walls and fewer interior obstructions, you can add many windows and skylights to provide more natural lighting. This holds down your electric bills, and reduce the heat buildup from electric lights in the summer.

You and a couple of friends should be able to enclose the entire shell of a dome home in two weekends. All of the construction members in the kit are pre-cut and color-coded. You can also select many options such as 2 x 6 studs for extra insulation thickness, special skylights, and entrance extensions to individualize the style and add more open areas.

Q - I am considering getting a new refrigerator and I want it to be energy efficient. One model has a small auxiliary door feature. How much will that feature save me so I can tell if it is worth the extra cost?

A - A small auxiliary door will save quite a lot of electricity over the life of your refrigerator. It saves energy because you only need to open the small door to get out frequently eaten foods. Therefore, less cold air is lost than if you opened the regular large door.

Based on a typical 16-cubic-foot refrigerator, opened an average 27 times a day, about 1,000 Btu of energy are wasted each day. The small auxiliary door would cut this loss and save several cents per day. This could add up to more than $100 saved over the life of the refrigerator.

Dear Reader,

Thank you for your interest in writing to me about energy efficient geodesic dome home kits. The list of manufacturers and literature are for your information only, and are not an endorsement of this type of product or a specific manufacturer.

Sincerely,

Jim

Jim Dulley

MANUFACTURERS OF DOME HOME KITS

DAYSTAR SHELTER, 9921 Central Ave. N.E., Blaine, MN 55434

GEODESIC DOMES, 10290 Davison Rd., Davison, MI 48423

MONTEREY DOMES, 1760 Chicago Ave., Riverside, CA 92517

OREGON DOME, 3215 Meadow Ln., Eugene, OR 97402

TIMBERLINE GEODESICS, 2015 Blake St., Berkeley, CA 94704

2243 Square Feet

3 Bedrooms	Laundry	
2 Baths	Walk-In Closet	
Living Room	Study	
Dining Room	Formal Entry	
Kitchen	Fireplace	
Family Room		

Alpine 40 Basic Home Package
4' Base Wall
5 Opening Extensions
3 Dormer Frame-In Packages
3 Medium Hexagon Skylights

2 Large Hexagon Skylights
5 Skylight Frame-In Packages
1 Endorsed Architectural Blueprint Package

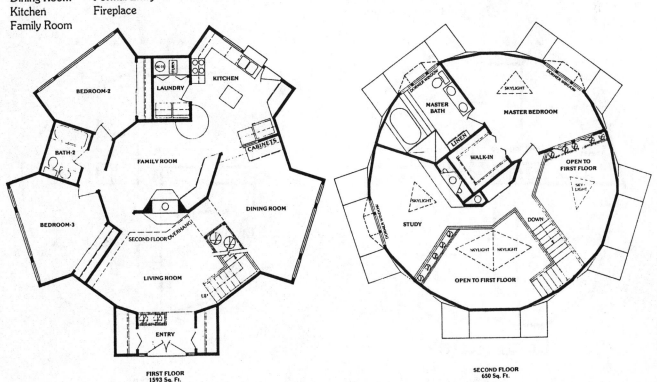

FIRST FLOOR
1593 Sq. Ft.

SECOND FLOOR
650 Sq. Ft.

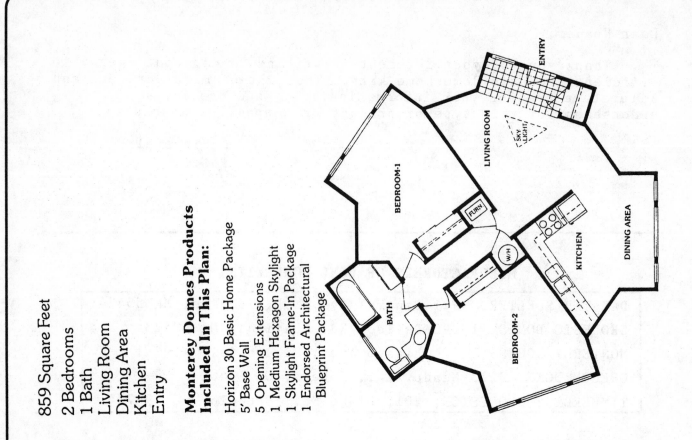

859 Square Feet

2 Bedrooms
1 Bath
Living Room
Dining Area
Kitchen
Entry

Monterey Domes Products Included In This Plan:

Horizon 30 Basic Home Package
5' Base Wall
5 Opening Extensions
1 Medium Hexagon Skylight
1 Skylight Frame-In Package
1 Endorsed Architectural
  Blueprint Package

1629 Square Feet

3 Bedrooms
2½ Baths
Living Room
Dining Room
Kitchen
Study
Laundry Room
Pantry
Entry

Horizon 40 Basic Home Package
4' Base Wall
3 Opening Extensions
2 Canopy Packages
3 Dormer Frame-In Packages
3 Medium Hexagon Skylights
3 Skylight Frame-In Packages
1 Endorsed Architectural
  Blueprint Package

FIRST FLOOR
1291 Sq. Ft.

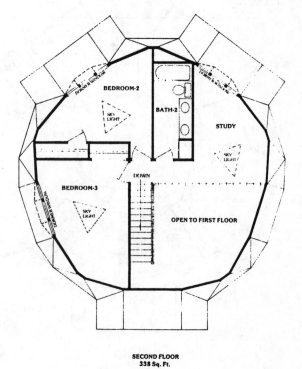

SECOND FLOOR
338 Sq. Ft.

1422 Square Feet

2 Bedrooms
2½ Baths
Living Room
Dining Room
Kitchen
Study
Walk-in Closet
Entry

Alpine 30 Basic Home Package
5' Base Wall
5 Opening Extensions
2 Dormer Frame-In Packages
2 Medium Hexagon Skylights
2 Skylight Frame-In Packages
1 Endorsed Architectural
  Blueprint Package

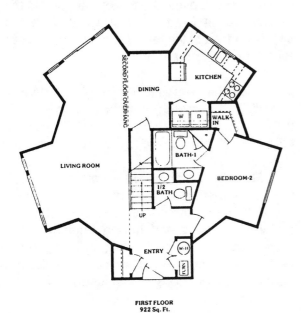

FIRST FLOOR
922 Sq. Ft.

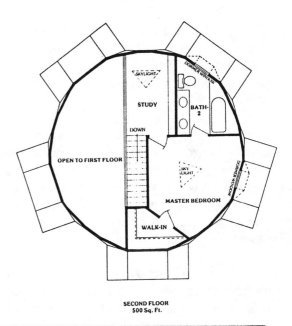

SECOND FLOOR
500 Sq. Ft.

3135 Square Feet

3 Bedrooms   Wet Bar
3 Baths   Spa
Living Room   Formal Entry
Dining Room   3 Fireplaces
Kitchen
Family Room

Alpine 45 Basic Home Package
3' Base Wall
5 Opening Extensions
3 Dormer Frame-In Packages
3 Medium Hexagon Skylights
  (2 Operable)

5 Medium Pentagon Skylights
8 Skylight Frame-In Packages
1 Endorsed Architectural
  Blueprint Package

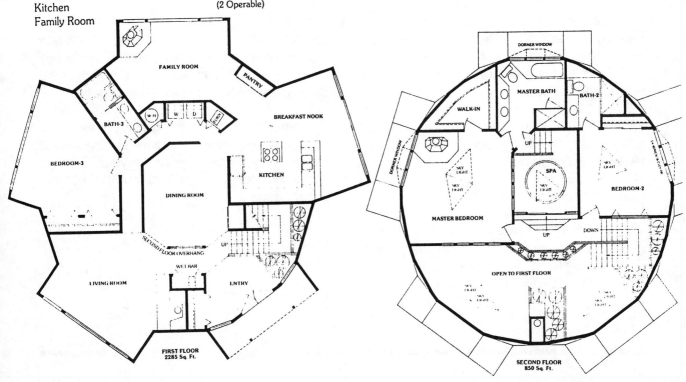

FIRST FLOOR
2285 Sq. Ft.

SECOND FLOOR
850 Sq. Ft.

Q - I am on a limited budget and I am interested in building one of those do-it-yourself insulated foam/concrete houses. How energy-efficient are they and are they easy and inexpensive to build?

A - The new types of insulated foam/concrete houses are extremely energy-efficient. They are very well-insulated with minimal air leakage and look like any conventionally-built house.

These houses are basically made of hollow insulating polystyrene foam blocks that fit together and become the concrete forms. Each foam block is roughly 10 inches square by 40 inches long and weighs only 1-1/2 pounds. The blocks for an entire house weigh only several hundred pounds.

Once the blocks are in place creating the foundation or walls, concrete is poured into the hollow openings from the top. This forms an extremely strong monolithic insulated concrete structure. The foam sections of the blocks on the inside and outside provide an insulation value of R-20. This is more than most conventional studded and insulated walls.

In addition to low-energy usage, strength, and termite resistance, these houses are very quiet. The combination of the heavy concrete mass and the foam on both sides stops much of the outdoor noise.

The concrete inside the walls also acts as a thermal mass to reduce the temperature swings inside the house throughout the day. This reduces the overall energy usage and increases your comfort level.

It is easy to build one of these houses yourself and greatly reduce the building costs. The blocks are made to snap together like a huge Lego set so you can build up the entire wall yourself. Then, with a small saw, you cut out the openings in the foam blocks for the windows and doors.

Once everything is ready, just have the concrete poured into the top openings and the hollow wall is filled. Cut small slots in the interior surface of the foam block to form chases for the wiring and plumbing.

The interior is finished by gluing drywall directly to the interior foam insulation surface with a special adhesive. The exterior can be finished with stucco, siding, brick, or stone.

For exterior siding, nails are pushed through the foam insulation from the inside hollow opening before the concrete is poured. After the concrete is poured, furring strips are hammered on over the nails sticking out and the ends are bent over. For a brick exterior, ties are pushed through the foam insulation as with the siding method.

Q - What is a desuperheater device that is used to heat hot water? I have heard that the heat for the hot water costs nothing.

A - Although a desuperheater sounds like something from a Star Trek movie, it is actually a simple device to heat your water. It attaches to your air conditioner and uses the waste heat to heat the incoming cold water supply.

These units give the greatest savings in hot southern climates where the air conditioner runs a great percentage of the year. Even in those climates, you still need another backup water heater.

Dear Reader,

Thank you for your interest in writing to me about insulated foam/concrete construction. The construction information, specifications and diagrams are for just one type of foam block construction method. You should contact all the manufacturers for detailed information on their individual designs and construction methods.

This information and list of manufacturers are for your information only and are not an endorsement of these types of products or a specific manufacturer.

Sincerely,

James Dulley

MANUFACTURERS

ARIZONA POLYTECH CORP., 101 S. 30th St., Phoenix, AZ 85034

BRANCH RIVER FOAM PLASTICS, 15 Thurber Blvd., Smtihfield, RI 02917

CONFORM, 1333 Lawrence, Expy., Santa Clara, CA 95051

CRETE-CORE CORP., 17 Tree Brook Dr., Rochester, NY 14625

SOUTHWEST FOAM FORM, 5150 F Edith, NE, Albuquerque, NM 87108

THERMAL WALL SYSTEMS, P.O. Box 2495, Naperville, IL 60566

THERMA-MANUFACTURING, 1435 Koll Cr., Suite 111, San Jose, CA 95112

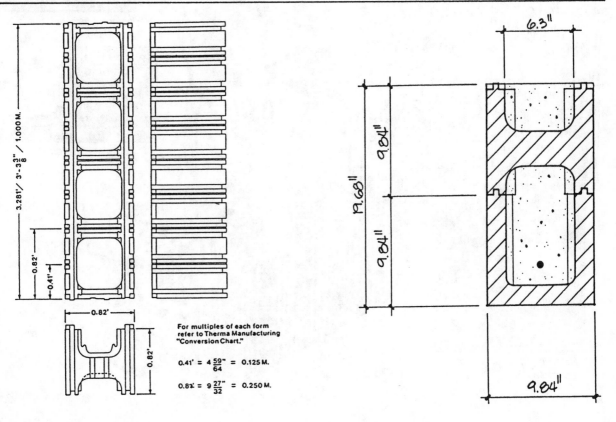

For multiples of each form refer to Therma Manufacturing "Conversion Chart."

$0.41' = 4\frac{59}{64}" = 0.125\,M.$

$0.82' = 9\frac{27}{32}" = 0.250\,M.$

Isoform is a unique and innovative insulated polystyrene concrete formwork which is pressed together by means of a patented tight-fitting interlocking system.

Isoform is designed to be built up one story at a time and then filled with concrete which flows around the formwork bridges to create a monolithic concrete wall.

Isoform can be used for most types of foundation work including stem-walls, pier and grade-beams, slab perimeter formwork, stepped foundations for hillside construction, and swimming pools.

Isoform will cover most applicable building codes and has great design flexibility. It can be engineered for most engineering applications and used for both residential and commercial construction.

Isoform saves time with its speedy assembly and light weight. This permanent insulated formwork simplifies installation for plumbing, electrical, and drywall trades.

Isoform saves energy with an R-Value of 17.95. It also saves energy better than a 2 x 6 wall and by thermal mass storage.

Isoform has been used in construction successfully worldwide for thirty years.

Isoform

THERMA MANUFACTURING

Isoforms interlock easily and stay in place to form straight, easy-to-maneuver forms. Any external finish can be bonded or fastened to Isoform.

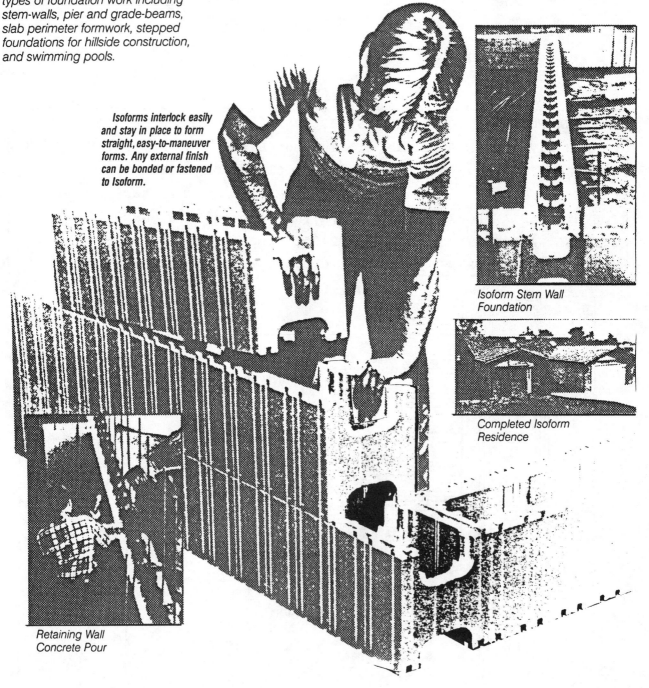

Isoform Stem Wall Foundation

Completed Isoform Residence

Retaining Wall Concrete Pour

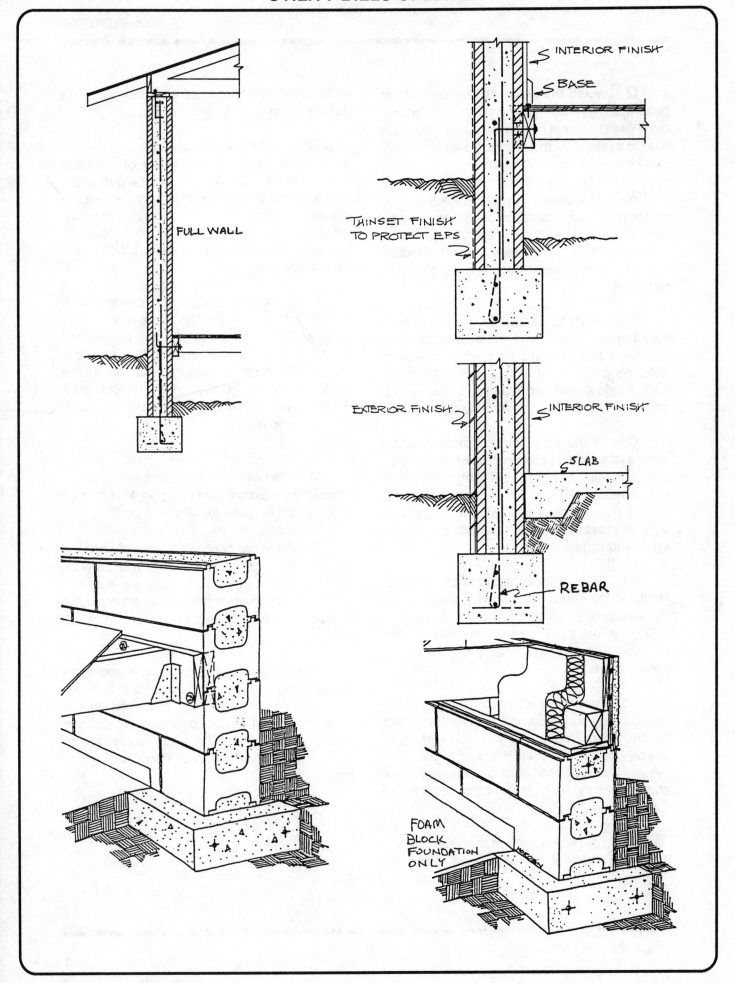

FULL WALL

INTERIOR FINISH

BASE

THINSET FINISH TO PROTECT EPS

EXTERIOR FINISH

INTERIOR FINISH

SLAB

REBAR

FOAM BLOCK FOUNDATION ONLY

Q - I would like to use some type of solar heating to keep our heating bills down, but we don't want to invest several thousand dollars in a large system. Is there a simple solar system that I can make myself?

A - A standard contractor-installed solar system can cost thousands of dollars, and can take many years to pay back its cost with energy savings. It is usually most effective when combined with water heating for year-round use.

If you want to use a solar system to heat your home and are on a limited budget, then you should be able to build a small air type of solar system yourself. With about $50 in materials, a little sweat and bruised knuckles, you can build one that will pay back its cost quickly.

One of the simplest and most effective solar systems is a solar window heater. You can use these in your south facing windows to get the most solar heat. On a bright winter day, a small do-it-yourself solar window heater can provide most of the heat needed for an average-sized room.

This solar window heater is basically an insulated flat wooden box with a glass top. You mount one open end of the box in your window and angle the other closed end down to the ground. This tilts and faces the glass top up toward the sun.

Split the solar box lengthwise with a horizontal plywood divider, so that you have two flat chambers inside. Paint the top surface of this plywood divider, which faces the glass, flat black. The divider should be several inches shorter than the box, leaving a gap at the lower outdoor end.

When the sun shines on the black divider, it gets hot and heats the air above it. Since hot air is less dense than cold air, it flows up and out the open end into your room.

The cooler room air, near your floor is drawn into the bottom chamber of the solar window heater. It flows around the gap at the bottom of the divider and into the hot sunny top chamber. When the sun shines very brightly, you'll be surprised at how much heated air flows out into your room. At night, block off the indoor opening.

For summertime use, you can mount a special vent door in the top of the box outside your window and close off the top indoor opening. When the sun shines, it will naturally create a breeze by exhausting warm air out the vent while drawing cool air in through your home. It works just like an exhaust fan, but it uses no electricity.

Q - We have a forced air furnace and it sometimes makes a loud banging sound when it comes on or goes off. What is causing it?

A - There can be several possible causes of that noise, and you should call your serviceman to have it inspected. One serious and potentially dangerous cause may be improper combustion or a leak in the combustion chamber.

The noise may also be what is known as "oil canning", which won't hurt your furnace. When the blower in your furnace kicks on, the air pressure in the ducts changes. If you have large flat ducts, the surfaces can buckle in and out like the bottom of an oil can causing that noise.

Dear Reader,

Thank you for your interest in writing to me about how to make an inexpensive solar window heater yourself. It can really add a lot of heat to a room on a sunny day.

Sincerely,

Jim

Jim Dulley

INSTRUCTIONS

The solar window heater is basically a wooden box with a glass top that collects heat from the sun. As the air inside gets hot, it flows out into your room, drawing in more cool room air to be heated.

Before you begin this project, make sure you wear enough safety clothing and safety glasses. You will be handling glass. Also, if you are going to use spray paint, use it outdoors and do not smoke while you spray it.

These are general instructions since everyone's application and design will be a little different. Other than the 3" and 4" dimensions shown in the diagram, the rest of the dimensions are not extremely critical to its effectiveness.

You will first have to determine the proper size of the box for your window. It should be slightly narrower than your window so it fits through the window and snugly against the sides of the window frame. You will use foam weatherstripping to seal it.

The angle of tilt (X° in the diagram) should be equal to the latitude for your area plus 15 degrees. The longer the box, the more surface area there is to collect heat. Use enough bricks under the outdoor end to get close to the proper tilt angle. Getting the exact angle is not critical to the performance.

Once you have determined the basic dimensions for the solar window heater, begin the build the plywood box. You can use 2 x 4 studs to make the basic frame, and then cover it with 3/8 inch plywood. Remember that the width will be 3/4 of an inch wider after the plywood sides are added, so make the frame small enough to fit into the window. Screws will hold up better than nails since it will get hot in the sun. Use silicone caulking to seal all the joints in the box. It must be airtight or it will lose more heat than it gains.

Leave the top of the box open for the piece of glass. It is a good idea to build a two inch wide plywood lip around the open top. This will add rigidity to the box, and provide support for the glass, without blocking much of the sun's heat.

For the most effective operation, you should line the inside of the box with reflective foam board insulation. This will reduce the heat loss from the cool room air in the bottom and the heated solar heated air to the cold outdoor air. In mild climates, the insulation is not necessary, but it will still help.

Make the plywood divider piece to fit as shown in the diagram. Attach a layer of foam insulation board to the underside of it and paint the top flat black. Mount the divider as shown in the diagram. Seal all around it with silicone caulking. It is very important that the air is forced to flow down around the end of the divider and back up under the glass.

Cut an opening in the solid horizontal top piece, by your window, to make the outdoor vent flap. Attach that piece with hinges to use as the vent door. Use foam weatherstripping around the edge to seal the flap when it is closed.

Make another flap door to mount on the inside opening from the upper chamber into your room. Mount it with hinges and use weatherstriping again to seal it. You should close it when the sun goes down and in the summertime. You can also add a small plywood apron where the bottom section comes into your window. This will make sure that only cool air from the floor is pulled into the heater.

The next step is to add the glass cover. **Use safety glass.** It may be easier and cheaper to use two or three pieces of glass instead of one. Have the glass cut to fit the finished box. Unless you're an accomplished cabinetmaker, the finished box will not end up exactly the same size as you planned.

Place the glass on the box and hold it in place with glazier points. Don't putty the glass in place. That won't hold up to the temperature changes of the box. Instead, use duct tape stapled to the sides of the box, or caulk the glass all the way around the edges so you get a good seal.

Paint the wood box with house paint before you put it into your window. Seal it against the window frame with adhesive foam weatherstripping.

In the winter, close off the indoor top flap at night. During the summer, you can store the solar window heater in your garage or basement. Or, close the top flap inside the house and open the outdoor top flap. Open the window on the other side of your room for cross-ventilation. Select a shady window for the coolest air to be drawn in.

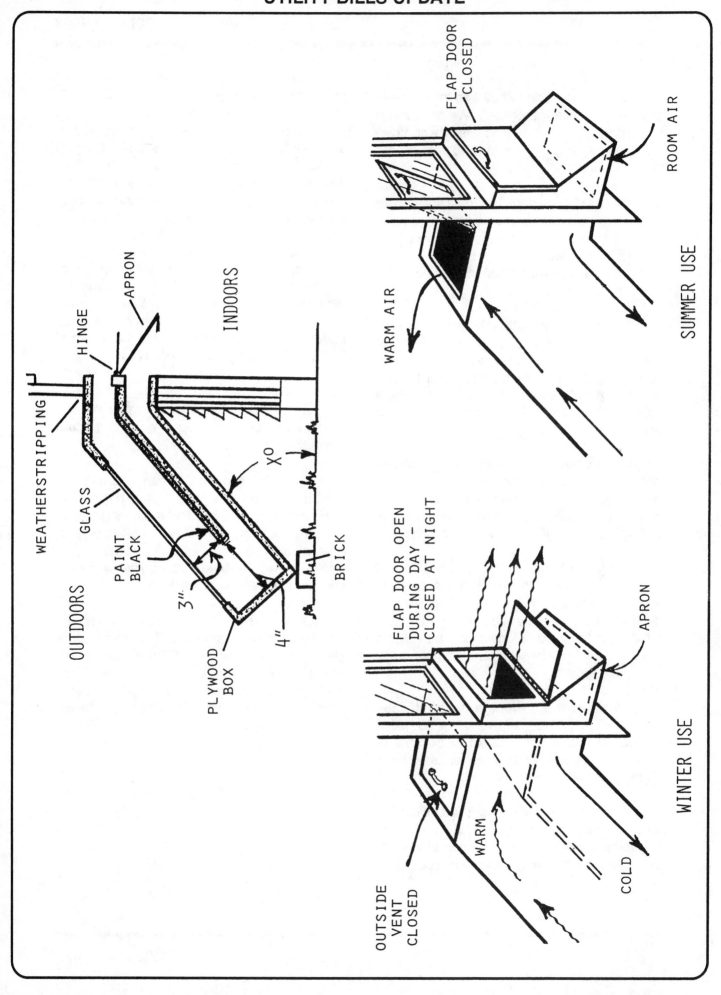

WEATHERSTRIPPING

HINGE

APRON

GLASS

OUTDOORS

PAINT BLACK

3"

PLYWOOD BOX

4"

INDOORS

X°

BRICK

FLAP DOOR CLOSED

WARM AIR

ROOM AIR

SUMMER USE

FLAP DOOR OPEN DURING DAY – CLOSED AT NIGHT

OUTSIDE VENT CLOSED

APRON

WARM

COLD

WINTER USE

Q - Is it possible to build an inexpensive solar water heater ourselves? We can't afford to spend the thousands of dollars for a contractor-installed one, but we want to reduce our water heating costs.

A - The simplest do-it-yourself solar water heating system is the passive breadbox design. It is extremely effective, and with your supplying the labor, it can be built over a weekend for less than $100 in materials, depending upon its size.

The hot water output from a breadbox solar water heater is greatest in the summer and least in the winter. Over the entire year, you can expect it to save an average of up to 50 percent of your water heating costs. For a large family, it can pay back its cost in less than one year.

A breadbox solar system looks just like its name suggests. It's basically one or two large water tanks mounted inside an insulated wooden box. You cover the top of the box with glass or a clear plastic sheet and tilt it so it faces the sun.

The water tanks, which you should paint flat black, work as both the solar collectors and the storage tanks. You can increase the efficiency of the system by laying shiny aluminum foil around the inside of the box. This reflects the solar heat to the water tank from the back and sides too.

Based upon an average daily hot water usage, a family of four will need one 80 gallon or two 40 gallon water tanks to be able to supply all its hot water requirements on a sunny summer day.

If you are lucky, you might find discarded water heater tanks for free in junkyards or at plumbing supply outlets. You can strip them down and cut the costs, otherwise, you'll have to buy the water tanks.

To be most effective, you should set up the plumbing to use the breadbox as a pre-heater for your standard water heater. This means that the cold inlet water line should first run to the breadbox heater, and then back out to your standard water heater.

Once you've made the insulated wooden box, locate it on the ground against the most southern wall of your home. This will minimize the heat loss from both the pipes and the back of the box. Tilt the box so that the glass surface makes an angle from the ground that is equal to the latitude degrees of your area.

Q - I watch a lot of TV at night. Will the amount of electricity it uses be less if I turn down the brightness knob?

A - A large color TV can use a lot of electricity, more than 200 watts, depending upon the type. You can feel the heat given off from the back of your TV which gives you an idea of how much electricity it uses. Just turning down the brightness a little won't cut your electric bills significantly.

Often you can still have an excellent TV picture at lower brightness if you use lower wattage light bulbs in your TV room. Better yet, turn off some of the lights. Adding all these wattage savings together over an entire year of TV watching can save quite a bit of electricity.

Dear Reader,

  Thank you for your interest in writing to me about how to make an inexpensive solar water heater yourself. The following breadbox design can be very effective and really reduce your water heating costs. During the coldest winter weather, you may find that you will have to drain it to avoid nighttime freeze-up problems.

  When you build this breadbox solar water heater, make it as simple as you possibly can, using as many material as possible that you already have on hand. The exact dimensions and shape are not critical to its performance.

  Set up the plumbing so that this solar water heater is used as a preheater for your regular water heater. When the sun can't supply enough hot water in the winter or on cloudy days, your regular water heater will kick on. Set the temperature dial on your water heater down so that the hot water temperature at your faucet is about 120 degrees.

Sincerely,

Jim Dulley

MATERIALS REQUIRED

2 x 4 lumber
2 x 2 lumber
Glass or clear acrylic glazing
Foil-faced Thermax insulation
Two water tanks
Pipe strapping
Copper plumbing and fittings
Corner flashing
Wood screws
Nails
Carpenter's wood glue
Flat black paint
Exterior house paint
Silicone caulk
Neoprene weatherstripping

INSTRUCTIONS TO MAKE SOLAR WATER HEATER

1) First you will have to get one or two water tanks depending on the size of solar water heater you want. Two 40 gallon tanks are generally adequate. Check at your plumbing supply outlet for old tanks. You'll have to strip down the tanks to remove the outer covering and the insulation. Once you have the actual tanks, you will be able to see what has to be done. Your plumbing supply dealer can explain the details to you.

2) Paint the stripped tanks with two coats of flat black paint.

3) Make the basic breadbox frame using 2 x 4 lumber as shown in the diagram. Size it big enough for the tanks and plumbing with at least one foot clearance between the tanks. You will need that clearance to gain additional exposure to the sun. Use screws and wood glue to assemble it.

4) Lay 2 x 4 tank supports across the bottom of the frame as shown in the diagram. Cut eight small pieces of the 2 x 4's to be used as the tank cradles. Nail the tanks cradles to the horizontal tank supports.

5) Cover the sides and back of the box with plywood sheathing. Use the silicone caulk at all of the joints and seams to seal the box tightly.

6) Make the top frame using the 2 x 2 lumber. Cut the glazing 1" smaller than the outside dimension of the cover to allow for any thermal expansion. Lay the glazing in a bead of silicone and cover it with another bead of caulk. Then screw the corner flashing down over it to the frame.

7) Avoiding the glazing, drill clearance holes through the flashing and the top frame. These will be used for screws to mount the glazing cover to the box.

8) Cut the foil-faced Thermax insulation and nail it in the bottom and sides of the box with the foil facing toward the inside.

9) Measure the location of the water tanks in the box, and make to necessary plumbing to fit. You should run the inlet and outlet pipes into the back of the box.

10) Lay the water tanks in their cradles in the box and tie them down with pipe strapping. Two straps over each tank should be adequate.

11) Cut exit holes in the bottom of the box for the pipes. Attach the pipes to the tanks. Put the weatherstripping over the top edge of the box, and screw the glazing cover over that.

12) Using the 2 x 4 lumber, make brackets to tilt the box up facing the sun. You should tilt it so that the back of the box makes and angle from the ground that is equal to your latitude angle for your area.

13) Set up the plumbing as shown in the diagram. If you are using two tanks, then pipe them in series with the hot outlet from the first one to the inlet for the second one.

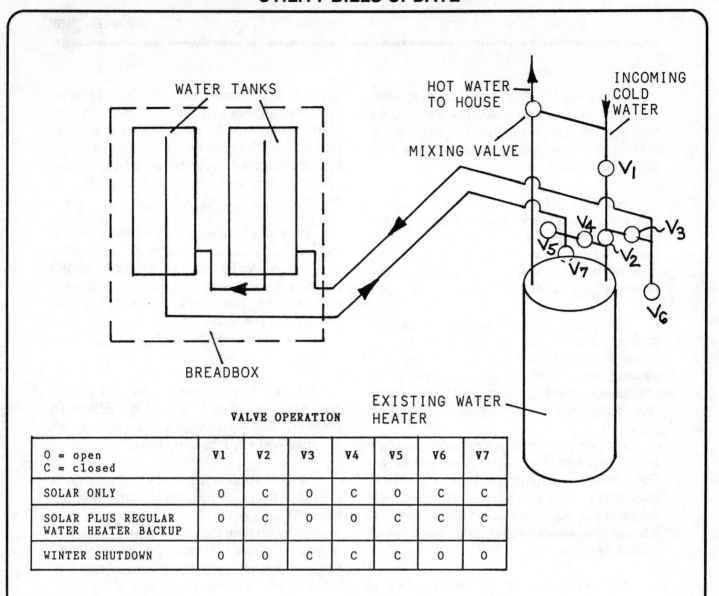

WATER TANKS

HOT WATER TO HOUSE

INCOMING COLD WATER

MIXING VALVE

V1
V4
V3
V5
V2
V7
V6

BREADBOX

EXISTING WATER HEATER

VALVE OPERATION

O = open C = closed	V1	V2	V3	V4	V5	V6	V7
SOLAR ONLY	O	C	O	C	O	C	C
SOLAR PLUS REGULAR WATER HEATER BACKUP	O	C	O	O	C	C	C
WINTER SHUTDOWN	O	O	C	C	C	O	O

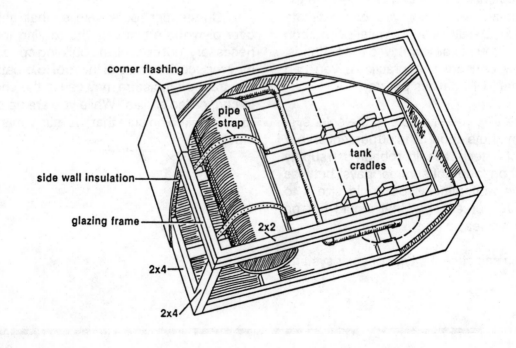

corner flashing

pipe strap

tank cradles

side wall insulation

glazing frame

2x2

2x4

2x4

Q - I always liked the idea of using solar energy to heat my domestic hot water, but I hear solar is dead due to the elimination of the tax credits. Is solar still a good investment, and how would I select a system?

A - Both the elimination of the solar income tax credits and reduced demand for solar systems have driven numerous manufacturers and dealers out of business. However, solar systems, especially ones to heat water, now may be a better buy than ever in the past.

Some of the manufacturers and dealers took unfair advantage of the tax credits to inflate their prices and their profits. Now the systems must be more reasonably-priced to offer an acceptable payback, and just the reputable companies are still in business.

A local solar consultant can often now find solar equipment for you at very reduced prices. Some solar water heating systems can offer a reasonably short payback period. For example, if you have an electric water heater, a solar system can save you up to several hundred dollars per year.

First, you should determine your hot water requirements, so you can properly size the solar system. Generally you can estimate about 15 to 20 gallons of hot water per person per day. If you install low flow shower heads, and follow conservation practices, you can reduce that to 10 gallons per day.

Generally, you should size the solar system to contribute about 50 to 60 percent of your annual hot water needs. It probably can supply most of it on long hot summer days, but less during the wintertime. You could size it to supply 100 percent, but that would not be economically feasible.

When selecting the type of solar system, consider a few simple, but not obvious points. In a thermosiphoning system, one with no pump to circulate the water, the water storage tank is mounted above the collectors. Will it fit in your attic or will it even fit through the access opening? Is your roof strong enough to support it?

With an active system, it's best to locate the storage tank near your existing water heater. Is there room for it? Will it be difficult to run the pipes from the basement to the roof? In general, will you have adequate solar access throughout the year? Neighbors may build near you and nearby trees will grow over time.

Q - We need to put a new roof on our house because it leaks water. Will putting 15 pound roofing felt down first under the asphalt shingles add any insulation value?

A - The roofing felt itself won't add much insulation value. In that location directly under the shingles, even high R-value won't help reduce much heat loss. The heavy insulation on your attic floor will handle that job quite well. Replace any cellulose insulation that had gotten wet, even if it has now dried out.

On steeper roofs, with asphalt shingles over plywood sheathing, the roofing felt isn't necessary, but consult the building codes. Felt may reduce the ability of the roof to breathe, so any trapped moisture may cause the shingles to curl, called smiles. While you are up on the roof, check to be sure that the attic vents aren't blocked.

Dear Reader,

Thank you for your interest in writing to me about solar water heating systems. The following formulas will show you how to calculate the cost of heating your water. Once you know that, you can compare to cost of a solar system to the cost of using a conventional water heater. You can also evaluate different-sized solar systems (the percentage of hot water usage it will supply), to see if the added cost of a bigger system will pay back.

The chart on the page 3 shows the average amounts of hot water used for various activites. A rule of thumb is that each person in a household uses about 20 gallons of hot water per day.

Sincerely,

Jim Dulley

HOT WATER ENERGY COST CALCULATIONS

1) First determine your energy cost per Btu of heat:
    your gas rate per therm/100,000 = cost per Btu - gas
    your electric rate per KWH/3,425 = cost per Btu - electric

2) Factor in the operating efficiency of your water heater:
    gas - cost per Btu X 1.5 = actual cost per Btu
    electric - cost per Btu X 1.05 = actual cost per Btu

3) Check the temperature of your cold water. It will vary somewhat throughout the year. For an average figure, contact your local waterworks.

4) Determine your desired hot water temperature. 120 degrees is usually adequate. With a dishwasher that doesn't have a water preheater, you will need 140 degrees.

5) Subtract the incoming cold water temperature from the desired hot water temperature to get the needed temperature rise.
    hot water temp. - cold water temp. = temperature rise

6) Calculate amount of Btu of energy used to heat your water:
    it takes 8.336 Btu to heat one gallon of water one degree.
    temperature rise needed X 8.336 = Btu/gallon of hot water.

7) Calculate the present energy cost per gallon of hot water:
    Btu/gallon of hot water X actual cost per Btu = cost/gallon

8) Calculate the total annual cost of your hot water:
    gallons of hot water used X cost/gallon = total energy cost

9) Calculate savings by using solar system:
    percentage of solar contribution X total energy cost.

Thermosiphon Water Heaters

Thermosiphon systems consist of a solar collector panel to absorb solar heat and a separate storage tank, either built-in at the top of the collector or placed inside the house, to hold solar-heated water. The solar collector is faced true south at an angle equal to the latitude. It must be mounted at least a foot below the storage tank to permit thermosiphoning - upward movement of of water by natural convection. When the water in the collector is heated, it becomes less dense and rises to the top of the storage tank. At the same time, cool water from the bottom of the tank flows into the bottom of the collector.

Although thermosiphon systems can be quite efficient and supply 40 to 60 percent of your hot water, two problems keep them from being used more often. First, because the storage tank must be installed above the collector, it is often placed on an upper floor or high in the attic above the roof rafter. In some cases, the roof or flooring may have to be reinforced because water tanks are quite heavy. Of course, the collectors can be placed on the ground if an adequate site is available.

Second, thermosiphon collectors in their simplest form contain no safeguard against freezing. This is important because water remains in the collector whenever convection stops (during sunless periods). If this water freezes it can expand with enough force to burst the piping or the tank. Freezing can be prevented by using movable insulation, an antifreeze/water solution or by installing a valve allowing the water to be drained at night. But operating a thermosiphon water heater is cheaper and easier in areas where freezing does not occur. If used elsewhere, the simplest solution is to drain them before the first frost.

Active Systems

Unlike passive systems, active domestic hot water systems use electrically driven pumps and valves to control the circulation of the heat absorbing liquid. This allows a greater degree of flexibility than their passive counterparts since the hot water storage tank does not have to be above or near the collectors. Also, active systems are designed to operate all year round without any danger of freezing.

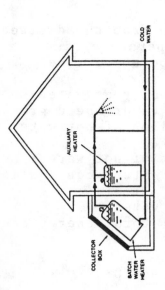

In a batch heater system, water flows through one or more tanks housed in a solar collector box. As warm water is drawn off the top of the tank, cold water automatically enters at the bottom.

Though there are dozens of solar collector manufacturers, each of whom has their own uniquely designed system, all the systems fall within four main categories: draindown, drainback, indirect and phase change.

Draindown

In a draindown system, water is pumped from the hot water storage tank up to the collectors and back again. It derives its name from the electrically powered draindown valve which is the key to its freeze protection system. When the sun is out, the valve is open and the pump circulates water through the pressurized solar loop. When there is not enough solar gain and the outdoor temperature drops near 32F (in clear, dry climates like Arizona and New Mexico, night sky radiation can draw enough heat from collectors to cause freezing at an ambient temperature of 40F), a sensor signals the central controller to close the valve. This causes the pressure in the loop to drop, and all the water in the collectors and the exposed plumbing empties out through a special opening into a house drain. When the temperature rises above 32F, the draindown valve will open and the pump will once again begin circulating the water.

Drainback

When the temperature falls near the freezing point the drainback system, like the draindown one just described, empties its collectors of water to avoid freeze damage. The difference between the two is that the water from the collectors in the drainback system empties back into a holding tank and is saved. Another difference is that the loop between the holding tank and the collectors is not pressurized. Therefore, when the thermostat signals the pump to turn off, the water drains by force of gravity. No electric valves are used which might fail.

Direct systems, whether pumped or thermosiphoning, cannot be used in areas where water is hard or acidic. Scale deposits would quickly clog the inside of the absorber tubing, and corrosion would render the system inoperable.

Indirect Systems

The best choice for hard water areas, or for people who do not want to have any worries about possible freeze damage of the collector array, is an indirect or closed-loop system. Instead of circulating water through the collectors, a fluid is used which will not freeze in the winter or boil in the summer. After the transfer fluid has been heated, it is sent through a heat exchanger which warms the household water. If the transfer fluid is toxic, a double wall heat exchanger must be used to insure that the water supply is not contaminated. Most local codes allow a single wall heat exchanger to be used when the transfer fluid is non-toxic. The single wall heat exchanger is usually placed inside the water heater for maximum transfer efficiency, but a separate unit outside the tank can be used to house the heat exchanger. Be sure that it is accessible and well insulated. The type of heat exchanger system chosen can markedly affect the overall efficiency of the solar system since heat exchangers range in efficiency from 90 percent down to 50 percent or lower.

While indirect systems offer the greatest flexibility in layout and installation, they are also the most expensive ones to purchase and install. Most active system are in the range of $3,500 to $6,000 in northern climates and $2,000 to $4,000 in the Sunbelt. The cost can be reduced if the homeowner purchases the system and installs it himself, but the homeowner should be sure that he has the skills needed to do a safe, successful job (see CAREIRS fact sheet FS 109 - Planning for a Homeowner Installation).

Phase Change Water Heaters

There has been a growing interest in these types of heaters because they offer automatic freeze protection, and are reported to be very reliable and highly efficient. Both active and passive phase change water heaters are available. These are closed loop systems which circulate a refrigerant, such as freon, through the collectors. As it is heated, the refrigerant quickly boils and turns to vapor which rises to the top of the collector. The vapor is carried to a heat exchanger inside the hot water storage tank (which on a passive system is directly above the collectors) where it gives off its heat, turns back to liquid and is sent back to the bottom of the collectors.

While phase change systems solve many of the problems related to passive and active heaters, they do have some draw-backs. They are more expensive, and, since they

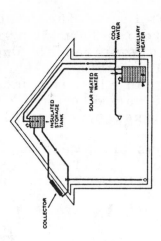

In a thermosiphoning system, cold water flows from the bottom of the tank to the bottom of the collector, and returns to the tank when warmed.

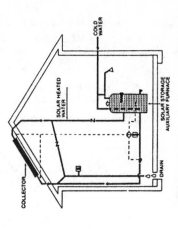

In a pumped draindown unit, solar heated water flows to the storage tank for direct use by the household. When the pump shuts off, whatever water remains in the collector drains away by gravity flow.

TYPICAL HOT WATER CONSUMPTION

Automatic washing machine, hot cycle	21 gal/load
Automatic washing machine, warm cycle	11 gal/load
Automatic washing machine, cold cycle	0 gal/load
Automatic dishwasher	15 gal/load
Dish washing by hand	4 gal/load
Food preparation (4 people)	3 gal/day
Household cleaning (4 people)	2 gal/day
Hand and face washing	2 gal/day/person
Wet shaving	2 gal/day/person
Tub bath	15 gal/bath
Showering, regular shower head	25 gal/shower
Showering, low-flow shower head	12 gal/shower

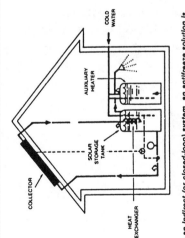

In an indirect (or closed-loop) system, an antifreeze solution is pumped through a heat exchanger, where it gives up its heat to the house water supply.

must be very carefully installed to ensure that the refrigerant does not leak, it is unlikely the homeowner would be able to cut costs by doing it himself. This is especially true of active systems which are more complicated to construct. While the basic technology behind phase change heaters is sound, the actual systems have not been time tested under real circumstances to see how they perform.

Basic Requirements

A solar energy system needs to be placed so that plenty of sunshine falls onto its collection surface. In order to ensure that your collector receives the greatest amount of sunlight:

- Aim it true south. Although collectors that are oriented within 15 degrees of true south receive the most sunshine, an unobstructed, generally south-facing surface is a potential collector location.

- Tilt it up at right angles to the sun. An angle equal to local latitude is the closest approximation to that tilt or slope on a year-round basis. This means that the ideal roof for mounting solar collectors is pitched about the same number of degrees as local latitude. The exact tilt of a collection area is not crucial; a variation of 10 degrees one way or the other to suit a roof's pitch makes almost no difference.

- Avoid shading, especially when the sun's rays are most intense, generally between 9 a.m. and 3 p.m.

Checking the House and Site

Now that it is fairly clear what is needed to make good use of the sun, it is necessary to check one's present home or future house site for any obstructions or restrictions that could prevent solar collectors from getting correct exposure to solar radiation. Things to consider include:

collector location;
access to sunlight; and
installation complication.

Any of these could hamper—and some might rule out—the installation of a solar energy system on the property.

Collector Location

The first thing to do is locate south. Though precision is not required at this point, one can easily find true south—which can vary by 20° from the magnetic south of the compass—by checking the north-south shadow cast at solar noon by a stick held vertical. Solar noon occurs exactly midway between sunrise and sunset—times that the local newspaper probably publishes.

Now look around for a generally unshaded, south-facing surface that is large enough for the collectors. For an active or thermosiphon system you will need space for 40 to 100 square feet of collectors (the average area needed for a typical single-family dwelling). If the home has no appropriate roof area, there may be good mounting surfaces on the south wall of an adjacent shed, garage or carport. Ground-mounted collectors on a support frame are another possibility. However, the use of a mounting frame or rack adds construction costs.

Access to Sunlight

Shading is most likely to come from two sources:

Parts of the house itself. Chimneys, dormers, overhangs and other elements can partially shade adjacent roof-mounted collectors.

Buildings or trees to the south. Obstructions like buildings or large evergreens that cause no interference in summer may cast long shadows when the winter sun is low in the sky. Trees that shed their leaves may still reduce the efficiency of the collectors in the winter.

Installation Complications

In a few cases, obstructions to sunlight provide less of an obstacle to a solar installation than certain limitations of an existing house. Here are some questions to consider now and possibly discuss later with an installer, particularly with respect to costs:

Piping or ductwork. How difficult will it be to route pipes or ducts from the basement or ground floor to the roof? Will sections of wall or floor need to be torn out?

Q - I want to make an inexpensive solar system to help heat my home. I heard that a water-type of collector is better than an air-type. Is that true and can I easily make a solar collector myself?

A - A solar collector that circulates water instead of air is generally more effective. Water can hold more solar heat energy than air and it offers a greater range of uses. It is possible to cut your utility bills by up to several hundred dollars per year with a do-it-yourself system.

In the summer, when you aren't heating your home, you may be able to use your solar collectors to heat your domestic water or your swimming pool. This year-round utilization yields the greatest total savings.

If you can do any simple plumbing, like replacing a kitchen faucet, you should be able to build your own solar collector inexpensively. All of the materials you need should be available at most hardware stores.

With some designs, you won't even need a pump to circulate the water. By locating a storage tank above the collector, the solar-heated water (hot water is less dense than cold water) naturally flows up to the tank.

You needn't mount your "homemade" solar collectors on your roof. A south-facing location on the ground near your house is fine. This provides easy access for keeping the glass top clean.

A typical do-it-yourself solar collector is basically a shallow insulated box with clear cover over it. Water, which flows through pipes inside the box, is heated by the sun.

Make the frame for the collector box with 2x6 lumber. Redwood works, but pressure-treated lumber is best. Cover the bottom of the frame with plywood to form the shallow box.

You can use standard wall-type of fiberglass insulation in the bottom of the box. It blocks heat loss out the back of the collector. The clear cover on top reduces heat loss to the cold outdoor air above.

For the simplest design, you can use copper piping which you paint black. The pipes run vertically in the collector with the inlet at the bottom. As the water heats in the copper collector pipes, it flows up and out the top of the collector.

For more effective operation, solder flat copper fins to the copper collector pipes. These fins increase the area exposed to the sun, so the collector's heat output is greater.

Q - Our toilet always seems to be hissing and gurgling. I am sure that it is wasting a lot of water. How can I fix it myself?

A - A leaky toilet can increase your water bills because it runs continuously. The noise is often caused by water leaking past a deteriorated stopper bulb in the tank. It may also be a bad float bulb or shut-off valve which lets the water level rise too high.

You can usually buy replacement parts to fix either problem. Simple installation instruction are shown on the packaging or check your library for "fix it" books. They all cover toilet repair.

Dear Reader,

Thank you for your interest in writing to me about how to make your own water-type solar collector. Making your own solar collectors can greatly reduce the cost of your total system. These types of collectors are well suited to space heating your house or for heating your hot water.

The design of solar collector described below is well suited for a thermosiphoning type of solar system. In this type of system, the hot water naturally flow up through the collector because hot water is less dense than colder water.

If you live in a cold climate, you will have to incorporate some type of freeze protection for your system. You should contact a solar designer to specify the proper size and system layout for your specific house, needs, and climate.

Sincerely,

Jim

Jim Dulley

DO-IT-YOURSELF WATER-TYPE SOLAR COLLECTOR

This type of solar collector utilizes a header/riser panel design. Copper pipes and absorber plates are energy efficient and copper is fairly easy to work with. The glazing cover can be made of many materials - glass (tempered and annealed or low-iron tempered and annealed), acrylic, polycarbonate, fiberglass reinforced polyester, or polyvinyl fluoride. Check with local plastic material suppliers for the non-glass glazing materials.

1) A good collector size is 96" by 48" outside dimensions. Materials for this size are easier to find.

2) Make the frame for the solar collector using 2x6 lumber. Standard lumber will work, but pressure-treated lumber is best. When using pressure-treated lumber, follow the suppliers guidelines for handling and safety precautions. You might want to consider treating the lumber after assembly. Therefore, the treating chemicals won't reduce the adhesion power of any glues that you use. Using dowels at the corner joints will increase the strength.

3) Nail and glue the plywood base on to the bottom of the frame. Drill several small weep holes in the back of the frame to let any moisture escape. Paint the inside and outside of the frame.

4) Cut a wood center support to fit across the frame. This supports the glazing in the center of the frame. Do not nail it into place yet.

5) You need 8 copper riser pipes and two header pipes. Make the header pipes using 3/4" copper pipe and the risers using 1/2" copper pipe. The header pipes should be cut to lengths of about 4-1/8" long to fit between the 3/4"x3/4"x1/2" tees. The riser pipes should be 91 inches long maximum. This will allow for expansion as the pipes heat in the sun. If they are too long, the header pipe will be too close to the inside of the frame. Trial assemble all the pipes together in the collector frame to make sure they fit properly.

6) Make the absorber plates using .020" copper sheet. They should be 90" long and 5-1/4" wide after they are formed with the groove for the riser pipe. Trim one of the center absorber plates narrower to leave clearance for the center wood support for the glazing. An easy way to form the groove is to make a simple 8-foot long wood jig. See the diagram. Press a 1/2" steel pipe down to form the groove in the copper.

7) Clean the copper risers and the grooves in the absorber plates with steel wool. Place the riser pipes in the plates. Using a propane torch, sweat solder into the joint attaching the risers to the plates. Make sure you get a continuous bead of solder connecting the two pieces. This is essential for good heat transfer from the absorber plates to the water.

8) Solder the tees and header pipe pieces to the riser/absorber plate assemblies. Cap off one end of both header pipes (the same end of each). The other ends are the inlet and outlet that extend through holes in the sides of the frame.

9) When the entire piping system is soldered and assembled, pressure test it with water and resolder any leaky spots.

10) Paint the copper assembly with high-temperature flat black paint to increase the solar heat gain. A flat black barbecue or automotive engine paint should work.

11) Use 3-1/2" foil-faced fiberglass or rock wool insulation batts in the bottom of the frame. Install the insulation with the foil facing upward. Staple the edges of the foil facing to the sides of the frame. This keeps it from settling when the collector is mounted up on an angle to face the sun. Seal the joints of the foil facing with duct tape.

12) Drill holes in the side of the frame for the inlet and outlet header pipes. Gently, slip the inlet and outlet pipes through the holes in the sides of the frame and lower the absorber assembly into the frame on top of the insulation. Using pipe strapping, secure the header pipes to the sides of the frame. Seal the gap between the inlet and outlet pipes and the frame.

13) Nail the wood support for the glazing across the center of the collector. You may have to notch it to clear the header pipes. Lay a bead of caulk along the top edge of the frame and the center support. Place the glazing on top of the frame. Lay another bead of caulk on top of the glazing and place aluminum angle over that. If you used plastic glazing you can drill through that and nail it on from the top. If you use glass, nail on the angle from the side.

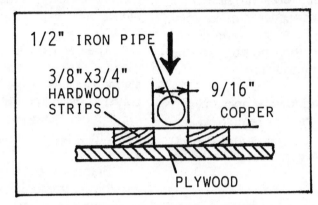

FORM ABSORBER PLATE

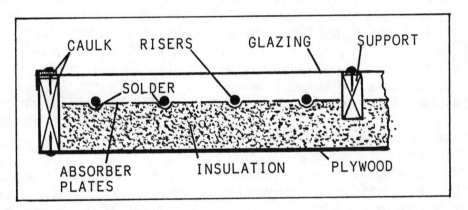

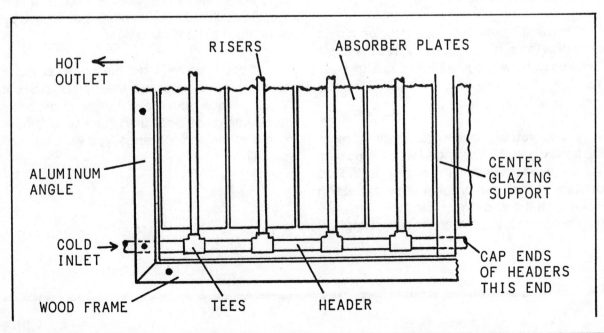

Q - My heating bills were high this winter and I like the idea of solar heating. There are trees and houses to the south of my home. How can I tell if they'll block too much sun for effective solar heating?

A - You should definitely first determine if you have adequate solar access to make solar heating feasible. Also, trees grow and neighbors build additions to their homes, so you must consider future changes too.

Even though you need solar access year-round for heating hot water for example, wintertime is the primary concern. The sun is lower in the winter sky and the chances of its being blocked are greatest.

First you must determine true 'solar' south, not magnetic south from a compass. The two can vary considerably. Your local weather report usually indicates the official times of sunrise and sunset. At the midpoint of those two times, lay a long board on the ground pointing in the direction of the sun. This is a good estimate of true solar south.

The actual position of the sun in the sky is different every day. It is lowest in the sky on December 21 and highest on June 21. Since it is past December 21, you can't measure the lowest position of the sun.

You will have to use sun position charts that show the sun's height (shown as the angle it makes with the ground) throughout the year. You can find them at your library or local weather service.

Next, you will have to determine whether the trees or nearby buildings will block the sun. This requires measuring the angle from the top of them to the location of your solar heating system. If the angle from the top of them to your solar site is lower than the lowest angle of

the sun on December 21 (from the solar chart), then the sun will not be blocked.

Measure the angle of the tops of the buildings and trees to the southeast and southwest too. As the sun position charts show, the sun is even lower in the sky in the morning and afternoon.

The easiest way to measure the angle of the tops of the buildings and trees is to make a simple device. Take a small protractor and punch a hole in the center point mark. Straighten out a paper clip and bend a hook in one end. Insert the paper clip hook through the hole.

Stand at the site of your solar system and turn the protractor with the circular side down so the paper clip hangs down across the angle markings. Look along the straight edge of the protractor to the treetops. The paper clip will hang straight down, showing the angle on the protractor scale.

Q - When I boil water for tea on my stove, is it better to start with cold or hot water from the tap?

A - Unless you have just used the hot water form the faucet, you should start with cold water. More hot water can be used and wasted to fill the hot water pipes than is used by your stove to heat the teapot.

If you have just used the hot water at the faucet, then the pipes are already filled with hot water. Since your water heater is probably more energy-efficient than the burner/teapot combination on your range, you will be ahead overall.

Dear Reader,

Thank you for your interest in writing to me about how to determine if you have adequate solar access. Check a map of the United States to find the latitude for your area. Then read the chart with the nearest latitude to determine the position of the sun throughout the year.

As was described in my column, hang a paper clip from the center of this protractor and sight along the flat bottom of the protractor to the top of nearby trees and buildings. The paper clip will hang down and show the angle. Then compare that angle to the sun's position from the appropriate chart.

Sincerely,

Jim Dulley

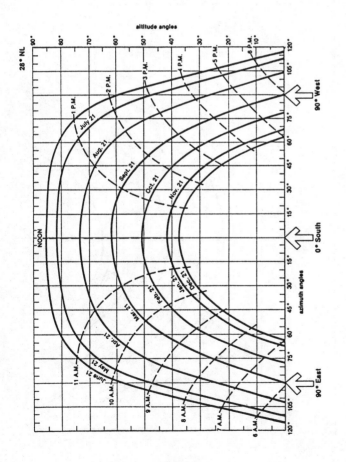

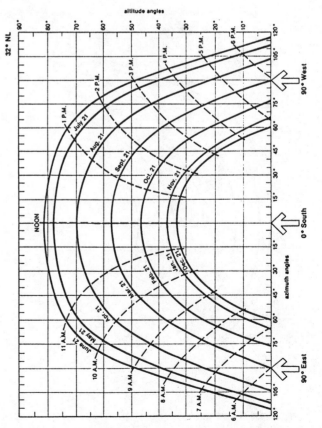

UTILITY BILLS UPDATE

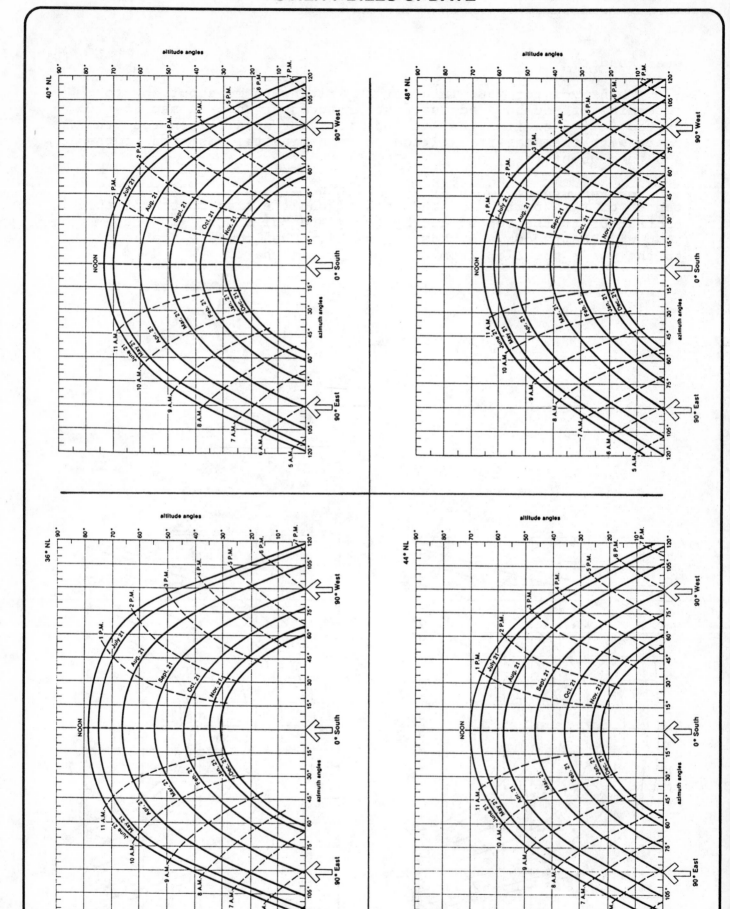

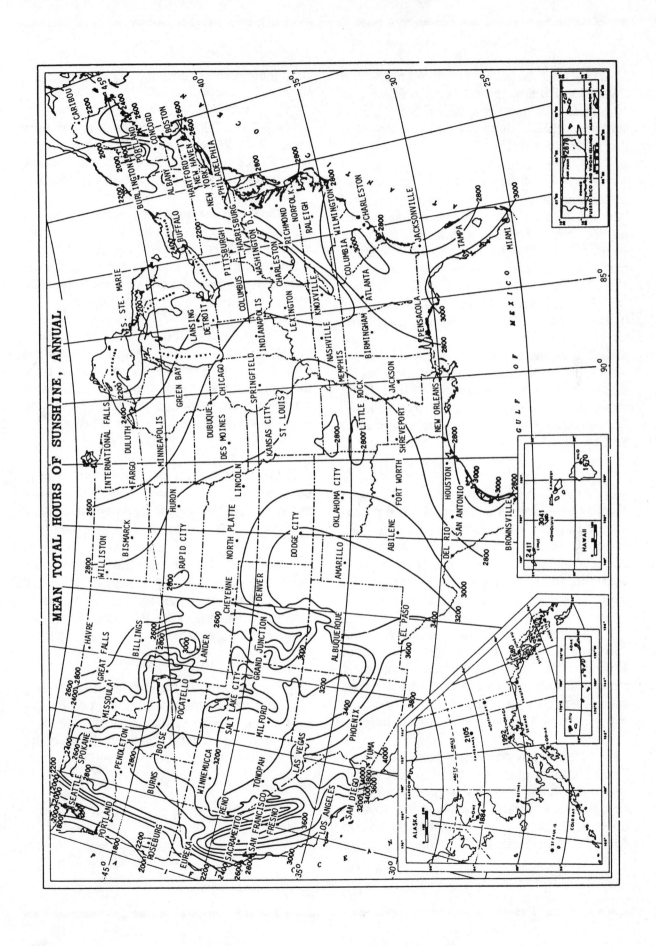

MEAN TOTAL HOURS OF SUNSHINE, ANNUAL

Q - I am redecorating my living room, and I want the lighting to be energy efficient, yet attractive. I've seen charts of recommended light intensity in foot-candles, but it's Greek to me. Can you explain it?

A - A well-thought-out lighting plan can not only enhance the decor and usefulness of your living room, but it can also reduce your electric bills. This is especially true in the summertime when the excess heat from lights makes your air conditioner run longer.

Professional designers use foot-candles of light intensity to plan lighting requirements for various rooms and tasks. They use light meters to measure the foot-candles. For example, 85 foot-candles are recommended for studying at a desk, as compared to only 12 foot-candles for general lighting in a hallway. Reading a book or magazine requires about 40 foot-candles.

Without a light meter, you can use a simple rule of thumb based on the amount of light output from light bulbs. Light output is measured in lumens, which is marked on the bulb carton. Most living rooms need a maximum of about 80 lumens of light output per square foot of floor area. For comparison, a dining room needs only 45 lumens per square foot.

A typical 40-watt light bulb produces about 450 lumens, and a 100-watt light bulb, about 1750 lumens. Therefore, the higher wattage is more efficient. A fluorescent tube is even several times more energy efficient than that, more than 2,000 lumens from 40-watt tube.

A 15-by-20 living room should have about 24,000 lumens of light output. Just total the lumen rating for all the lights in each room. A 12-by-12 dining room would need a total of about 6,500 lumens. To be most attractive and energy efficient, select a combination of standard incandescent and fluorescent lighting.

For example, use lamps with three-way bulbs (50-200-250-watts) on each end of your sofa. Two 75-watt reflector bulbs above a fireplace or piano and a 40-watt fluorescent tube under a drapery cornice are very effective.

Only use the three-way bulbs where you will need to vary the light intensity often. They are not as energy efficient as a larger single-wattage bulb. Also, install solid-state dimmer switches, not the inexpensive resistor-type, on the lights used for overall room lighting.

Carefully plan the location of your wall switches and the wiring layout. Locate the switches together where you most often enter the room. That will make it convenient to switch on only the lights that you need and to switch them off again when you leave the room.

Q - I installed an insulated metal door to save energy. Each time I paint it, the paint seems to start peeling off within a year. It starts by the plastic trim pieces. What should I do?

A - A common cause of the problem is the difference in thermal expansion of the metal door and the trim pieces. Since the door exterior is insulated from the indoors, its temperature changes dramatically throughout the day.

Remove the trim and paint it separately next time. Since there won't be a continuous skin of paint over the joint between the door and the trim, there won't be the stresses of the temperature changes on that area.

Dear Reader,

Thank you for your interest in writing to me about developing a lighting plan for your home. The chart below for recommended lumen light output per square foot of various rooms is only an average figure. Depending on the activities you do in a room, you may need different levels of lighting. That is where the use of dimmers and three-way bulbs will give you the added flexibility.

The bottom chart shows the lumens output for standard incandescent light bulbs. The chart on page 2 show the lumens outputs for fluorescent lights of various sizes and types. You should use a combination of the two to get the most energy efficient and attractive lighting plan.

Sincerely,

Jim Dulley

LIGHTING LEVEL RECOMMENDATIONS

ROOM	LUMENS PER SQ. FT.
LIVING ROOM	80
DINING ROOM	45
KITCHEN	80
BATHROOM	65
BEDROOM	70
HALLWAY	45
LAUNDRY	70
WORK BENCH AREA	70

LIGHTING OUTPUT FOR INCANDESCENT BULBS

WATTS	LUMENS	AVERAGE LIFE - HR
25	235	2,500
40	455	1,500
60	870	1,000
75	1,190	750
100	1,750	750
150	2,880	750
200	4,010	750

FLUORESCENT LIGHTING

GENERAL SERVICE Watts	Tube Diameter	Tube Length	Lumens Deluxe Colors*	Lumens Standard Colors*	Average Life-Hours
15	1"	18"	610	870	7,500
15	1½"	18"	540	800	9,000
20	1½"	24"	850	1300	9,000
30	1"	36"	1540	2300	18,000
40	1½"	48"	2150	3150	20,000

U-SHAPED Watts	Tube Diameter	Tube Length	Lumens Range	Average Life-Hours
40	1½"	22¼"	1980-2900	12,000

CIRCULAR Watts	Tube Diameter	Circle Diameter	Lumens Range	Average Life-Hours
20	2"	6½"	650-825	12,000
22	2¼"	8¼"	800-1000	12,000
32	2¼"	12"	1300-1900	12,000
40	2¼"	16"	1900-2600	12,000

SUNLAMPS Watts	Tube Diameter	Tube Length	Average Life
20	1½"	24"	5000 applications
40	1½"	48"	15 minutes per start

BUG LAMPS Watts	Tube Diameter	Tube Length	Average Life-Hours
20	1½"	24"	9,000
40	1½"	48"	20,000

GERMICIDAL Watts	Tube Diameter	Tube Length	Average Life-Hours
4	⅝"	6"	6,000
6	⅝"	9"	7,500
8	⅝"	12"	7,500
15	1"	18"	7,500
20	1½"	24"	9,000
30	1"	36"	7,500
40	1½"	48"	20,000

PLANT-GROW Watts	Tube Diameter	Tube Length	Average Life-Hours	Lumen Output
15	1"	18"	7,500	410
20	1½"	24"	9,000	600
40	1½"	48"	20,000	1,600

LIGHTING LAYOUT

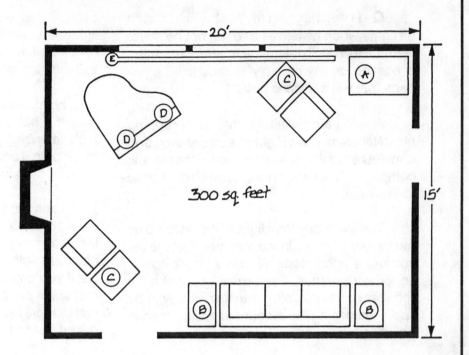

Lumens

A. One 200-watt inside frosted bulb at 3,940 lumens in a study lamp 3,940

B. Two (50-200-250-watt) Soft White 3-way bulbs at 4,110 lumens each in two senior table lamps 8,220

C. Two (50-100-150-watt) Soft White 3-way bulbs at 2,190 lumens in two chairside table lamps 4,380

D. Two 75-watt reflector spotlights ceiling recessed at 860 lumens each over the piano keyboard ... 1,720

E. Three 40-watt Deluxe Warm White fluorescent tubes at 2,080 lumens each in a drapery cornice 6,240

Total Lumens Provided 24,500

SWITCH & WIRING LAYOUT

General Outlets

o Ceiling surface fixture outlet

○ Ceiling recessed fixture outlet

⊖ Continuous wireway for fluorescent lighting on ceiling, in coves, cornices, etc. (Extend rectangle to show length of installation.)

Convenience Outlets

⊖ Duplex convenience outlet

⊖ₐₐ Duplex convenience outlet for grounding-type plug

⊖ᵥₚ Weatherproof convenience outlet

⊖ₛ Combination switch and convenience outlet

⊙ Floor outlet

Switch Outlets

S Single-pole switch

S₃ Three-way switch

S₄ Four-way switch

Sₒ Automatic door switch

Sᵥₚ Weatherproof switch

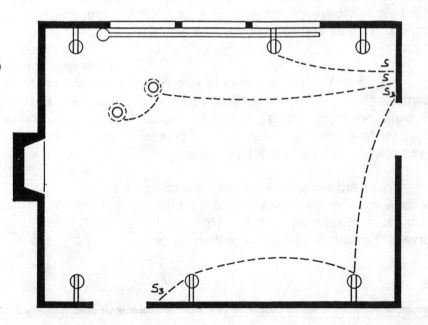

Q - I keep nagging my husband to switch off lights when he leaves a room, but he never learns. How can I determine how much lighting is costing on my monthly electric bills? Perhaps that will convince him.

A - You are definitely justified in nagging him. Needless use of lights wastes energy and contributes to the peak demand for the electric company. This causes long-term electric rates to increase.

The electricity from light bulbs ends up as heat in your home. In the summer, that makes you more uncomfortable and your air conditioner work harder. Each extra light that is on requires more coal, oil, or nuclear energy to be used, increasing the amount of environmental pollution.

You can easily calculate how much each light bulb used is costing you. A 100-watt bulb uses one-tenth of a kilowatt-hour (KWH) of electricity for each hour it is on. First check the electric rate per KWH in your area. It should be listed on your monthly electric bill.

You'll have to multiply the wattage marked on the top of the bulb by the electric rate in cents per KWH. Divide that by 1,000 to get the operating cost per hour. When you add up all the bulbs that are on throughout a 24-hour period, you'll be surprised at the total electric cost.

For example, with an electric rate of 7 cents per KWH, each 100-watt light bulb costs .7 cents per hour. Using just one additional bulb for four hours per day, would increase your electric bill by about $10 per year.

There are several things you can do to reduce your lighting costs. Keep the bulbs, shades, and reflectors clean. This can increase the light output by more than 15 per-cent, so you won't have to switch on additional lights. Install solid state dimmers with a built-in on-off switch, so you don't have to change the intensity adjustment when you switch it off.

Light bulbs lose brightness as they get old. If a hallway bulb (where you don't need high intensity) burns out, replace it with an older bulb from the family room. Put the new brighter bulb in the family room lamp.

There are newer energy efficient "watt saver" bulbs available. They use about 5 to 10 less watts to give the same amount of light as standard bulbs. This doesn't sound like much, but if you count up all the bulbs in your home, that small per-bulb-savings will add up to several dinners out at the restaurant for your family over a year's time.

Q - We have weatherstripped our front door with spring metal strips, but we still get a draft past the metal door latch plate. Can we seal that area with the spring metal too?

A - A common problem area is the metal striker plate in the door frame where you can't attach the spring metal strip in the same way. Spring metal strips are designed to be installed so that the edge of the door slides against the strip, compressing it for a seal.

Try mounting a short piece of the spring steel strip against the door stop in the frame, across from the metal striker plate. It will seal fairly well, but there will still be some air leakage around the ends of the short strip. Make it about two inches longer than the striker plate so that the outside air has a longer path to travel around it to get indoors.

UTILITY BILLS UPDATE

Dear Reader,

Thank you for your interest in writing to me about how to determine your annual lighting costs. You will probably be surprised at how high it is. During the summer, all that electricity ends up adding more heat to your home.

The worksheet below will show you how to calculate the annual cost for use each bulb in your home. Then just sum them for a total annual cost.

Under column "A", list the wattage of each bulb. Under column "B", estimate how many hours you use that bulb each <u>week</u>. Then divide that number of hours by 84. Under column "C", enter the cost from the chart on Page 2 for that wattage bulb and your electric rates. Under column "D", multiply the number in "B" by the number in "C". That will give you the annual electricity cost for each bulb.

Sincerely,

Jim Dulley

WORKSHEET

"A"	"B"	"C"	"D"
WATTAGE	(HOURS/WEEK)÷84	COST FROM CHART	ANNUAL COST ("B"x"C")
watts	hours	$ per 84 hours	$

ANNUAL LIGHTING COST COMPARISON

KILOWATT HOUR (KWH) COST RATE (¢)

WATTS	2	2.5	3	3.5	4	4.5	5	5.5	6	6.5	7	7.5	8	8.5	9	9.5	10
15	1.31	1.64	1.97	2.29	2.62	2.95	3.28	3.60	3.93	4.26	4.59	4.91	5.24	5.57	5.90	6.22	6.55
25	2.18	2.73	3.28	3.82	4.37	4.91	5.46	6.01	6.55	7.10	7.64	8.19	8.74	9.28	9.83	10.37	10.92
35	3.06	3.82	4.59	5.35	6.12	6.88	7.64	8.41	9.17	9.94	10.70	11.47	12.23	12.99	13.76	14.52	15.29
40	3.49	4.37	5.24	6.12	6.99	7.86	8.74	9.61	10.48	11.36	12.23	13.10	13.98	14.85	15.72	16.60	17.47
60	5.24	6.55	7.86	9.17	10.48	11.79	13.10	14.41	15.72	17.04	18.35	19.66	20.97	22.28	23.59	24.90	26.21
75	6.55	8.19	9.83	11.47	13.10	14.74	16.38	18.02	19.66	21.29	22.93	24.57	26.21	27.85	29.48	31.12	32.76
80	6.99	8.74	10.48	12.23	13.98	15.72	17.47	19.22	20.97	22.71	24.46	26.22	27.96	29.70	31.45	33.20	34.94
90	7.86	9.83	11.79	13.76	15.72	17.69	19.66	21.62	23.59	25.55	27.52	29.48	31.45	33.42	35.38	37.35	39.31
100	8.74	10.92	13.10	15.29	17.47	19.66	21.84	24.02	26.21	28.39	30.58	32.76	34.94	37.13	39.31	41.50	43.68
105	9.17	11.47	13.76	16.05	18.35	20.64	22.93	25.23	27.52	29.81	32.10	34.40	36.69	38.98	41.28	43.57	45.86
135	11.79	14.74	17.69	20.64	23.59	26.54	29.48	32.43	35.38	38.33	41.28	44.23	47.17	50.12	53.07	56.02	58.97
150	13.10	16.38	19.66	22.93	26.21	29.48	32.76	36.04	39.31	42.59	45.86	49.14	52.42	55.69	58.97	62.24	65.52
160	13.98	17.47	20.97	24.46	27.96	31.45	34.94	38.44	41.93	45.43	48.92	52.42	55.91	59.40	62.90	66.39	69.89
175	15.29	19.11	22.93	26.75	30.58	34.40	38.22	42.04	45.86	49.69	53.51	57.33	61.15	64.97	68.80	72.62	76.44
200	16.94	21.84	26.20	30.58	34.94	39.32	43.68	48.04	52.42	56.78	61.16	65.52	69.88	74.26	78.62	83.00	87.36
215	18.78	23.48	28.17	32.87	37.56	42.26	46.96	51.65	56.35	61.04	65.74	70.43	75.13	79.83	84.52	89.22	93.91
250	21.84	27.30	32.76	38.22	43.68	49.14	54.60	60.06	65.52	70.98	76.44	81.90	87.36	92.82	98.28	103.74	109.20
300	26.20	32.76	39.32	45.86	52.42	58.96	65.52	72.08	78.62	85.18	91.72	98.28	104.84	111.38	117.94	124.48	131.04

Using this chart, you can determine the cost of lighting your home. First, list all of the light bulbs in your home, each with wattage. Determine the approximate number of hours each is used during a 24-hour period. Find the column corresponding to your utility rate. Extract the figure in that column on line with the wattage of the first bulb. It is a dollar figure for 12 hours of use, seven days a week for a year. If you estimate use at five hours daily, multiply it by 5/12. Repeat the calculation for all bulbs. Total the figures to find the yearly cost.

Chart adapted from North American Philips Lighting Corp.

Comparison of Light Efficiency

Just as an automobile's fuel efficiency is measured in miles per gallon, lamp efficiency is measured in terms of lumens per watt—in other words, the amount of light produced for each watt of electrical power consumed. In some cases, different types of the same kind of lamp may vary in efficiency because of their construction. Replacing one lamp with another that produces more lumens per watt can provide you with the same amount of light for less money.

EFFICIENCIES OF DIFFERENT LAMPS
(LPW = LUMENS PER WATT)

LOW PRESSURE SODIUM
183 LPW
100 LPW

HIGH PRESSURE SODIUM
140 LPW
63 LPW

FLUORESCENT
100 LPW
35 LPW

MERCURY VAPOR
63 LPW
31 LPW

INCANDESCENT
22 LPW
7 LPW

Q - I want outside storm windows for my home, and plan to make them myself to save money. Can you tell me several ways to make them?

A - There are many types of storm windows that you can make yourself at only a fraction of the cost of contractor-installed ones. These homemade storm windows can be very energy efficient and can pay back their cost with lower utility bills in about a year.

Exterior storm windows are the easiest to make because you don't have to be as concerned about a totally smooth and finished look. Since they are on the outside, they keep your primary windows warmer and reduce any moisture condensation problems.

The simplest outside do-it-yourself storm window is just a single piece of clear rigid acrylic plastic sheet with foam weatherstripping as a seal. Size the plastic sheet about two inches larger than the window opening.

Cut lengths of 1/2 x 1-inch wood to make support pieces for the perimeter of the plastic pane. Drill through the wood and the plastic sheet into the outside wall around your window. Attach self-adhesive foam weatherstripping to the plastic and screw the entire assembly to the wall, compressing the weatherstripping for a good seal.

Another inexpensive method is to build a light wood frame, sized larger than your window opening. Staple 6 mil polyethylene film to the frame. Using the foam weatherstripping as a seal, screw on the frame over your window. The film is cloudy, so you won't want it for all your windows.

The most attractive and durable do-it-yourself storm windows closely resemble some contractor installed storms. These are sized smaller to fit inside the window trim, and use glass panes for clarity. You can make these using either single or double panes.

You will probably want to use double pane storms only on second floor or other windows where you won't need a clear view. With homemade double pane storms that aren't hermetically sealed, fog may develop between the panes. This won't effect the energy savings, just the view.

You should make a durable wooden frame, using 1 x 2-inch clear dry pine. Attach a small wooden face strip around the inside edge of the frame to position the pane of glass. Lay a bead of silicone caulking on the face strip, and set in the glass pane. Attach another face strip on the other side of the glass to hold it in place.

Q - We have our furnace thermostat located near a cold air return register. Should we move the thermostat to another location to get it out of that cool breeze?

A - The location for your thermostat, near the cold air return register, is not bad. Often, thermostats are mounted on walls near a corner or away from the natural air flow patterns, making them less sensitive. Curtains, furniture, and lamps can all effect these air flow currents.

Your thermostat senses the actual temperature of the room air, so there isn't any wind chill effect by being located near the register. Since there is more air movement, you should take off its cover several times a year, and carefully clean off any dust with a soft brush.

Dear Reader,

Thank you for your interest in writing to me about how to make your own storm windows. There are several types that you can make and they can pay back their cost quickly with the energy saings.

Whenever you are handling glass, make sure that you are wearing the proper safety equipment. Always wear heavy work gloves, work shoes, and long sleeves. When you're cutting the glass or the wood, wear safety glasses or goggles to protect your eyes.

The first type shown below is the easiest to make and can be used on all of your windows, since these storms won't distort your vision through them. Since they are made of acrylic plastic, you must be careful not to scratch them. The second type shown will distort the view, so my only want to use them on certain windows. The plastic film is not totally clear.

Also the final type shown using glass may develop some fog between the double pane design. The single pane ones, although they are not as energy efficient, will not distort the view and will remain totally clear.

Sincerely,

Jim

Jim Dulley

INSTRUCTIONS

DESIGN #1: See Diagrams on page 2.

1) Measure the window opening on the outside wall.
2) Cut the acrylic sheet (Plexiglas) two inches larger in both dimensions.
3) Cut four 1/2 x 1 inch wood support strips. Make them 2 inches shorter than the plexiglas sheet.
4) Using some strips of double sided tape, stick the wood strips around the edges of the plexiglas sheet.
5) Drill clearance holes through the wood and plexiglas at three locations on each side.
6) Have a helper hold this assembly against the wall over the window, and mark the location of the holes on the wall.
7) Drill holes through the siding into the sheathing beneath. For a masonry house, you'll need to drill a larger hole and install anchors for the mounting screws. Paint the wood.
8) Attach the foam weatherstripping to the plexiglas, opposite the wood strips, and screw the storm window tightly to the wall.

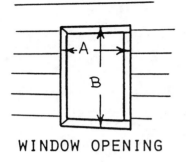

WINDOW OPENING

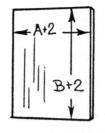

ACRYLIC SHEET

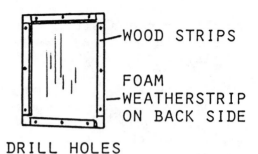

DRILL HOLES

WOOD STRIPS

FOAM
WEATHERSTRIP
ON BACK SIDE

DESIGN #2: See diagrams below.

1) Measure your window opening on the outside wall.
2) Make a rectangular wood frame that is 2 inches longer and
   wider (inside of frame) than the window opening. 1 x 2 inch
   lumber should be adequately strong. Paint the wood frame.
3) Using a scizzors, cut out a rectangular piece of 6 mil thick
   polyethylene plastic film. 4 mil is also available, but it's
   not as strong, so make sure that you are buying the 6 mil
   thickness.
4) Lay the film over the wood frame and center it evenly as much
   as possible.
5) Using a heavy-duty stapler, staple one side of the piece of
   film to the wood frame..
6) You'll need a helper for this. Hold the film taut in all
   directions, but not too tight that you stretch it.   Then
   staple the other three sides to the wood frame. Cut off the
   excess film.
7) Drill through the wood frame and locate the hole positions as
   in the above design.
8) Attach the foam weatherstripping to the back of the frame, and
   screw the frame to the wall.

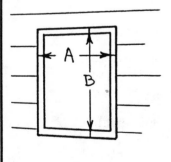

WINDOW OPENING

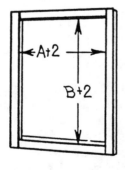

WOOD FRAME

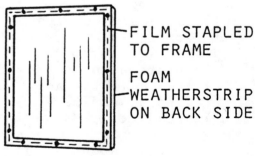

DRILL HOLES

FILM STAPLED
TO FRAME

FOAM
WEATHERSTRIP
ON BACK SIDE

DESIGN #3: See diagrams below.

1) Build a frame for the storm window using 1-1/8 x 2-1/2 inch clear dry pine. Size the frame to fit inside the exterior trim of the window opening. Use half lap joints at the corners for extra strength.

2) Attach one set of face strips (1/2 x 1/2 inch for single glazed or 1/4 x 12 inch for double glazed – see diagram) with nails and waterproof glue.

3) Cut the sheets of glass 1/4 inch smaller than the opening in the frame to provide for a 1/8 inch gap all around the glass.

4) For the double glazed strom window, use silicone sealer to stick the two panes of glass together with the 1/4 x 3/16 inch spacer strip in between them. The spacer strip should be recessed about 1/16 inch from the edge. Let this unit dry for a day.

5) Lay the window frame horizontally with the attached face strip down. Set the glass assembly in the frame against the face strip and position it to have an even 1/8 inch gap all around.

6) Fill the 1/8 inch gap with more silicone sealre, making sure that it fills the gap completely. Then attach the other face strip.

7) Prime and paint the frame with a good quality exterior paint.

8) Attach the appropriate brackets to mount the storm window in the window opening. Seal around the storm window frame with caulking cord. You can pull the caulking cord away each year when you want to open your windows.

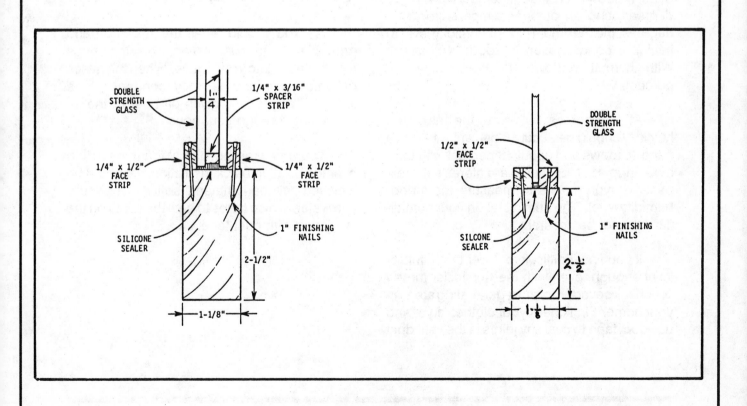

Q - I have a problem with my windows sweating during the coldest winter weather. It is annoying and is causing damage to the windows and walls. What can I do to stop the condensation?

A - Condensation is not only an annoying problem, but possibly a very expensive one. The minor surface damage you see may be only the tip of the iceberg. There may be progressive damage to the lumber and other supporting structure inside your walls and attic. Even if you don't notice condensation, excess indoor moisture may be penetrating your walls.

Condensation occurs when warm humid indoor air contacts a cold surface like a window or wall. Controlling the indoor humidity level is the least expensive method to reduce condensation. Installing replacement double pane thermal windows is another method.

You should lower the indoor humidity level as the outdoor temperature drops. With single pane windows, an indoor temperature of 70 degrees, and an outdoor temperature of 30 degrees, the maximum indoor humidity level to minimize condensation is about 30 percent. With thermal windows, the maximum is 60 percent.

At 10 degrees outdoors, the maximum humidity should be about 18 percent with single pane windows and about 43 percent with thermal windows. Most hardware stores sell inexpensive hygrometers to measure the indoor humidity level. The humidistat on your humidifier may not be accurate.

If you find it difficult to lower the humidity level enough, even with the humidifier turned off, check several moisture-generating areas in your home. First check your clothes dryer and use duct tape to seal any joints in the vent duct where moist air may leak out into your home.

Your kitchen is major moisture generator. When you cook or wash dishes, switch on the exhaust vent fan. If you can close a door to the kitchen, crack open a window just a little. This keeps heated room air from being drawn from the rest of your house when the fan is on.

After you finish showering in the bathroom, don't turn off the vent fan immediately. It takes a while for the moisture level to decrease. Let the fan run for about five minutes longer with the door closed.

Crawl spaces are a common source of moisture. Even though the ground seems dry, it still gives off a lot of moisture. Cover the ground with 4- or 6-mil polyethylene plastic film if your local building codes approve.

Q - We have a heat pump outdoors. There a thin layer of black foam insulation over the pipe leading into our house, but the insulation is torn in spots. How can I repair the insulation?

A - You should repair the insulation and probably add more insulation. The pipe brings the hot gases into your house. When the gases get into your furnace, they condense to a liquid. This process gives off heat to the air circulating through your house.

You can wrap additional foam insulation over the existing black insulation. It should be a closed-cell foam material so it won't adsorb rain water. It also helps to seal the joints on the insulation with duct tape.

Dear Reader,

Thank you for your interest in writing to me about condensation on windows and walls. Even if you don't see the condensation, it may be occurring inside your walls.

Briefly, condensation is caused by warm room air coming in contact with the cold glass or wall surface. As the warm air cools, it can't hold as much water vapor as it does when it is warm. Therefore, the water vapor condenses where the air is the coldest, on cold windows or uninsulated walls.

The following charts show the maximum indoor humidity level without condensation forming on your windows. As it gets colder outdoors, the glass surface also gets colder. Therefore, you must lower the indoor humidity level as it gets colder outdoors. With double pane thermal windows, the interior glass surface stay warmer than with single pane windows. That it why you can have a higher indoor humidity level without condensation.

The figures on these charts are approximate levels for good quality windows. It assumes insulating values of R-1 and R-2 for single and double pane windows respectively. Depending on the type of window frame material and condition of your windows, the actual allowable humidity level varies somewhat. There is a greater difference among double pane windows due to the effect of the width of air gap, low-e or standard glass, spacer material, etc.. Use the humidity levels in the charts as a starting point.

Sincerely,

Jim Dulley

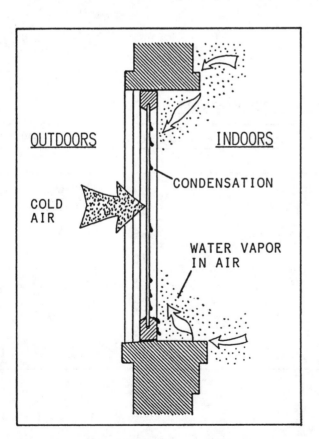

OUTDOORS   INDOORS

CONDENSATION

COLD
AIR

WATER VAPOR
IN AIR

MAXIMUM INDOOR HUMIDITY LEVELS TO CONTROL CONDENSATION

The following charts are based on an indoor temperature of 70°F and a wind speed of 15 miles-per-hour.

SINGLE PANE WINDOWS

OUTDOOR TEMPERATURE	MAXIMUM INDOOR HUMIDITY LEVEL
^{O}F	%
-30	3
-20	6
-10	8
0	13
10	20
20	26
30	32
40	44

DOUBLE PANE WINDOWS

OUTDOOR TEMPERATURE	MAXIMUM INDOOR HUMIDITY LEVEL
^{O}F	%
-30	27
-20	30
-10	35
0	40
10	46
20	52
30	59
40	68

ALTERNATE WINDOW CONDENSATION/HUMIDITY LEVEL CHART

You can use this chart to determine the indoor humidity level at indoor temperatures other than 70°. Select the indoor temperature on the horizontal scale on the chart on the right. Follow this vertically until it meets the outdoor temperature curve that you are concerned about.

Then follow that intersection point horizontally over the the chart on the left. Follow it until it intersects with the type of window curve (single, double, triple pane, etc.). Then follow that point down vertically to read the maximum allowable indoor humidity level without condensation. These are approximations, so use them as a starting point to control window condensation.

For example, if you have double pane windows, and indoor temperature of 60°, and an outdoor temperature of 10°, proceed as follows. Follow the 60° indoor temperature line up until it intersects the 10° outdoor temperature curve. Follow that horizontally to the left until it intersects the B-curve (double pane windows). Read the indoor humidity level below it - 54%.

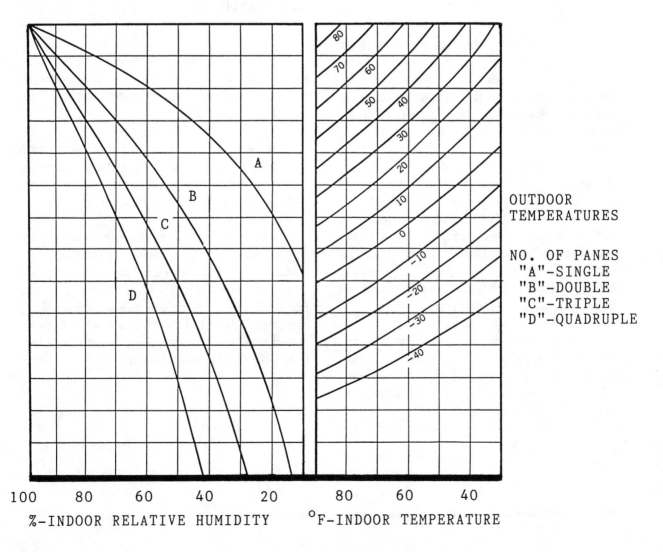

OUTDOOR
TEMPERATURES

NO. OF PANES
"A"-SINGLE
"B"-DOUBLE
"C"-TRIPLE
"D"-QUADRUPLE

100   80   60   40   20   80   60   40

%-INDOOR RELATIVE HUMIDITY   °F-INDOOR TEMPERATURE

Q - Are window coverings, like insulating shades and shutters very effective and worth the expense? I have priced some and they are fairly expensive to have installed.

A - Insulating window shades or shutters can be very effective and can save a lot of energy. In addition to cutting your utility bills, they can make you much more comfortable by blocking the radiant heat loss from your body to the cold window. Also, on extremely hot summer days, they can block much of the heat from entering your home.

Insulating shutters, mounted on the inside of your windows, offer the greatest energy savings, especially at night. Leave them open in the day to gain the sun's direct heat and reduce the need to switch on your electric lights.

These insulating shutters will add about R-7 insulation value to your present windows, now only about R-2, even for thermal windows. The cost of these shutters varies greatly depending upon the materials, decorative qualities, and insulation values.

With careful shopping and by installing the insulating shutters yourself, you can reduce the cost and get a good payback on your investment. The only tools you will generally need are a drill, screwdriver, stapler, and the instructions. When installing them, be careful to properly align them with the window frame. This minimizes the flow of heated room air against the cold window glass.

Insulating window shades provide about half of the energy savings of shutters, but they cost a lot less. They are usually more convenient to open and close, and more attractive. Many types are available, from simple roll-up quilts, to ones that operate like a rolltop desk.

Before you purchase any shutters or shades, be sure to check some actual installations in homes. Most dealers will show you several. Often, small scale sales samples can be misleading in appearance and operation.

If you are handy with a needle and thread, you can make a very effective and inexpensive insulating window shade yourself. To make this insulating Roman shade, just sew several layers of insulating material into an envelope of fabric to match your room's decor.

Attach eyelets for quilting and drawstrings to raise and lower it. Then screw it to wooden support pieces and mount it to the frame of your window. For added energy savings, you can mount side boards on hinges to hold it tightly against your wall when it's down to help block the cold air.

Q - We are about to select a new bathroom cabinet. Is there a difference in the electrical usage between fluorescent and incandescent bulbs? T. H.

A - A fluorescent light will use about one fourth as much electricity as a standard incandescent light bulb. In most areas of your home, fluorescent lights are the best choice.

However, in your bathroom, you may be better off with the standard incandescent light bulbs. Even though incandescent bulbs will cost more to operate, they are not on very long. For applying makeup, the quality of the light is important. Although there are special fluorescent lights made to approximate normal lights, they may not be adequate for you.

UTILITY BILLS UPDATE

Dear Reader,

Thank you for your interest in writing to me about how to make the insulating roman shade yourself. It has three layers - a layer of fiberfill, a layer of heavy inner-facing, and an envelope of fabric. This insulating shade can really cut the heat loss through your windows.

Sincerely,

Jim Dulley

MATERIALS LIST

Muslin, duck, kettlecloth
1/2" thick fiberfill
Heavy inner-facing
1/2" diameter plastic rings
crochet thread
nylon cord
1/4" & 1/2" screw eyes
1-1/2" size spring hinges
1 x 2 lumber
1/2 x 3/4 lumber
1-1/4 flat head
staple gun
2" size cleat

INSTRUCTIONS

Measure the height of window from the tip edges of window sill to the inner edge of upper casing. Measure width of window sill between inner edges of window casing.

Layout fabric and cut two rectangles whose dimensions are:
5-1/2 " wider than the width measurement
3-1/2 longer than the height measurement.

Pin fabric pieces together so that right sides face in. Leaving the top open, sew one side and bottom. On the other side, leave a 1-1/4" opening near the bottom edge for the weight stick. Turn the shade right side out and press.

SEE DIAGRAM #1

Sew seam 1-1/4" above bottom edge of shade. Cut the weight stick 2" less than width of shade so the weight stick will not rub against window casing. Insert the weight stick and sew the seam closed by hand.

SEE DIAGRAM #2

Place the heavy inner-facing and fiberfill on top of it.
Fold these layers in half lengthwise. You can also wrap this
with optional thin shiny mylar material to help to reflect the
radiant heat. Then stuff the materials into the shade. The
inner layers must fit tightly against the side and bottom seams.

Sew a 1/2" seam across the top edge of the shade cover and
trim away the excess fiberfill stuffing. Leave at least 1/4" of
material above seam to allow room for attaching the shade to the
mounting strip.

SEE DIAGRAM #3

Make marks on the back side of the shade for quilting. The
first row of vertical stitches should be 2" in from the bottom
edge. Allow 8" between stitches in the vertical rows. The
next rows of vertical stitches should be 2" in from the left side.
Mark as many rows as will fit, allowing 6" to 8" between rows.

With the front sie of the shade facing you, staple the top
to the mounting strip. Insert the screw eyes onto the top edge
of the strip. The screw eyes should line up with the vertical
rows of marks. Also, insert one 1/4" screw eye per vertical row
through the fabric into the weight stick at the bottom.

Thread two strands of crochet thread through a neddle. Quilt
where you marked the shade by pushing the needle from the back
of the shade. Leave a 2" tail of thread on back. Push the
needle back through and slip a plastic ring over needle. Secure
it by tying threads around the ring.

SEE DIAGRAM #4

Cut the nylon cords measuring twice the length plus the width of
the shade. Cut as many cords as there are vertical rows. Tie
each cord to the screw eye in the weight stick and thread the
cords up through the plastic rings. Each cord is threaded
through the screw eye at the top of the vertical row and through
all the screw eyes to the left.

SEE DIAGRAM #5

Cut two 1 x 2's each 4" shorter than the shade. Attach two
hinges to each side clamp - 3 to each if the side clamp is longer
than 60". Mount the side clamps to the window casing, so it
covers at least 1" of the shade when closed. Attach one
additional screw eye to the outside of the opened left side
clamp and thread all the cords through it. Attach the cleat
under the sill, and tie the cords to it when the shade is open.

With the back side of the shade facing you, turn the shade
upside down - mounting strip toward the floor and weight stick
up. Place the raw stapled edge of the shade to the window casing
and attach with screws. Adjust the shade so the edges are placed
evenly over the side window casing and so the bottom edge of the
shade extends 1" below top edge of sill.

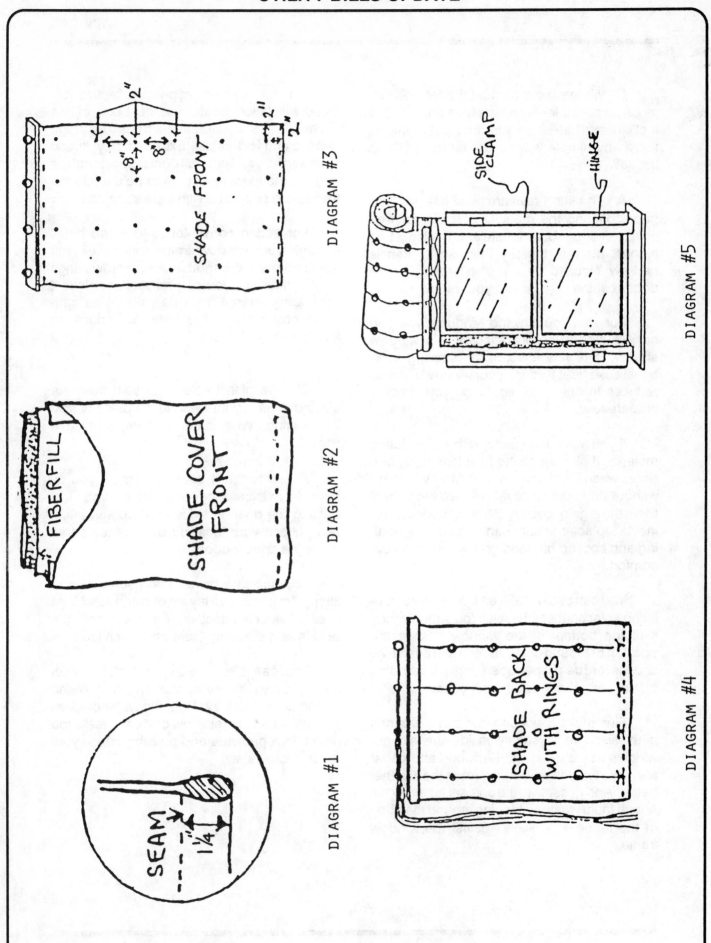

DIAGRAM #3

SHADE FRONT

2"

2"

2"

8" 8"

DIAGRAM #2

FIBERFILL

SHADE COVER FRONT

DIAGRAM #5

SIDE CLAMP

HINGE

DIAGRAM #1

SEAM

1¼"

DIAGRAM #4

SHADE BACK WITH RINGS

Q - We leave our window shades open as much as possible to get heat from the sun, but it still doesn't shine very far into our room. Is there any simple way to get more sunshine inside?

A - The sun's rays are most intense near noon, offering the greatest potential for free solar heating. Unfortunately, it is also at its highest point in the sky then, so it often is partially blocked by a roof overhang and it doesn't shine very far into your room.

For your south-facing windows, you can easily build and install a reflective solar window shutter. It is very effective for directing additional solar heat through your windows. It also reduces the need for lights, so your electric bills are less.

If you make the shutter with an insulating material, it also stops the heat loss back outdoors when it is closed at night. Most windows, without any special covering, lose more heat than they gain over a 24-hour period. An insulating solar shutter can reduce your heating and cooling bills and greatly improve your comfort.

You can easily make an inexpensive insulating solar shutter yourself. You should hinge it at the bottom of the window. Since the position of the sun changes, you can adjust the shutter for the proper open angle depending on the time of day and month of year.

First make a wooden frame of 1 X 2-inch pine, sized to fit snugly inside the exterior window frame opening. Redwood and cedar are more expensive, but they resist the weather better. Add gussets to the corners for strength. Attach foam weatherstripping around the edge of the frame so it seals against the window frame.

You can use any type of reflective foil-faced insulation board for the body of the shutter. Polyisocyanurate foam has a very high R-value and is durable. Extruded polystyrene is also effective. Apply foil duct tape around the edge of the foam insulation to hold it into the frame, and support it with pipe strapping.

For added convenience, drill two holes through your window frame, opposite each upper corner of the shutter. Attach drawstrings to the shutter so you can adjust it, or close it completely at night, from the inside. Use tight-fitting grommets in the holes to reduce air leakage through them.

Q - We plan to duct the vent from our electric dryer indoors with just a piece of flexible ducting. What is the best way to make a filter?

A - Although it saves energy, if you already have excess indoor moisture problems, ducting the dryer indoors may worsen them. Also, check your local building codes about venting a dryer indoors.

You definitely have to add some type of filter. Stretching two layers of nylon stockings over the duct is effective. Clean out both the built-in and stocking filters after each load.

You can also run the end of the duct straight down into a very shallow pan of water. As the air bubbles through, the water catches the lint. It must be shallow or it can create too much back pressure and possibly cause your dryer to overheat.

Dear Reader,

　　Thank you for your interest in writing to me about how to make reflective insulating shutters for your windows. They are easy to make and can increase the solar gain into your windows and reduce the heat loss back outside at night.

　　When making this shutter, it is important that it fits tightly inside and against the sides of the window frame to reduce air leakage when it is closed. Select straight lumber and measure carefully. If you want the shutter to cover the entire window, make it several inches larger than the window opening so it rests against the wall surface when it is closed.

Sincerely,

Jim

Jim Dulley

MATERIALS REQUIRED

1" x 2" lumber
3/4" wood screws
1 pair of chrome plated or galvanized hinges
Pipe strapping
2" wide shiny foil or duct tape
1/2" plywood
1" thick foil-faced rigid insulation board
Waterproof glue
Staples
Heavy string
Closed-cell adhesive-backed foam weatherstripping
Spring-loaded cleats from a marine shop

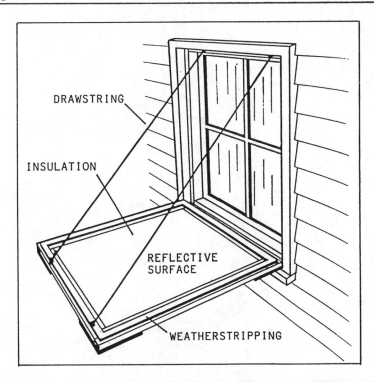

DRAWSTRING

INSULATION

REFLECTIVE SURFACE

WEATHERSTRIPPING

DO-IT-YOURSELF INSTRUCTIONS

A) Saw the 1" x 2" lumber to make the frame for the shutter. Make them the proper length and height to fit snugly in the window opening.

B) Notch the ends of the pieces of lumber for lap joints when you assemble the frame. This gives strong and smooth corner joints.

C) Assemble the frame using wood screws and waterproof glue. Measure across the diagonals of the frame to make sure that it is square before you drill the holes for the screws. Then clamp the frame assembly and allow it to dry.

D) You can add stiffness to the frame by making triangular gussets for the four corners of the frame assembly. The gussets will also support the reflective foam insulation board. Make them 4" to 5" long on the sides. Drill holes and use glue and screws to secure them to the frame assembly.

E) Paint the frame assembly with good-quality wall paint to match your house. Make sure to get good coverage over all the joints since this will be exposed to the worse winter weather.

F) After the frame has dried, you can cut the reflective foam insulation to fit it. Lay the frame flat with the gussets against the table. Carefully measure the inside dimensions of the frame. You can usually cut the foam insulation with a sharp knife. Cut slowly and carefully.

G) Lay the piece of insulation into the frame against the gussets. The reflective side of the insulation should be facing upward.

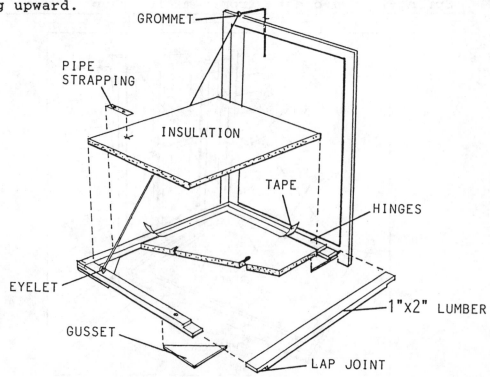

H) Using the foil duct tape, lay a strip overlapping the foil and the frame. This will seal the edge of the foam insulation and help to hold it in place. Use the tape on both sides of the frame and insulation joint. You can use staples to better secure the tape to the frame and insulation.

I) Cut 2" lengths of the pipe strapping. These will be used to help hold the insulation into the frame. Cut enough to space them about every 2-1/2 ft. around the frame. Mount them so they extend about 1-1/4" out over the insulation.

J) Stick the adhesive-backed foam weatherstripping around the edge of the frame where it will lay against the window frame. That will produce a good seal when it is closed.

K) Have a helper hold the assembled shutter up against the window where it will be mounted. Mark the locations for the hinges to be attached to the shutter frame and the window frame. It should be hinged at the bottom.

L) If you want the operate the shutter from outdoors (this is easiest method), attach the boat cleats to the wall above the window.

M) Attach small eyelet to the top of the shutter frame and tie the strings to them. Run the other end of the strings through the cleats above them. You can then adjust the angle that the shutter is opened for the maximum heat gain or close it tightly at night.

N) If you plan to operate the shutter from indoors, then you will have to drill two hole through the window frame opposite the eyelets on the top of the shutter frame. Drill the holes big enough to install plastic grommets for the string to slide through. That will reduce wear on the string and reduce air leakage through the holes.

O) Feed the strings through the grommets into your house. The strings should be about three times the height of the shutter. Tie the indoor ends of the strings to a 1" dowel and glue them so they won't slide around the dowel. You will roll the string up on the dowel to control the position of the shutter on the outside. Hammer a small nail partially into the center of the dowel.

O) Using the pipe strapping, make an upside-down J-hook to mount under your window sill inside your house. That will hold the dowel. You wind up the strings on the dowel to position the shutter and then hook the nail in the dowel under the pipe strapping J-hook to hold that position.

Q - I used my wood burning fireplace (open hearth) several times last winter. I wondered if I should have the chimney cleaned or can I easily clean it myself?

A - Spring is the best time to have your chimney cleaned. Chimney sweeps are less busy now. If any problems with the chimney are discovered, you will have ample time to have it repaired. Also, buying your firewood now gives it time to "season" before next fall.

Although typical open hearth fireplaces usually burn hot enough to minimize creosote buildup, it can accumulate. Creosote is a combustible product of incomplete combustion of wood. Unburnt wood gases coat the chimney wall and gradually build up to form a hard black coating.

When the creosote ignites inside your chimney, it can burn slowly, often without your even noticing it. If your chimney is in need of repair, the fire can eventually burn through to your house wall. Many lives are lost each year due to chimney fires.

The best way to minimize creosote buildup is burning good hot fires and not using high-creosote forming types of firewood. Generally, the softer, higher-moisture content types of firewood tend to form more creosote.

If you haven't had your chimney checked for years, it is best to hire a qualified chimney sweep. It usually costs about $50 and it is $50 well spent. The chimney sweep can also inspect your chimney after the cleaning for any needed repairs.

After that initial inspection, you can clean it yourself. One excellent cleaning method is a two-person brush. This special brush has a long rope tied to each end. With one person on the roof and one at the hearth, pull the brush up and down through the chimney.

For one-person operation, you can tie a heavy weight to the bottom of the brush. From up on the roof, drop the weight and brush down the chimney and work it up and down. You can also buy brushes with handle extensions that you can slowly work up the chimney from the hearth.

There are also other "homemade" methods such as hanging chains down the chimney and banging them around. Another method is pulling a small tree up and down through the chimney. If you are going to clean it yourself, stick with the wire chimney brush.

Q - Our house was drafty during the colder winter weather even when it wasn't windy outdoors. Now in the milder weather, I don't seem to notice it. What causes that winter draft?

A - Just the larger temperature difference between indoors and outdoors draws air in during the winter. Since warm indoor air is less dense, it rises and leaks out through cracks in the ceilings and walls. This draws in denser cold outdoor air causing a draft.

In the milder weather, doors are opened more and the house is less stuffy. Therefore, people tend not to run kitchen and bathroom exhaust fans as much. Also, any outdoor air that does leak in, especially along the floor, is not as cold, so you don't notice it as much.

Dear Reader,

Thank you for your interest in writing to about how to clean your chimney. It is very important to keep your chimney clean for efficient operation of your fireplace and for safety. Creosote in your chimney can cause a chimney fire and risk the safety of your family.

The following are a list of low-creosote forming firewoods - APPLE, ASH, BEECH, BIRCH (WHITE), CHERRY, DOGWOOD, ELM, EUCALYPUS, HICKORY, LOCUST (BLACK), LIVE OAK, AND PERSIMMON. Generally, harder woods tend to burn cleaner. Although soft woods have a slightly higher heat content, they are also more resinous. These unburnt resins contribute to much of the creosote buildup.

It is also very important to use only well-seasoned firewood. Some green wood can be up to 50% moisture by weight. This moisture cools the fire and contributes to creosote formation. Even the low creosote forming woods create creosote if they are burned when green.

The two diagrams below show the commonly accepted methods to build a fire. These provide for easy starting and a hot clean burn. The one on the left is called the English method and the one on the right is called the Teepee method.

Sincerely,

Jim Dulley

INSPECTING YOUR CHIMNEY

First you should inspect your chimney to see if it needs cleaning. From the hearth inside your house, look up into your chimney using a flashlight. Gently scrap around the opening and the damper. If you find a lot of soot and creosote here, you can be pretty certain that there is creosote buildup further up in the chimney. Creosote will look and feel like a black peanut brittle material.

If you don't find creosote or soot, go up on your roof and check from the top of your chimney. ALWAYS WEAR HIGH-FRICTION SOFT-SOLED SHOES AND HOOK YOURSELF TO THE CHIMNEY OR ROOF WITH AN APPROVED SAFETY LINE. Shine a flashlight into the chimney from the top. If you don't find any creosote there either, your chimney is probably clean.

Even if it is clean, it is still a good idea to slowly lower a burlap bag filled with rocks or chains and tied to a rope into the chimney. This will dislodge and bird or squirrel nests. First, cover the heath opening of your fireplace with a sheet of plywood or heavy plastic film to keep any dirt from coming out into your room.

Then build a small fire in the fireplace and hold a few wet rags over the top of the chimney to block the smoke. Look for any spots where the smoke is escaping through leaky spots in the chimney. Check for leaks quickly and then remove the rags or your house will fill with smoke.

CLEANING YOUR CHIMNEY

The two general methods to clean a chimney yourself are using a special wire chimney cleaning brush or tire chains. The chains are either hanging loose or in a burlap bag. There is less chance of damage to the lining of the chimney if the chains are in a bag.

BRUSH CLEANING

Using a special wire chimney brush from the top of the chimney is one of the best methods to clean your chimney. On the following page, I have shown diagrams of several types of chimney brushes and a sketch of how to make a simple adjustable chimney brush to clean in the corners of a rectangular chimney. You can find chimney brushes at most fireplace stores.

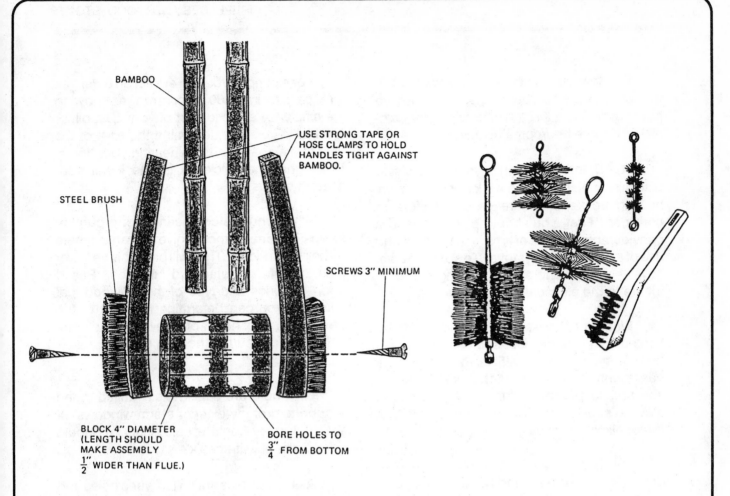

BAMBOO

USE STRONG TAPE OR HOSE CLAMPS TO HOLD HANDLES TIGHT AGAINST BAMBOO.

STEEL BRUSH

SCREWS 3″ MINIMUM

BLOCK 4″ DIAMETER (LENGTH SHOULD MAKE ASSEMBLY $\frac{1}{2}$″ WIDER THAN FLUE.)

BORE HOLES TO $\frac{3}{4}$″ FROM BOTTOM

A two-person operation is most effective with one person at top and bottom to work the brush up and down. When doing this, cover a large area of the floor around the fireplace opening. The dust and soot carry a long way. Rotate the brush a partial turn each time you drag it up and down.

For a one-person operation, hang a 20-pound weight on the end of the brush and work it up and down from the top of the chimney. With this method, you can cover the opening of the fireplace to block the dirt from getting into your room.

TIRE CHAIN CLEANING

This method is fairly similar to using a brush except that you rotate the chains around as you lower them into the chimney. Usually the weight of the chains is enough to make them drop. You should drop them a couple of inches and abruptly stop them so they bounce around a little. This breaks the creosote loose from the chimney lining. Putting the chains in a coarse burlap bag protects the chimney lining better, but you will have to work longer to break the creosote loose.

FINAL INSPECTION

When creosote stops falling out of the chimney, inspect it with a flashlight again. If the light shines almost to the bottom of the chimney, it is probably clean. If it is still dirty, the soot and creosote will absorb the light several feet down into the chimney. Therefore, run the brush or chains through it several more times and check it again.

Q - How can I determine if it is worthwhile to switch to a wood burning stove to help to heat our house? It is a typical two-story colonial with three bedrooms upstairs.

A - Before you begin your analysis to determine if burning wood will lower your annual heating costs, there are several factors to consider. First, you should plan to spend a considerable amount of time with the care and use of a wood burning stove. To some people, however, these chores are relaxing and contribute to the pleasure of wood burning.

Since your house was not designed to be heated with a single heat source, like a wood burning stove, it will be difficult to distribute the heat evenly throughout your house. Therefore, you should probably plan to use the wood stove to supplement your present furnace, not totally eliminate its use.

The best way to use wood to heat an entire home is with a wood burning furnace. It is usually located near your current furnace and is connected to the same hot air duct system. When your wood furnace can not supply enough heat, your regular furnace kicks on.

It is a somewhat involved process to calculate whether or not heating with wood is less expensive than using your existing heating system. You must determine the current cost of the heat from your furnace, and then compare that to the cost of the heat from the wood burning stove.

Since your furnace is not totally energy efficient, some of the energy you buy from the utility company is lost up the flue. Your furnace contractor should be able to estimate the efficiency of your furnace.

For example, you can expect an older gas furnace to be in the 60 percent range. Knowing the efficiency and the cost of your gas, oil, or electricity, you can determine the cost of the heat that actually ends up heating your home. The higher the efficiency is, the lower your heating cost is.

When you are comparing wood burning stoves, the dealer should give you an estimate of their efficiencies. They will probably be lower than that of most standard furnaces. Based upon the price and type of the firewood that you buy, you can determine the cost of the same amount of heat from firewood and compare it to your current heating costs.

Q - There are small holes drilled in the very bottom of my exterior storm windows. It seems like they would let cold air get in. Should I seal them off with caulk?

A - Those holes are called weep holes and they are necessary. You can't totally stop water vapor from getting in between the storm and your primary window. It passes through tiny cracks and straight through the interior wall surface materials.

When it's very cold outside, this water vapor condenses in the windows and these holes let it escape. Since the holes are small and at the bottom, very little air leaks in through them. Colder air naturally settles to the bottom anyway. With no entrance holes at the top, there won't be any convective air currents set up.

Dear Reader,

Thank you for your interest in writing to me about how to evaluate if wood heat is right for your home. The following worksheet analyzes the economics of burning wood as compared to using a conventional furnace, but there are also other factors to consider. It is a lot of work to heat your home with firewood and it is a fairly dirty form of heat.

When you have a wood burning stove installed, be sure that you have been very careful about the fire safety and adequate clearances. If your area has building and heating systems codes and inspections, definitely pay the small fee and have it inspected. Wood burning stoves are one of the primary causes of house fires.

Use the charts on the following pages to determine the efficiency of your current heating system, and the cost of your current heat. I have also the included the following chart to show you the relative heat contents of various types of firewood.

Sincerely,

Jim

Jim Dulley

Heat Value Per Cord
(In BTU Per Cord)[1]

High	Medium	Low
24–31	20–24	16–20
Live oak	Holly	Black spruce
Shagbark hickory	Pond pine	Hemlock
Black locust	Nut pine	Catalpa
Dogwood	Loblolly pine	Red sider
Slash pine	Tamarack	Tulip poplar
Hop hornbean	Shortleaf pine	Red fir
Persimmon	Western larch	Sitka spruce
Shadbush	Juniper	Black willow
Apple	Paper birch	Large-tooth aspen
White oak	Red maple	Butternut
Honey locust	Cherry	Ponderosa pine
Black birch	American elm	Noble fir
Yew	Black gum	Redwood
Blue beech	Sycamore	Quaking aspen
Red oak	Gray birch	Sugar pine
Rock elm	Douglas fir	White pine
Sugar maple	Pitch pine	Balsam fir
American beech	Sassafras	Cottonwood
Yellow birch	Magnolia	Basswood
Longleaf pine	Red cedar	Western red cedar
White ash	Norway pine	Balsam poplar
Oregon ash	Bald cypress	White spruce
Black walnut	Chestnut	

1) Assume 80 cubic feet of solid wood per cord and 8600 BTU/lb. of oven dry wood.

WOOD HEAT EVALUATION WORKSHEET

1) Heating fuel you now use _____

2) Fuel unit _____

3) Number of Btu's per fuel unit - Chart A _____

4) Number of fuel units you used last year _____

5) Money that you spent for this fuel _____

6) Potential Btu's in the fuel you used (#3 x #4) _____

7) Efficiency of your heating system - Chart B _____

8) Btu's you actually received (#6 x #7) _____

9) Percentage of the heat load you want from wood _____

10) Convert to percentage (#9 ÷ 100) _____

11) Type of wood you will burn _____

12) Cost of one cord of wood _____

13) Potential heat content in cord of wood - Chart A _____

14) Number of cords containing enough heat
    to heat for your home (#8 ÷ #13) _____

15) Number of cords to supply the heat
    you need (#14 x #10) _____

16) Type of wood burning device you install _____

17) Efficiency rating of device - Chart B _____

18) Number of cords you will need to buy (#15 ÷ #17) _____

19) Money you will spend on wood (#18 x #12) _____

20) Proportional cost of heat (#5 x #10) _____

21) Annual savings from burning wood (#20 - #19) _____

UTILITY BILLS UPDATE

CHART A – HEAT CONTENT PER FUEL UNIT

FUEL	UNIT	BTU/UNIT
Oil	gallon	138,700
Kerosene	gallon	138,500
Natural Gas	therm	100,000
"	cu. ft.	1,025
Electricity	kwh	3,414
Hardwood	cord	19,000,000
Mixed Woods	cord	17,000,000
Soft Woods	cord	15,000,000
Propane	cu. ft.	2,500
"	gallon	91,000
"	pound	21,500
Coal	ton	27,000,000

CHART B – HEATING SYSTEMS EFFICIENCY RATINGS

FUEL	HEATING DEVICE	EFFICIENCY
Oil or Kerosene	New high efficiency	.85
	Recently tuned with flue damper	.7
	Without flue damper	.6
	Average untuned	.5
Electricity	Resistance type	.95
	Heat pump	1.75
Natural gas or Propane	New high efficiency	.92
	Good condition with stack damper	.8
	Average condition	.7
	Untuned	.6
Coal	New high efficiency	.7
	Good with flue damper	.6
	Without flue damper	.55
Wood	High efficiency wood stove or furnace	.74
	Standard wood stove	.5

Q - Sometimes when we use our wood burning fireplace to help heat the living room, it does not draw well and smoke comes out into the room. How can we make it draw better?

A - A common cause of poor draw in a fireplace is improper design. Sometimes if the opening height is too large, just adding a narrow metal trim strip across the top of the opening can dramatically improve the draw. If a fireplace has good draw, it will not dump smoke into your room.

There are many design dimensions that should be considered for a fireplace and the proper relationship among them is important. Most critical is the relationship between the opening width, height, and depth.

A rule of thumb is that the opening height should be between 2/3 and 3/4 of the width and the depth should be 1/2 to 2/3 of the height. You should follow FHA or your local code requirements for the size of the flue.

The height and position of your chimney relative to your roof and trees can effect the draw. A strong wind blowing in a particular direction may create a downward draft into your chimney. You can get chimney caps and wind deflectors to minimize the effect of the wind.

You should have your chimney checked and cleaned. Open fireplaces generally burn hot enough to minimize creosote buildup, but a bird or other animal's nest in the chimney may be obstructing the flow.

If you have an airtight house, the smoke may be caused by an inadequate supply of air. Try opening a window in your living room and see if that helps. Also try to determine if it smokes more when the clothes dryer or kitchen or bathroom exhaust fans are running.

The best method to provide combustion air and to increase the overall energy efficiency of your fireplace is to provide outdoor combustion air. Without it, your fireplace draws heated air out of the rest of your house. The room with the fireplace stays warm, but the other rooms get chilly.

You can run a duct from outdoors under the floor to the fireplace. You should put a damper baffle in it or have a tight-fitting cover so you can close it off when there is no fire. If your house is built on a slab, just crack a window open a little in that room and close doors leading to other rooms. This reduces warm room air loss.

Q - Our home is designed with the furnace ducts running through the crawl space. We have insulated the sides of the foundation wall. Should we insulate the floor above the crawl space too?

A - The additional energy savings from insulating your floor above the crawl space probably won't give a good payback. If the entire foundation wall is insulated, the uninsulated ground surface should not absorb a significant amount of heat.

Even though your crawl space is insulated, it would be a good idea to insulate any hot water pipes running through it. You also should have caulked around the sill perimeter where the walls rest on the top of the foundation. This is a common source of outdoor air leaking into your home.

Dear Reader,

    Thank you for your interest in writing to me about fireplaces. The following charts and diagrams show the proper design dimensions for a fireplace. The proper relationship among these dimension is important to make the fireplace draw well. Also, check with your local building and fire inspectors for any special requirements that they might have.

Sincerely,

Jim

Jim Dulley

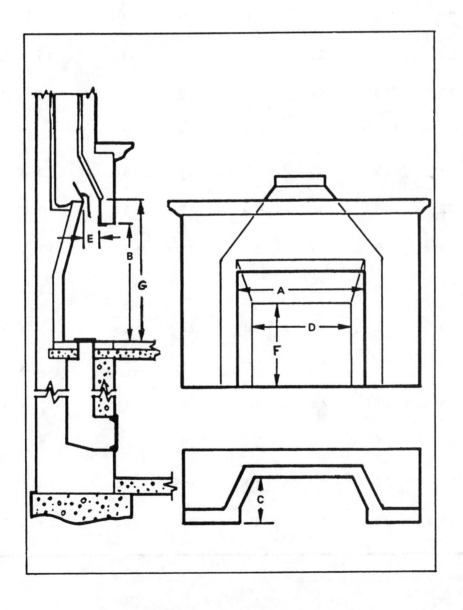

PROPER RELATIONSHIP OF DIMENSIONS FOR A FIREPLACE
(INCHES)

A	B	C	D	E	F	G	FLUE
24	28	16	16	9	14	32	8.5 X 8.5
26	28	16	18	9	14	32	8.5 X 8.5
28	28	16	20	9	14	33	8.5 X 13
30	30	17	22	9	15	33	8.5 X 13
32	30	17	24	9	15	34	8.5 X 13
34	30	17	26	9	15	35	8.5 X 13
36	31	18	27	9	16	36	13 X 13
38	31	18	29	9	16	36	13 X 13
40	31	18	31	9	16	36	13 X 13
42	31	19	33	9	16	36	13 X 13
44	32	19	35	10	17	37	13 X 13
46	32	19	37	10	17	38	13 X 13
48	33	20	38	10	17	38	13 X 18
50	34	21	40	10	18	39	13 X 18
52	34	20	42	10	18	39	13 X 18
54	35	21	44	10	18	40	13 X 18
56	36	21	46	10	19	41	18 X 18
58	36	22	47	10	19	41	18 X 18
60	36	22	49	10	20	41	18 X 18

TIPS FOR USING YOUR FIREPLACE EFFICIENTLY

1) If possible, duct outdoor combustion air to the fireplace and close doors leading to other rooms of your house.

2) If you can't duct in combustion air, crack open a window a little in that room and close doors.

3) Use a fireplace screen with glass doors. The glass doors will reduce the amount of heated room air that is drawn up the chimney.

4) When installing the screen, try to make as tight a fit as possible to the front of the fireplace so the air loss is minimized.

5) When burning a fire, close the vent openings through the glass doors somewhat, but not completely. The fire needs adequate combustion air to burn properly and cleanly.

6) Don't build too large a fire. This wastes additional heated room air. Just build one big enough to be aesthetically pleasing and provide some heat. An open hearth fireplace contributes very little net heat to your house.

7) Stir up the coals before going to bed at night. Try to make sure that the fire is totally out. Close the vents in the fireplace screen completely. In the morning, also close the flue damper.

8) While the fire is burning, periodically stir up the coals so the red hot ones are exposed through the ashes. This will radiate more heat into your room.

9) Clean out your fireplace after each fire. With less ash in the fireplace, more of the red hot coals will be exposed. Use a metal ash bucket that has the bottom raised from the floor. Even though the ash seems to be out, there many still be some hot coals mixed in.

10) Set your furnace (not a heat pump) thermostat a little lower while you are burning the fire. This keeps the furnace from kicking on as often as heated room air is being drawn up the flue. You can set the thermostat back up after your close off the fireplace screen vents.

Q - I want to plant some trees in my yard to improve the appearance, but I don't want to locate them improperly for energy-efficiency. Where should I locate them and will it effect my utility bills much?

A - Proper selection and location of trees can have a significant impact on both the heating and cooling costs for your home. For example, in the summer, one large tree can provide the cooling equivalent of several 10,000-Btu air conditioners. In the winter, they help block the wind.

Try to select fast growing trees, suitable to your climate and soil conditions. The height and shape at maturity and the density of the foliage are also important considerations for cutting your utility bills.

When locating your trees, the primary concerns are access to the sun and the blocking of the wind during the winter, and blocking the sun and access to the breezes in the summer. For the greatest windbreak effect in the winter, locate them close to your house.

Evergreen-types of trees are a good choice for the north and northwestern sides of your house. Those are the directions of the prevailing cold winter winds. In the winter, with the sun always in the south, the evergreens won't block the warming rays.

Deciduous trees, ones that lose their leaves in the winter, are best for other locations. They block the sun in the summer, yet let it shine through in the winter. In the summer, the evaporation of water from the leaves can lower the air temperature around them by ten degrees.

For morning shading, place a tree due east. A 30-foot tree about 15 feet from your house is usually best. If you don't have that much space, a smaller tree located closer to your house will work.

Since the sun is higher in the sky by late morning, locate a taller tree, about 35 to 40 feet high, no more than 20 feet to the southwest of your house. An adequate roof overhang is most effective to the direct south.

Trees planted directly to the south generally don't help much. In the summer, the noontime sun shines over them and they may block the prevailing southern breezes. Also, in the winter, even though they drop their leaves, the trunk and branches can block up to 60 percent of the sun's heat.

Three trees to the west are effective. Locate two of them opposite the ones on the east. A third fuller and shorter tree, located slightly north of west, can block the very late afternoon summer sun.

Q - I have heard that you should close off heating and cooling registers in unused rooms to save energy. Will that reduce the efficiency of my furnace or air conditioner by reducing the air flow through it?

A - It's true that a heat exchanger and air-conditioning evaporator coils in your furnace need a certain amount of air flow for maximum design efficiency. However, unless you close off the majority of your registers, the total air flow will not change significantly.

You may realize slightly increased noise from the open registers caused by more air being pushed through the fewer open registers. If your ductwork is properly-sized, you probably won't notice that small sound difference.

Dear Reader,

    Thank you for your interest in writing to me about trees to landscape your house. The map below shows the hardiness zones for trees. A tree should survive the winters in the zones of the number listed by it and zones of higher numbers.

Sincerely,

Jim Dulley

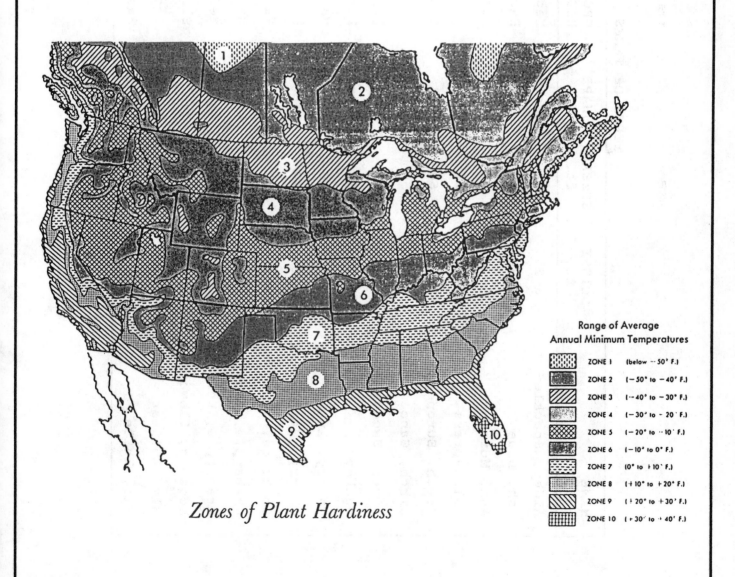

Zones of Plant Hardiness

**Range of Average
Annual Minimum Temperatures**

	ZONE 1	(below -50° F.)
	ZONE 2	(-50° to -40° F.)
	ZONE 3	(-40° to -30° F.)
	ZONE 4	(-30° to -20° F.)
	ZONE 5	(-20° to -10° F.)
	ZONE 6	(-10° to 0° F.)
	ZONE 7	(0° to +10° F.)
	ZONE 8	(+10° to +20° F.)
	ZONE 9	(+20° to +30° F.)
	ZONE 10	(+30° to +40° F.)

TYPES OF TREES

NAME	HEIGHT ft.	SPREAD ft.	SHAPE	GROWTH RATE	DENSITY	SOIL	ZONE
Alder, Speckled	8-25	12	Ascend	Medium	Medium	Moist	3
Ash, Blue	70-80	60	Round	Fast	Heavy	Any	2
Ash, Moraine	35-40	20	Narrow	Fast	Medium	Moist	5
Baldcypress	50-80	25	Round	Medium	Light	Moist	4
Beech, European	60-80	60	Oval	Slow	Heavy	Light	4
Birch, Canoe	60-70	30	Narrow	Medium	Medium	Moist	2
Birch, Sweet	40-55	45	Round	Medium	Medium	Any	3
Buckeye	18-20	15	Round	Fast	Light	Rich	4
Cherry, Autumn	25-30	20	Round	Medium	Dense	Any	5
Cherry, Sargent	40-50	40	Round	Fast	Medium	Any	4
Corktree, Amur	30-45	30	Round	Fast	Medium	Dry	3
Crabapple, Carmine	30-45	30	Round	Medium	Dense	Any	4
Crabapple, Red Jade	20-25	25	Round	Medium	Medium	Any	4
Dogwood, Flowering	20-25	15	Oval	Slow	Medium	Rich	4
Elm, Chinese	40-50	30	Round	Fast	Medium	Any	5
Fir, White	40-50	30	Pyramd	Fast	Medium	Any	3

TYPE OF TREE

NAME	HEIGHT ft.	SPREAD ft.	SHAPE	GROWTH RATE	DENSITY	SOIL	ZONE
Goldraintree	30-35	20	Round	Fast	Medium	Any	5
Hawthorn, Lavalle	20-30	20	Round	Fast	Dense	Any	4
Hemlock, Canadian	50-70	30	Pyramd	Medium	Dense	Moist	3
Katsura Tree	30-40	30	Round	Fast	Medium	Moist	4
Linden, American	60-80	55	Oval	Medium	Dense	Loose	2
Magnolia, Sweetbay	10-20	15	Flat	Slow	Open	Moist	5
Maple, Norway	50-60	40	Oval	Medium	Dense	Moist	3
Oak, Pin	40-70	45	Pyramd	Fast	Medium	Moist	4
Pine, Austrian	50-60	35	Pyramd	Fast	Dense	Any	4
Pine, Eastern White	50-80	55	Pyramd	Medium	Medium	Moist	3
Redbud	20-25	12	Round	Medium	Dense	Moist	4
Silverbell	30-35	20	Narrow	Medium	Medium	Loose	5
Spruce, Blue	80-95	25	Pyramd	Slow	Dense	Moist	3
Sweetgum	60-70	40	Pyramd	Medium	Dense	Moist	5
Yellowwood	35-50	40	Oval	Medium	Dense	Moist	3
Zelkova, Japanese	50-80	60	Vase	Fast	Dense	Moist	5

Q - I am planning to do some landscaping with shrubs close to my house. Are there any things that I should consider from an energy-saving standpoint before I begin?

A - Landscaping with shrubs near your house can have a significant impact on your utility bills throughout the year. Also, a properly-landscaped lot can increase the resale value of your house.

Planting special "dwarf" shrubs near your house increases the energy efficiency of your house in several ways. First, the shrubs tend to block the force of the wind. Since the sill, where the walls rest on the foundation, is a major air leakage source, the low shrubs form a very effective windbreak. This yields both winter and summer savings.

If you live in a cold climate with much snowfall, the snow can build up against the shrubs. This provides an even more effective windbreak and the shrubs and snow create an insulating barrier to the cold.

In the summer, much heat is reflected and radiated from sidewalks and patios in through your windows and walls. A leafy barrier from a shrub can block much of this reflected radiant heat from reaching your house. The leaves from the shrubs, from evaporation of moisture, also cool the air near your house.

Try to select shrubs which retain their foliage throughout the year or have a fairly dense branch structure. This provides for better protection from cold winter conditions. For example, boxwoods stay green and you can prune the branches for an effective and attractive size and shape.

Dwarf shrubs are especially good for under windows because they don't grow tall at maturity. If they stay under about three feet in height, they generally won't block the sun in the winter. In the summer, with the sun higher in the sky, even taller shrubs would not offer much sun control.

Before you plant your shrubs, make sure the ground slopes away from your foundation to avoid water leakage problems. Also plant them far enough from the wall so the foliage does not contact it. If the wall retains too much moisture, the insulation can become less efficient and structural damage can occur.

Q - After this winter, I am considering getting exterior storm windows for my house. What is the difference between double and triple track storm windows and which type is best?

A - From an energy efficiency standpoint, they are the same. The only difference is in the convenience of moving the screen.

With double track storm windows, there is an upper and a lower storm sash, one in each track. The screen is in the other half of one of the tracks. When summer comes, you must remove the lower glass storm window sash from the track and slide the screen down in the track to cover the opening.

With triple track storms, each storm window sash and screen has its own track. When summer arrives, you just slip the lower storm sash up and the screen down without having to remove either. If you are trying to gain some solar heat in the winter, you should take the screen section out.

Dear Reader,

    Thank you for your interest in writing to me about dwarf shrubs to landscaping your yard. Planting small shrubs near your house will help reduce your utility bills and improve the appearance of your home. After reviewing this list of shrubs, contact a local nursery to determine which shrubs are suitable for your climate. I have used the botanical name because the common names vary from area to area.

    The height and width at maturity are shown in inches in the chart below. The reference number by each name is indicated on the diagrams of the leaves and blooms.

Sincerely,

Jim Dulley

DWARF SHRUBS

NAME	HEIGHT in.	WIDTH in.	GROWTH RATE
DECIDUOUS			
1) BERBERIS THUNBERGLI	30	48	SLOW
2) CHAENOMELES JAPONICA	42	48	FAST
3) COMPTONIA PEREGRINA	48	72	MEDIUM
4) CORNUS STOLONIFERA	24	24	MEDIUM
5) COTONEASTER HORIZONTALIS	30	78	MEDIUM
6) DAPHNE BURKWOODII	48	72	SLOW
7) DAPHNE CNEORUM	12	36	SLOW
8) DAPHNE GIRALDII	30	48	SLOW
9) FORSYTHIA VIRIDISSIMA	24	36	SLOW
10) FOTHERGILLA GARDENII	36	42	SLOW
11) GENISTA TINCTORIA	36	36	MEDIUM
12) HYDRANGEA ARBORESCENS	42	48	FAST
13) HYPERICUM FRONDOSUM	24	48	MEDIUM

UTILITY BILLS UPDATE

NAME	HEIGHT in.	WIDTH in.	GROWTH RATE
BROAD-LEAVED EVERGREENS			
14) ARCTOSTAPHYLOS UVA-URSI	6	120	SLOW
15) BUXUS MICROPHYLLA	12	48	SLOW
16) BUXUS SEMPERVIRENS	36	36	SLOW
17) ILEX CRENATA	36	48	SLOW
18) MAHONIA AQUIFOLIUM	30	48	SLOW
19) MAHONIA REPENS	10	24	MEDIUM
20) PAXISTIMA CANBYI	18	24	MEDIUM

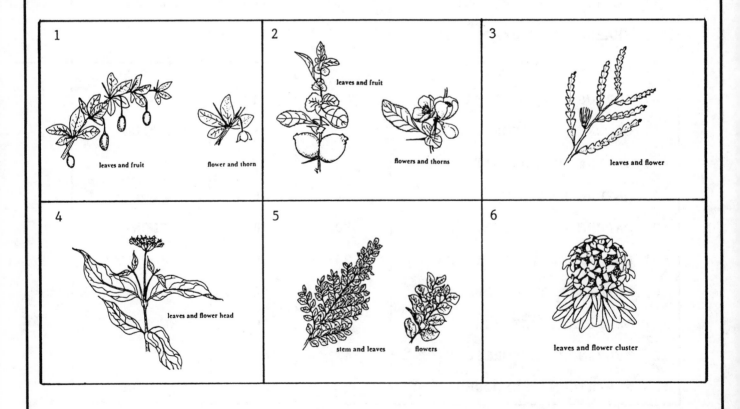

1

leaves and fruit   flower and thorn

2

leaves and fruit

flowers and thorns

3

leaves and flower

4

leaves and flower head

5

stem and leaves   flowers

6

leaves and flower cluster

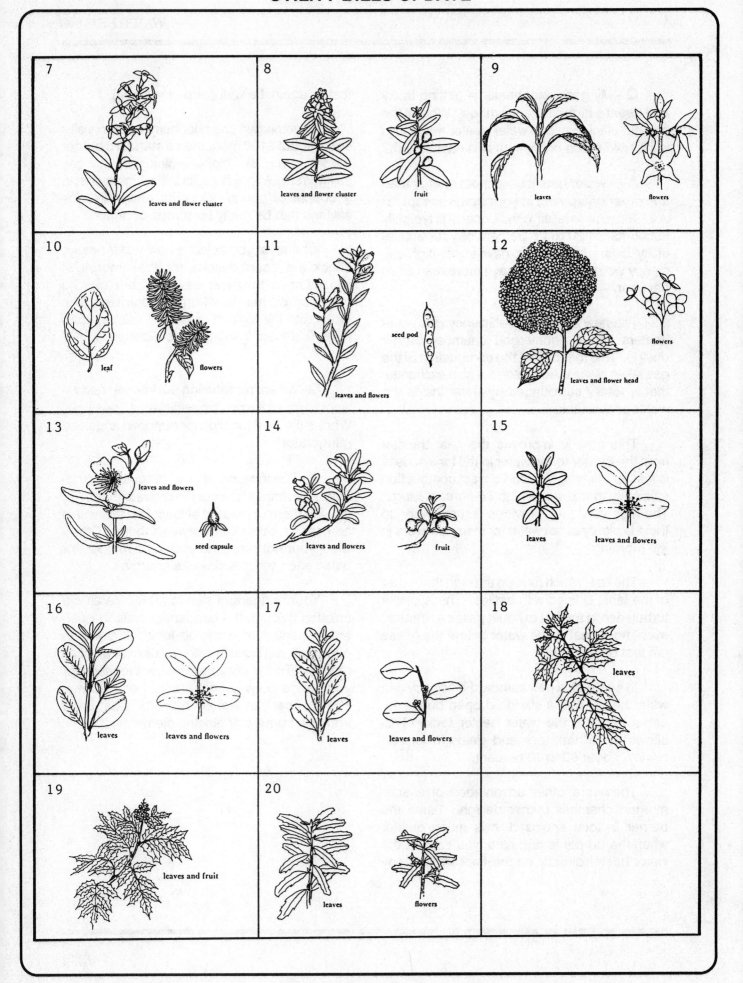

Q - My gas water heater is getting leaky and I want a high-efficiency model. What is the highest-efficiency gas water heater made and will it save much on my gas bills each month?

A - A water heater uses more energy than any other equipment in your home except for your furnace and air conditioner. It typically accounts for 20 to 25 percent of your annual utility bills. Installing a new super-high-efficiency water heater can save more than $100 per year.

The new super-high-efficiency gas water heaters use a submerged chamber burner design. This means that the combustion of the gas takes place inside a special heat exchanger that is totally surrounded by water inside the water heater tank.

This greatly improves the heat transfer from the burner to the water in the tank so less is lost up the flue. You can expect combustion efficiency in the super-high 85-percent range. The high efficiency provides fast recovery so there is plenty of hot water for many showers in the morning.

The flue, which runs up through the center of the tank, is lined with baffles. These cause turbulence in the hot exhaust gases to transfer even more heat to the water before the gases are lost up the flue.

In contrast, a new standard-efficiency gas water heater has a standard open burner located beneath the water heater tank. This allows more heat loss and yields lower efficiency, about 60 to 70 percent.

There are other advantages of a submerged chamber burner design. Since the burner is total enclosed, it is much quieter when the burner is on. Also, you can set the water heater directly on the floor without any feet or against a wall (zero-clearance).

A submerged chamber burner water heater costs about $100 more than a standard burner model. With the higher efficiency, the gas savings should pay back its initial higher cost in a couple of years. Over its entire life, the savings can be many hundreds of dollars.

Whenever you select a new water heater, check the specifications for the amount of insulation in the tank walls. There can be considerable heat loss from the tank itself. The tanks with the highest insulation values, up to R-16, use foam insulation, not fiberglass.

Q - We are remodeling our kitchen and we want to make it as energy efficient as possible. What is the best location for our new range and refrigerator?

A - The location of your range and refrigerator can impact the cost to operate them. Try to keep them separated at least two feet with a counter or cabinet in between them. Otherwise, your hot oven and your cold refrigerator battle each other and waste energy.

Your refrigerator needs adequate air circulation through the condenser coils to operate efficiently. You should locate it along an open wall, not back in a corner or near a hot air register. To the contrary, the best location for your range is away from breezes or windows. The air flow can literally blow the heat away from the burners or electric elements.

UTILITY BILLS UPDATE

Dear Reader,

Thank you for your interest in writing to me about the submerged burner chamber type of gas water heaters. They are very energy-efficient with efficiencies in the 85% range.

Standard burner high-efficiency gas water heaters have efficiencies in the 77% range and low-cost water heaters are in the 65% range. The chart below shows the estimated annual operating costs of the three types of water heaters mentioned above for a typical family. Check your local gas company for the natural gas rates or LPG costs in your area.

This literature and list of manufacturers are for your information only and are not an endorsement of this type of product or a specific manufacturer or model.

Sincerely,

Jim Dulley

MANUFACTURERS

A. O. SMITH CORP., P.O. Box 1499, Camden, SC 29020
"Subchamber"   (803) 432-3266

MOR-FLO INDUSTRIES, 18450 S. Miles Rd., Cleveland, OH 44128
"Nautilus"   (216) 663-7300

ESTIMATED ANNUAL OPERATING COST - $

TYPE	NATURAL GAS COST PER THERM - $						
	.50	.60	.70	.80	.90	1.00	1.10
SUBMERGED BURNER CHAMBER	144	173	202	230	259	288	317
STANDARD HIGH-EFFICIENCY	160	192	224	256	289	321	353
LOW-COST	189	227	265	303	341	379	417

These operating costs are based on a 40-gallon tank size and a daily hot water usage rate of 64.3 gallons. To determine the operating costs using LPG, multiply the above cost in the "$1.00" column times 1.1 times the cost of a gallon of LPG in your area.

NAUTILUS II ®

The advanced submerged combustion chamber gas water heater.

15555/MOR
BuyLine 1741

RESIDENTIAL GAS WATER HEATERS

The Nautilus II is an improved, second-generation version of our original Nautilus water heater. It is designed for higher recovery, lower operating costs, yet the Nautilus II is well within the price range of most families. And that investment is protected for years by Mor-Flo®/American® choice of warranties.

The combustion chamber of the Nautilus II is submerged and completely surrounded by water and utilizes our new jet flame burner that propels the flame directly into the open area of the submerged combustion chamber. As a result, the inner walls of the chamber are engulfed by an intense, powerful flame, thereby assuring uniform heat with maximum heat transfer.

Specifications

Model No.	Limited Warranty Years	Insulation R-Factor	Gallon Capacity	Gas BTU Input Natural/ Propane	G.P.H. Recovery @ 90° Rise Natural/ Propane	Recovery Efficiency	A	B	C	D	F	Approx. Shipping Weight in Pounds
GXN363V	10	8.3	30	36,000	41.2	85%	56	53	16	3	47	158
GXN363SV	10	8.3	30	30,000	34.3	85%	44	40¾	18	3	35	160
GXN463V	10	8.3	40	38,000	43.5	85%	56	53	18	3	47	170
GXN463SV	10	8.3	40	32,000	36.6	85%	44⅜	41¼	20	3	35¼	172
GXN563V	10	8.3	50	40,000	45.8	85%	54¾	51½	20	3	45¾	201
GVN363	5	8.3	30	36,000	41.2	85%	56	53	16	3	47	156
GVN363S	5	8.3	30	30,000	34.3	85%	43⅞	40¾	18	3	35	158
GVN463	5	8.3	40	38,000	43.5	85%	56	53	18	3	47	168
GVN463S	5	8.3	40	32,000	36.6	85%	44⅜	41¼	20	3	35¼	170
GVN563	5	8.3	50	40,000	45.8	85%	54¾	51½	20	3	45¾	199
GXN2F463V	10	16.6	40	38,000	43.5	85%	56	53	20	3	47	180
GXN2F563V	10	16.6	50	40,000	45.8	85%	55	51½	22	3	45¾	213
GVN2F463	5	16.6	40	38,000	43.5	85%	56	53	20	3	47	177
GVN2F563	5	16.6	50	40,000	45.8	85%	55	51½	22	3	45¾	210

All dimensions shown in inches.

☐ **E** — All gas heat inlets are 17¼" from floor
☐ Through the wall — direct vent models and other sizes available soon

GXN Models feature larger anode rod, special contrasting paint with vinyl front panel, installed temperature and pressure relief valve and heat traps — 10-year limited warranty.
GVN Models feature standard anode rod, white paint with blue trim — 5-year limited warranty.

In keeping with our policy of product improvement, specifications are subject to change or modification.

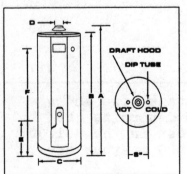

85% efficiency on Nautilus II models compared to only 70% on standard models. This means over 21% more water is heated for the same cost. This saves money each time water is heated.

UTILITY BILLS UPDATE

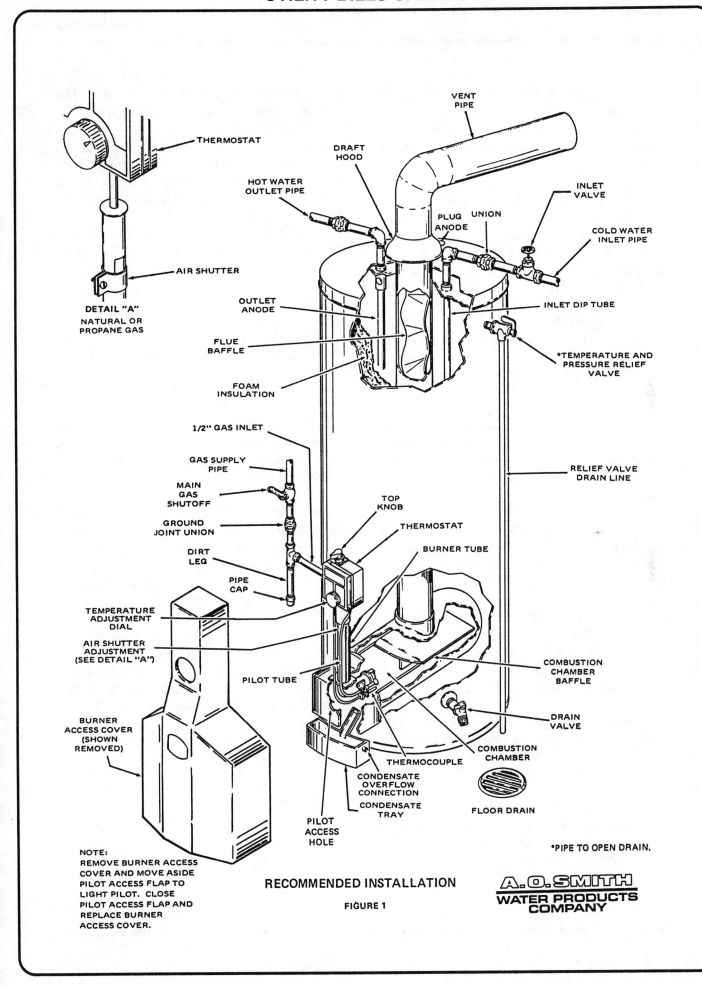

THERMOSTAT

AIR SHUTTER

DETAIL "A"
NATURAL OR
PROPANE GAS

VENT PIPE

DRAFT HOOD

HOT WATER OUTLET PIPE

PLUG ANODE

UNION

INLET VALVE

COLD WATER INLET PIPE

OUTLET ANODE

INLET DIP TUBE

FLUE BAFFLE

*TEMPERATURE AND PRESSURE RELIEF VALVE

FOAM INSULATION

1/2" GAS INLET

GAS SUPPLY PIPE

MAIN GAS SHUTOFF

GROUND JOINT UNION

DIRT LEG

PIPE CAP

TOP KNOB

THERMOSTAT

BURNER TUBE

RELIEF VALVE DRAIN LINE

TEMPERATURE ADJUSTMENT DIAL

AIR SHUTTER ADJUSTMENT (SEE DETAIL "A")

PILOT TUBE

COMBUSTION CHAMBER BAFFLE

DRAIN VALVE

BURNER ACCESS COVER (SHOWN REMOVED)

THERMOCOUPLE

CONDENSATE OVERFLOW CONNECTION

CONDENSATE TRAY

PILOT ACCESS HOLE

COMBUSTION CHAMBER

FLOOR DRAIN

NOTE:
REMOVE BURNER ACCESS
COVER AND MOVE ASIDE
PILOT ACCESS FLAP TO
LIGHT PILOT. CLOSE
PILOT ACCESS FLAP AND
REPLACE BURNER
ACCESS COVER.

*PIPE TO OPEN DRAIN.

RECOMMENDED INSTALLATION

FIGURE 1

A.O. SMITH
WATER PRODUCTS
COMPANY

Q - I think it might cut my utility bills to add insulation to my old water heater tank. I have some fiberglass wall insulation let over from another job. Can I use it on my water heater tank?

A - If you have an old water heater, chances are there is inadequate insulation in the tank walls. A poorly-insulated water heater tank can lose up to 30 percent of the water's heat to the surrounding air. This can total to several hundred dollars wasted over the life of a water heater.

One quick test to determine if your water heater could use additional tank insulation is to place the back of your hand against the upper side of the tank. If it feels warm, then it is losing too much heat.

If you have some old wall insulation, you can save the cost of purchasing a special water heater insulation jacket. Insulation with a foil or kraft paper backing is easiest and cleanest to use.

With an electric water heater, it is a very simple job to add tank insulation. Cut the insulation into lengths to fit horizontally around the circumference of the tank.

With the kraft paper on the outside, staple the ends of the paper together. You will need several lengths to cover the entire tank. Cut a circular piece of insulation for the top. Slit it so it fits around the inlet and outlet water pipes.

Insulating a gas water heater is a little trickier. You must be careful not to block the combustion air inlet and the draft diverter at the top of the tank around the flue.

You can use bent coat hangers to form long vertical hooks that hold the pieces of insulation in place. Using coat hangers, make a support circle around the flue pipe a couple of inches smaller in diameter than the tank. This rests on the top of the tank to support the hooks and insulation.

Make four hooks from coat hangers that, when bent around the support circle, hang down about 14 inches. Make another set of four 14-inch-long hooks and hang them from the first set. Continue this until you are about one foot from the floor. The last set of hooks will be shorter.

Wrap a length of insulation around the tank and hooks and staple the paper backing together. This should rest in the top set of hooks. Continue down attaching lengths of insulation until the entire tank is covered.

Q - I have a heat pump. My house always seems to stay warm, but when I put my hand by the warm air register, it feels chilly. How can it keep my house warm?

A - The heated air output from your heat pump is cooler than that from an electric, gas, or oil furnace. Its temperature, as it reaches your hand, is lower than your body temperature. The slightly cooler air feels even cooler because of the wind chill effect.

Since you keep your house in the 68 to 70 degree range, the air output is hot enough to keep it warm. Heat pumps tend to run longer and move more air than other furnaces because the air coming out isn't as hot.

Dear Reader,

Thank you for your interest in writing to me about how to insulate your water heater tank. Using your water heater efficently can yield substantial annual savings on your utility bills. The simplest method to insulate it is to buy an insulation jacket at your hardware store. As discussed in my newspaper column, you can also use standard fiberglass wall insulation.

The following instructions and diagrams show how to do it yourself with fiberglass wall insulation. If you are insulating a gas water heater, be careful **NOT TO BLOCK THE COMBUSTION AIR INLET OR THE DRAFT DIVERTER OPENING AROUND THE FLUE.** If you are insulating an electric water heater, **SWITCH OFF THE ELECTRIC POWER TO IT FIRST** at the fuse or circuit breaker box.

Sincerely,

Jim Dulley

MATERIALS REQUIRED

Metal coat hangers
Fiberglass wall insulation batts
Staples
Duct tape
Pliers
Wire cutters
Scissors
Knife
Stapler

INSTRUCTIONS FOR INSULATING YOUR WATER HEATER

1) For a standard-sized water heater, untwist about 12 metal coat hangers. Using the pliers, straighten them as much as possible. You will use these to form the hooks that support the insulation around the tank.

2) Measure the diameter of the top of the water heater tank.
   Using the coat hangers, form a circle, three inches smaller
   in diameter, around the flue on top of the tank. This will
   be used to support the coat hanger hooks below.

3) Once the circle is formed, use the duct tape to secure it to
   the top of the tank. (See diagram "A".) Clean the dust off
   the top of the tank first, or the tape will not stick well
   enough.

4) Bend four coat hangers into the hook shape shown in diagram
   "B". The 3-inch dimension is used for standard 3-1/2 wall
   insulation. If you are using thicker insulation, increase
   that dimension accordingly.

5) Bend the straight end of the coat hanger hooks around the
   wire support circle on top of the tank. Just a single-bend
   loop will be adequate. Tape the hooks to the side of the
   tank. (See diagram "C".)

6) Measure the circumference of the water heater tank. Cut a
   length of insulation to that length plus four inches. One
   easy method to cut fiberglass batts insulation is to lay it
   on a cutting board and lay another board across it. (See
   diagram "D".) Wear a mask to avoid breathing the fiberglass
   dust.

7) Using a scissors, cut the insulation back 2 inches on each
   end of the length of insulation, leaving the paper backing
   intact. (See diagram "E".) You will use this 2-inch flap to
   staple the ends together.

8) Place the insulation around the tank in the hooks. The paper
   facing on the insulation should be to the outside. Using the
   stapler, staple the ends of the paper facing together. (See
   diagram "F".) Don't try to pull it too tight, or you will
   compress the insulation and reduce the overall R-value
   somewhat.

9) Make another set of four hooks and hang them from the first
   top set of hooks. Follow the same procedure for making and
   attaching the fiberglass insulation. (See diagram "G".)
   Continue this procedure until the tank is covered to about
   six inches from the floor.

10) Using the scissors, cut back the insulation at least three
    inches from access openings, pipes, combustion air inlet, and
    thermostat. Using the pliers, bend under the exposed ends of
    the wire hooks.

DIAGRAMS

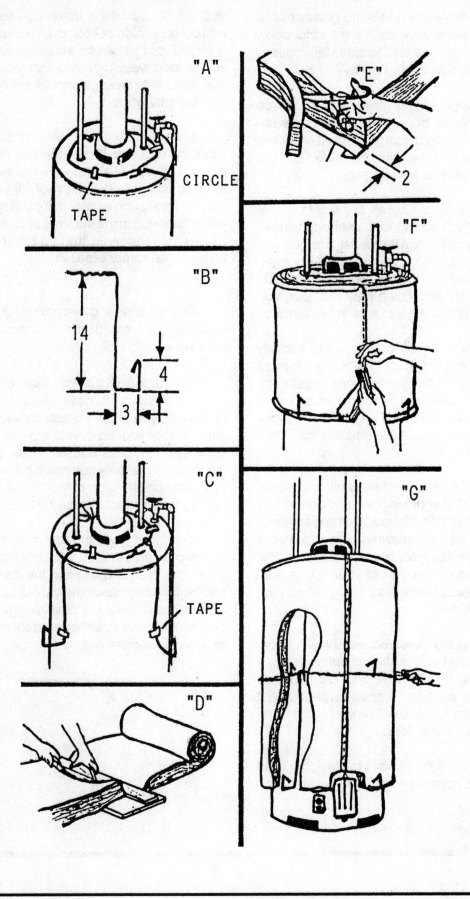

Q - We have a large sliding glass door to our patio. It always seems drafty by that door, even though we have tried to carefully weather-strip it. What else should we try?

A - A large sliding glass door is a large energy consumer both in the winter and summer. This is due to the large amount of sliding and mating edges that must be sealed and the large glass surface area.

The majority, but not all, of the draft is from outdoor air leaking indoors. Although these leaks make you chilly in the winter, they rob you of a lot of your energy dollars in the summer. Often, because the cool air from your air conditioner tends to drop down near the floor, you aren't as aware of the leaks as in the winter.

Some of the chilly drafts are not actually caused by air leaks at all. The warm room air near the large glass window tends to get cold, even with thermal glass. This cold air is heavier than the rest of the heated room air, so it sinks to the floor and causes an apparent cool draft from outdoors.

You should also carefully caulk and weatherstrip the rest of your windows and doors. Any air that leaks in through your sliding glass door must push out air somewhere else from your house. Otherwise, your house would explode. By tightening up the rest of your house, you may find that it feels less drafty near your sliding glass door.

Blocking the direct force of the wind from blowing against your sliding glass door helps considerably. The amount of cold outdoor air leaking in through just a small unsealed spot can be increased several times by the wind blowing against the door.

One of the easiest ways to block the wind is to build a covered windbreak around your door. It is basically a three-foot wide framed wall on each side of your door, covered with a shingled roof. It can be attractive and provide additional privacy too. Your increased comfort and utility bills savings should justify the minimal material costs.

In the summer, in addition to blocking the wind, the roof acts like an awning to block the hot sun. It also provides an excellent location to hang plants under the roof. If you rely on natural ventilation or fans for cooling, you can either remove it in the summer or build a hinged shutter or window in the side that faces the prevailing summer breezes.

Q - I have a gas clothes dryer and I wondered if I could vent it indoors without causing a problem?

A - Although the products of complete gas combustion are basically carbon dioxide and water, you should check your local codes first. Indoor venting of any type of gas appliance often violates codes. Also, your dryer owner's manual may comment on indoor venting. Altering the type of venting designed by the dryer manufacturer may void its warranty.

Venting a dryer indoors may exacerbate any excess indoor moisture problem you may now have. You should keep the lint filter clean and periodically check the vent duct too. It can gradually over time become clogged with lint. This blockage can impede adequate air flow for energy-efficient drying.

Dear Reader,

Thank you for writing to me about how to block the wind and sun from coming in your sliding glass patio door. Even the best doors get leaky. By blocking the force and pressure of the wind, the leakage can be minimized. It can also be effective for growing hanging plants and for shelter from the rain and sun for your pet.

Sincerely,

Jim Dulley

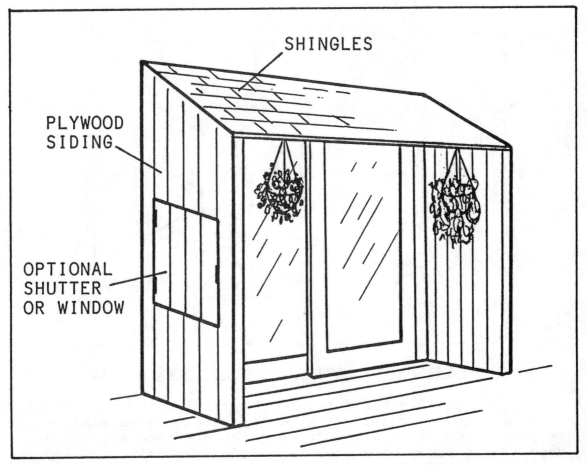

WIND SHELTER BLOCKS CHILLY DRAFTS THROUGH DOOR

MATERIALS LIST

```
2x4 lumber
1x6 lumber
3/8" exterior grade plywood
5/8" plywood siding
roof shingles
metal flashing
roofing tar
building paper
narrow metal strip
galvanized nails
```

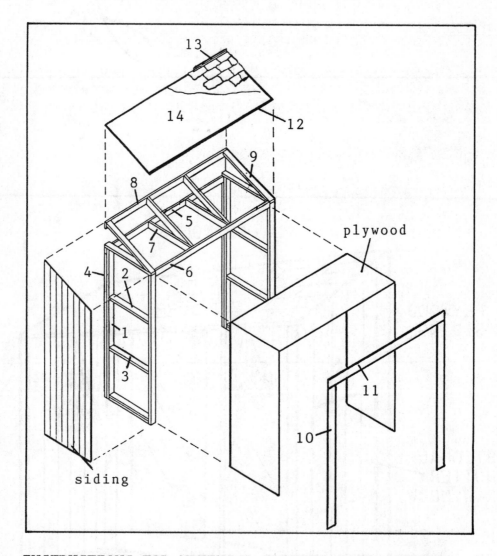

INSTRUCTIONS FOR MAKING A SLIDING DOOR SHELTER

a) Before starting to build this shelter, plan the size and slope of roof that you want. It will depend on the size and style of your house. Also consider the orientation to the sun. A door facing toward the east or west will require to deeper shelter to block the sun. (The sun is lower in the sky in the morning and afternoon.) Determine the type of plywood siding that will look best. Cedar siding is also an option.

b) You should determine if you want a window or shutter in one of the sides of the shelter. Depending on your house orientation, it may allow for more natural ventilation in the summer.

c) First you should assemble the frames for the side walls of the shelter. It is usually easiest to assemble these flat on the ground. Cut the vertical pieces (1) from the 2x4 lumber to a length to give adequate headroom under the shelter. Cut the horizontal pieces (2,3) to provide the depth of shelter you want.

d) Nail the horizontal and vertical pieces together to form two side walls. If you plan to add a window or shutter, cut and nail the header supports in the side wall for it.

e) Cut vertical door opening pieces (4) and the cross piece (5) from the 2x4 lumber. Nail these to the house around the sliding glass door opening. These will be used to attach the shelter to the house.

f) Nail the side wall frames to the door opening pieces (4,5).

g) Cut a piece of 2x4 lumber for the front roof support (6) and nail it the top of the side wall frames. This will tie the ends together. Add two cross supports (7) from the top piece (6) to piece (5).

h) After you have determine the pitch of the roof that you want, cut and nail the horizontal roof support (8) to the house. Locate the wall studs before you drive in the nails.

i) Cut the roof rafters (9) and nail them to the roof support (8) and to the front support (6). You may want to bevel the ends of the rafters to the angle of the roof.

j) Cut the 5/8" siding to make the covers for the side walls. Nail these covers to the side wall frames.

k) Cut the 3/8" plywood for the inside surface of the side walls and underneath the roof. Nail these pieces into place.

l) Cut trim pieces (10,11) from the 1x6 lumber and nail them to the front of the shelter.

m) Cut a piece of the 3/8" plywood (14) to use for the roof sheathing. Nail it in place over the roof frame. Cover the roof sheathing with building paper. Nail a metal drip strip (12) to the lower end of the roof.

n) Cover the roof with shingles. Lighter-colored shingles will not get as hot in the summer. Nail metal flashing (13) against the house. Seal it with roofing tar.

o) Finish the shelter with good-quality exterior grade paint or stain.

Q - My two-car garage is attached to my home. It is awfully cold when I work in it during the winter and the family room next to it feels cold too. Will installing an insulated garage door help reduce the heat loss?

A - An insulated garage door can have a significant effect on the heat loss from your garage and from the rest of your house. It can reduce your heating and cooling cost and improve your comfort level. This is especially true if you have a built-in garage with a room above it.

A standard garage door has an insulation value of only about R-2 at best. A top-of-the-line insulated garage door has an R-13 insulation value and seals much better to reduce cold air leakage. The combined effect reduces heat loss by more than 90 percent.

Before you go to the expense of installing an insulated garage door, caulk and weather-strip any windows and doors to the garage to reduce air leakage. Also try to get some insulation in the garage ceiling if possible.

Not all insulated garage doors are created equally, so check the specifications. There are a significant differences in the design and construction which effect the savings and comfort you will realize.

First, check the amount of insulation and how it is installed. The higher the insulation R-value, the better. Foamed-in-place insulation is better than cut-foam insulation board which just attach to the back of the door panels. Foamed-in-place insulation, which is injected in between the indoor and outdoor panels, eliminates void spots and adhers to the panels.

A good-quality insulated steel garage door has a plastic non-heat-conducting thermal break that separates the indoor and outdoor metal panels. This eliminates the direct path for heat loss.

Having seals around the garage door and between each section are very important to minimize the cold air leakage. Some doors use a seal that is attached to the fixed garage door frame. Others use rubber-type seals that move up and down with the door. In addition to minimizing air leakage, the seals help keep rain water out of your garage.

The best type of horizontal seal between each door section utilizes a compressible rubber-type hollow tube or gasket. Also, the panels should fit together with an overlap, called a ship lap joint. Some doors use only one or the other, but a combination of both is best.

Q - I just bought an older house and I wanted to add some attic insulation. Is it necessary to remove the old rock wool insulation before adding the new insulation?

A - If the old insulation is not damp or badly deteriorated, you should be able to add new insulation over it. You should check under the old insulation for a vapor barrier. If is has none, you may need additional attic ventilation to minimize the chance of condensation.

Since it is old insulation, it could have some asbestos mixed with it. Wear a mask and protective clothing when you are near it. Before you work up there, you should have a sample of the old insulation tested for asbestos. Polarized light microscopy tests cost about $30 to $40 and it is well worth the small expense.

Dear Reader,

Thank you for your interest in writing to me about insulated garage doors. When you select an insulated garage door, check the specifications for the insulation value and the type of seals that are used.

This product information and specifications are for your information only, and are not an endorsement of this type of product or a specific manufacturer or model.

Sincerely,

Jim

Jim Dulley

MANUFACTURERS

GENERAL DOOR, Monroe & Radcliff Sts., Bristol, PA 19007

HAAS DOOR CO., 26202 Glenwood Rd., Perrysburg, OH 43551

OHD THERMOCORE, 3200 Reach Rd., Williamsport, PA 17701

SALEM DOOR MFG., 11235 Sebring Dr., Cincinnati, OH 45240

TAYLOR BLDG. PROD., 631 N. First St., West Branch, MI 48661

WAYNE DALTON, P.O. Box 67, Mt. Hope, OH 44660

Specifications

Architectural Specifications for Foamcore Raised Panel Sectional Overhead Doors

Furnish and install upward-acting sectional, overhead Wayne-Dalton "Foamcore" door, manufactured by Wayne-Dalton Corp., Mt. Hope, Ohio — sold and installed by Wayne-Dalton distributors.

Sections

All door sections shall be of steel/polyurethane/laminate sandwich type construction. The exterior skin will be hot-dipped galvanized steel pre-painted with a two-coat, two-bake paint system featuring an extended warranty. The steel skin will be woodgrain textured. Interior skin will be a polylaminate with white polyester finish. Muntins and stiles will be pre-painted, hot-dipped galvanized steel. The cavity between inner skin and exterior skin will be completely filled with a tightly packed polyurethane core, having a total thickness of 9/16". A total door section thickness will be 2".

Seals

The door will be equipped with shiplap section design and a factory installed astragal on the bottom section.

Track and hardware

Hot-dipped galvanized track will be 2". Doors are bracket mounted. All brackets shall be made from hot-dipped galvanized steel. Hinge rollers shall be 2" 7-ball. Optional torsion springs will be wound from oil tempered wire.

Lites

Optional SSB lites available in molded high-impact polymer frames.

Sizes

The Foamcore Raised Panel door is available in standard widths of 8', 9', 16' and 18'. Available heights include 6'6", 7' and 8'.

Wind load

Doors shall meet or exceed standards established by ANSI Bulletin A216.1 1977 and NAGDM publication 102-1976.

Warranty

Wayne-Dalton Corp. and its subsidiaries back all of their doors and hardware fittings with a LIMITED WARRANTY against defects in workmanship and materials. A copy of this warranty is available upon request.

Take a good look !

Thermacore® panels are manufactured using a unique, patented method of polyurethane foam and galvanized steel lamination. These panels are produced on a computerized, television-monitored line under strict quality control at one of the most modern facilities in the world.

Years of development, research and testing resulted in a panel that can withstand extraordinary punishment and still function like new. Moreover, our specially-formulated polyurethane *will not absorb water,* which eventually may add weight to the door and cause maintenance problems. Also, the Thermacore door will not swell, stick, warp, or rot.

The advantage to you: a lightweight, extremely rugged door panel with an insulation R-value of 13.0 (comparable to a solid brick wall 57" thick!) that will save you energy dollars year after year.

And, in the event your door becomes accidentally damaged, service is fast, easy and inexpensive. Our distributors carry a complete inventory of replacement panels which they can install with ordinary hand tools in a matter of minutes.

If security is a concern, Thermacore panels provide a hard-to-break-through barrier to unwanted intruders. These doors are so tough and rugged that they may well outlast the house they are installed in. In fact, the same type of Thermacore panel is in use around the world by industry, service stations, warehouses, fire stations and other high-use operations. Now, this commercial quality panel is available to you.

Because we're so confident in the qualtiy of our product, we offer what no one else in this industry can: **a FIVE YEAR limited delamination warranty** as well as a **ONE YEAR limited warranty on parts and labor.***

Your savings on energy bills and maintenance can pay back your investment in a short time and go on paying dividends for years to come, as well as adding value to your home. When considering a garage door, consider a door that will benefit you -

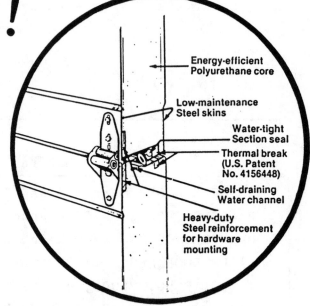

Energy-efficient
Polyurethane core

Low-maintenance
Steel skins

Water-tight
Section seal

Thermal break
(U.S. Patent
No. 4156448)

Self-draining
Water channel

Heavy-duty
Steel reinforcement
for hardware
mounting

THERMAC■RE®

Manufactured by
O.H.D. Thermacore, Inc.
3200 Reach Rd., Williamsport, PA 17701 • (717) 326-7325

A part of the Dallas Corporation

STANDARD SIZES AVAILABLE
Width: 8', 9', 10', 12', 16', 18', 20', 22'
Height: 6'6", 7', 7'6", 8'
Other custom sizes available; contact dealer.

COLORS
Factory-painted in your choice of brown or white which can be field painted.

HARDWARE
All hardware necessary for installation (including track, hinges, lock assembly with key, rollers, brackets, cables, pulleys, handles, and fasteners) is made of high quality materials to insure reliable performance and long life.

OPTIONAL WINDOW LITES
Window lites, 25" x 8", are available factory-installed using double thermal glazing.

OPTIONS
• Draw bar reinforcement plate for electric door operator
• Exhaust port • Deluxe step handle
• Jamb sealing and/or top sealing for optimum insulation value.
Sealing between sections and bottom seals are standard.

* Contact factory for details.   Technical changes may be made without prior notification.

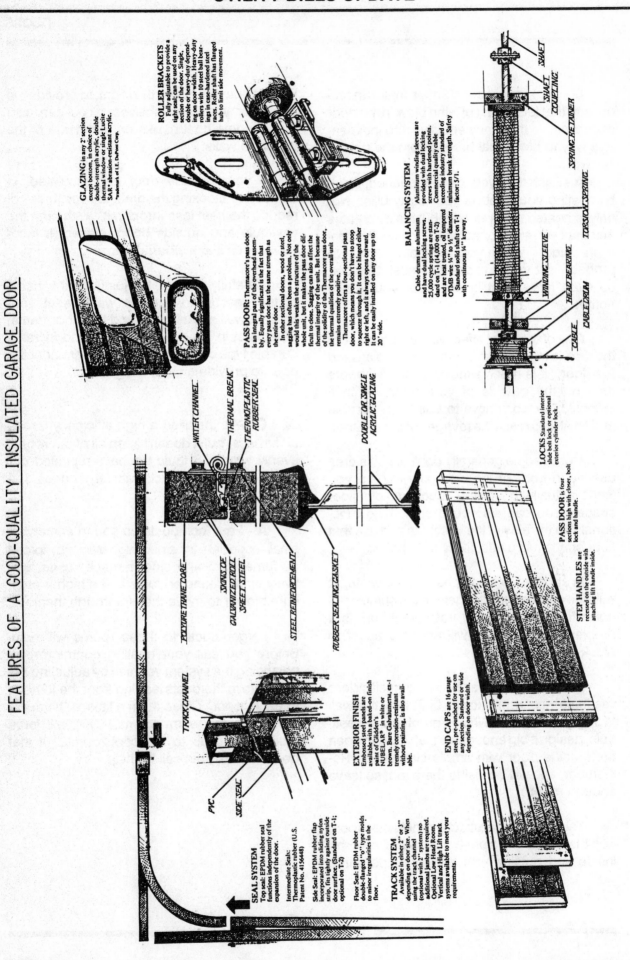

FEATURES OF A GOOD-QUALITY INSULATED GARAGE DOOR

ROLLER BRACKETS
Fully adjustable to provide a tight seal; can be used on any section of the door. Single, double or heavy-duty depending on door width. Heavy-duty rollers with 10 steel ball bearings in case-hardened steel races. Roller shaft has flanged hub to limit side movement.

GLAZING in any 2″ section except bottom, in choice of double-strength acrylic, double thermal window or single Lucite SAR* abrasion-resistant acrylic.
*trademark of I.E. DuPont Corp.

PASS DOOR: Thermacore's pass door is an integral part of the overhead assembly. Equally significant is the fact that every pass door has the same strength as the entire door.

In other sectional doors, wood or steel, sagging has often been a problem. Not only would this weaken the structure of the whole unit, but it makes the pass door difficult to close. Sagging can also affect the thermal integrity of the unit. But because of the solidity of the Thermacore pass door, the thermal qualities of the overall unit remains extremely positive.

Thermacore offers a four-sectional pass door, which means you don't have to stoop to squeeze through it. It can be hinged either right or left, and it always opens outward. It can be easily installed on any door up to 20′ wide.

SHAFT
SHAFT COUPLING
SPRING RETAINER
TORSION SPRING
WINDING SLEEVE
HEAD BEARING
CABLE DRUM
CABLE

BALANCING SYSTEM
Aluminum winding sleeve are provided with dual locking screws with hardened points. Commercial quality cable exceeding industry standard of 25,000-cycle springs are standard on T-1 (14,000 on T-2) OTMB wire (treated, oil tempered OTMB wire ¼″ to ½″ diameter. Standard solid shafts on T-1 with continuous ¼″ keyway.

WATER CHANNEL
THERMAL BREAK
THERMOPLASTIC RUBBER SEAL
SKINS OF GALVANIZED ROLL SHEET STEEL
POLYURETHANE CORE
STEEL REINFORCEMENT
RUBBER SEALING GASKET
DOUBLE OR SINGLE ACRYLIC GLAZING

LOCKS Standard interior slide bolt lock or optional exterior cylinder lock.

PASS DOOR is four sections high with closer, bolt lock and handle.

STEP HANDLES are recessed on the outside with attaching lift handle inside.

END CAPS are 16 gauge steel, pre-punched for use on any section. Standard or wide depending on door width.

TRACK CHANNEL
PVC
SIDE SEAL

EXTERIOR FINISH
Embossed steel panels are available with a baked-on finish paint of Glidden's NUBELAR® in white or brown. Bare Galvalume™, extremely corrosion-resistant without painting, is also available.

SEAL SYSTEM
Top seal: EPDM rubber seal functions independently of the expansion of the door.

Intermediate Seals: Thermoplastic rubber (U.S. Patent No. 4156448)

Side Seal: EPDM rubber flap incorporated into sliding nylon strip, fits tightly against outside door surface. (Standard on T-1; optional on T-2)

Floor Seal: EPDM rubber double-flanged "o" type molds to minor irregularities in the floor.

TRACK SYSTEM
Available in either 2″ or 3″ depending on door size. When using the track channel (optional with 2″ system) no additional jambs are required. Optional Low Head Room, Vertical and High Lift track systems available to meet your requirements.

Q - Our kids are constantly running in and out and that lets a gust of wind blow in the door each time. Is there any effective and inexpensive way to block that breeze from the door?

A - Each time your door is opened, it can be costing you a lot on your utility bills. Not only is heated room air lost, but it also creates that draft you mentioned which makes you feel even colder. When you feel colder, you will probably set your furnace thermostat higher, so even more heat is lost from your entire home.

One of the most effective methods to stop the draft is to install an indoor vestibule around the door. It is much simpler to put it indoors than on the outside of your door. With it indoors, you won't have to build it as durable and finish it to resist the ravages of the weather.

Most people generally don't use this area directly in front of the door anyway, so you won't actually be losing much usable floor space. You can also build something functional into the side of the vestibule and use that floor space more effectively than before.

In addition to saving heat in the winter, it will also reduce the heat gain in the summer. If noise from the street or your neighbors is a problem, the vestibule will act as a buffer to block much of it.

One common type of do-it-yourself indoor vestibule has a bookcase built into the wall facing your room. When you plan the vestibule, design it big enough so that you can open the outside door with ample clearance. Remember, you will be inside there too, so leave enough room.

You basically construct a mini-framed room with the 2 X 4's and a pre-hung door. Cover the inside and outside with drywall or paneling.

Extend one wall facing the room, to provide the depth for your bookshelves. You can also mount some coat hooks on the inside of the vestibule walls.

If your primary door isn't insulated, in addition to blocking the draft, the vestibule will reduce the heat loss through it. With both the vestibule and outside doors closed, it functions much like a storm door.

Carefully caulk all the joints on the inside of the vestibule where its walls meet your present wall and also around the door frame. Weatherstrip the pre-hung door and install a durable type of threshold on the floor under the door to provide a more airtight seal.

Q - We installed a high efficiency forced air furnace, but it doesn't keep all of our rooms evenly warm. Should we have replaced our four inch diameter ducts with larger ones during installation?

A - Four inch ducts do sound somewhat small, especially for a new high efficiency forced air furnace. Some older furnaces used relatively small diameter ducts and a higher pressure blower to move the air through them.

Larger ducts to those rooms will help. Before you call your heating contractor, try balancing the system yourself by adjusting the dampers in the ducts leading from the furnace to each room. Close them a little in the ducts leading to the warm rooms. That will force more heated air to the cool rooms. If that doesn't help, then call for help.

Dear Reader,

    Thank you for your interest in writing to me about how to make an indoor bookcase/vestibule. It can really save a lot of energy, and make your home feel much tighter. By blocking the cold draft, you should be able to set your thermostat a little lower and further cut your heating costs.

Sincerely,

Jim

Jim Dulley

MATERIALS LIST

Lumber - 2x4's
          1/2" Plywood

Drywall

Drywall Tape

Pre-hung Door

Door Threshold

Wood Trim Molding

Bookshelf Supports

Bookshelf Clips

Angle Brackets

Latex Caulk

Weatherstripping

Interior Paint

Nails

Screws

<u>BUILDING INSTRUCTIONS</u>

1) First, check which way your ceiling joists run because you
   will want to nail the top plates of the vestibule to them.
   Nail the three top plates (1,2,3) to the joists.

2) Cut and pull back the carpeting and carpet pad where the
   vestibule will be built. Mark the location of the soleplates
   (4,5,6) on the floor directly under the top plates on the
   ceiling. Nail the soleplates to the floor.

3) Following the diagram, nail the studs (7) between the top and
   soleplates.

4) Attach the door header pieces (8) in between the studs (7) as
   shown. Also nail the header for the bookcase (9,10) in place.
   Brace these headers with studs (11). Nail pieces (12,13) into
   place for added support.

5) Next make the bookshelf divider using 2x4's (14,15). Center
   the divider in the bookshelf opening and nail it the the frame
   and floor. Attach the halves with angle brackets.

6) Cut away the section of the soleplate under the door opening
   to make room for the pre-hung door. Nail the pre-hung door
   into place.

7) Finish the walls with drywall and tape all the joints. Do the
   inside too for a more finished look.

8) Attach the adjustable shelf supports to the sides of the shelf
   opening and to each side of the divider.

9) Cut the shelves from the 1/2" plywood and finish them. Attach
   the clips for the shelf supports and slide in the shelves.

10) Cut the door trim to size and nail it around the door.

11) Install a door threshold under the door. You will probably
    have to cut off the bottom of the door for clearance. A
    vinyl bulb type of threshold would be a good choice.

12) Caulk all the joints and weatherstrip the door. Then paint
    the vestibule with interior wall paint.

13) Lay the carpeting back against the vestibule and cut it for a
    snug fit. Finish it off with a molding around the bottom of
    vestibule.

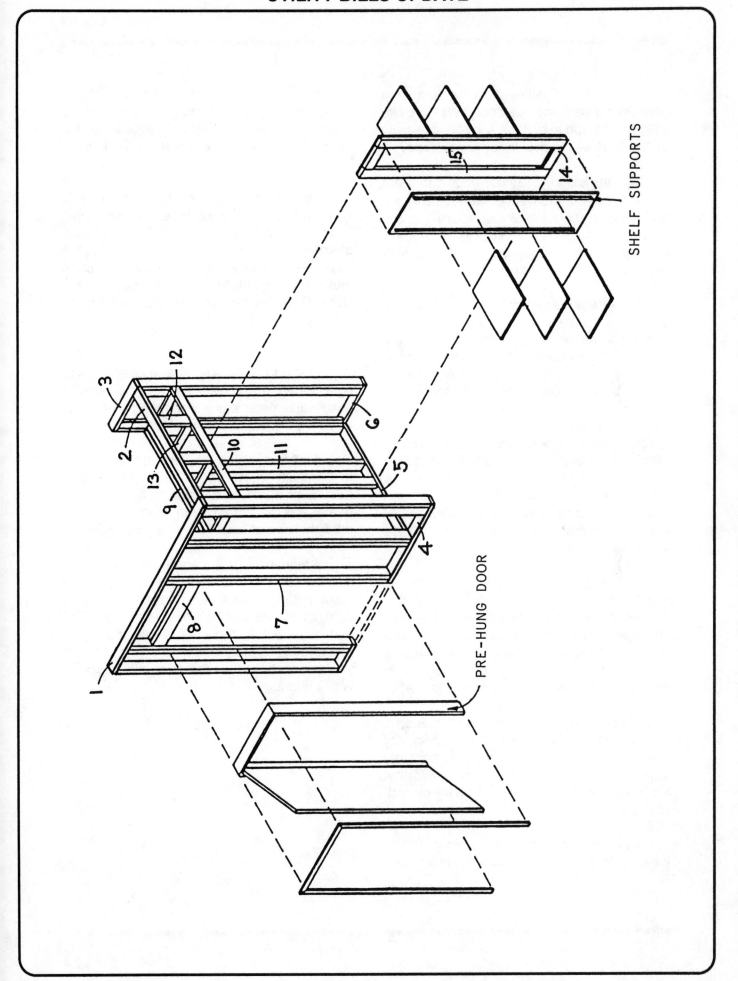

SHELF SUPPORTS

PRE-HUNG DOOR

Q - We are getting a chilly draft from beneath our front and side doors. We have two children that run in and out a lot. What would be the best way to seal those leaky areas?

A - Air leaking in under your doors not only makes you uncomfortable, but increases both your heating and air-conditioning costs. The energy savings from sealing those leaks can pay back the material costs for door threshold seals in a couple of months.

There are many types of door threshold seals and the best choice depends on your specific home. Although there are many variations, the most common types you will find at your hardware or home center store are the sweep, door shoe, vinyl bulb, and interlocking.

The sweep threshold seal is the easiest to install yourself. It is a flexible rubber-type blade which is screwed through slotted holes to the lower edge of your door. After you mount it, slide it down until it firmly touches the floor. Then tighten the screws to fix it in position. As it wears, you can loosen the screws and slide it down a little farther.

Although you must remove your door to install it, a door shoe would be a good choice with active children. It is a flexible vinyl bulb strip that mounts on the underside of the door and seals against the floor or wooden threshold. Since it is under the door edge, it is protected from the pitter-patter of little feet.

If your floor or threshold at the door is worn low in spots so that neither a sweep nor a door shoe will seal well, a vinyl-bulb threshold is best. This is an aluminum threshold that screws to the floor directly beneath the closed-door position.

Once you screw down the threshold, slide the vinyl bulb seal into its slot. It should touch the bottom of the door when it's closed. When your door is opened, the vinyl bulb is exposed and susceptible to damage. If it gets damaged, you can easily slide in an inexpensive replacement bulb.

One of the most effective and durable types of threshold seals, the interlocking type, is also the most difficult to install. A specially-shaped aluminum threshold is screwed to the floor. It has a lip and groove to mate with an aluminum strip that is mounted beneath the door. Both pieces have to be carefully aligned so they interlock properly.

Q - I had all the electrical appliances and lights turned off the other day and the wheel in my electric meter was still spinning pretty fast. Does my aquarium use much electricity?

A - An aquarium can be a significant user of electricity in the home. It has an electric heater, air pump, and intensive lighting. The heater and the air pump run continuously and the light is on at least 12 hours each day.

A typical 20-gallon aquarium uses about 600 kilowatt-hours of electricity each year. In some houses, that can account for nine percent of the total electric bill. A large aquarium can actually use more electricity than your refrigerator. Unfortunately, there isn't much you can do to reduce the electricity usage of your aquarium.

UTILITY BILLS UPDATE

Dear Reader,

Thank you for your interest in writing to me about door threshold weatherstripping. It can reduce the air leakage underneath your door. You can purchase most threshold weatherstripping at most discount department, hardware, or home center stores.

The chart below shows the advantages and disadvantages of common types of threshold seals. Page 2 and 3 show diagrams and installation instructions. These are simple general instructions designed to help you determine if you can do the job yourself. For the actual installation, refer to the detailed instruction on the product packaging.

This Update information is for your information only and is not an endorsement of these types of products or specific products or manufacturers.

Sincerely,

Jim Dulley

ADVANTAGES AND DISADVANTAGES OF TYPES OF THRESHOLD WEATHERSTRIPPING

SWEEP
Advantages - Easy to install, low cost, easily replaced, moderate durability, use with even (unworn) floor.
Disadvantages - May drag on carpet, door must be even, moderate sealing quality, visible on bottom of door.

DOOR SHOE
Advantages - Low cost, very durable, very airtight seal, not visible on door, rain drip cap available.
Disadvantages - Must remove and trim door to install, floor or threshold must be even.

VINYL BULB & THRESHOLD
Advantages - Useful where no present threshold or floor is worn, vinyl seal is easily replaced, attractive appearance.
Disadvantages - Exposed vinyl bulb is susceptible to wear, must remove and bevel bottom of door, higher cost.

INTERLOCKING
Advantages - Excellent seal, very durable, attractive, rain drip cap available.
Disadvantages - Must remove door to install, must be properly aligned, higher cost.

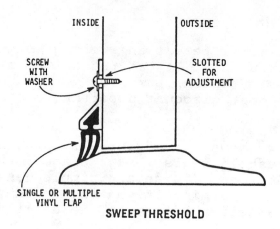

SWEEP THRESHOLD

1) Make sure that the floor or threshold is even so the sweep seals against it.
2) Measure the width of your door and saw the sweep to a length about one-eighth inch shorter.
3) Center the sweep on the bottom of your door so it just touches the floor or threshold.
4) Mark the location of the slotted holes on your   door.
5) Remove the sweep and drill holes in the marked spots.
6) Screw the sweep into place, leaving the screws loose.
7) Slide the sweep down so it rest firmly against the floor or threshold. Tighten the screws.

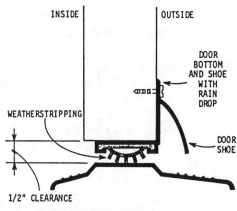

VINYL-BULB DOOR OVER THRESHOLD

1) Make sure that the floor or threshold is even so the shoe seals against it.
2) Measure up from the floor or threshold up and mark a line about 1/2" high on the door.
3) Remove the door and saw along the marked line.

5) Center the door shoe over the bottom of the door with the rain drip cap to the outside.
6) Mark the mounting holes on the bottom of the door.
7) Remove the door shoe utnd drill the holes.
8) Screw the door shoe into place and replace the door.

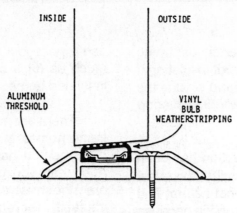

VINYL-BULB THRESHOLD

1) Saw the threshold to fit in the door opening on the floor.
2) Slip the vinyl bulb into the threshold and measure its height above the floor.
3) Mark the height of the uncompressed threshold on the bottom edge of the door.
4) Remove the door form the hinges.
5) Saw the bottom of the door on an angle so that it will slightly compress the vinyl bulb when the door closes.
6) Mark and drill mounting holes in the floor. Screw the threshold in place.
7) Snap the vinyl bulb in the slot in the threshold.
8) Replace the door on the hinges.

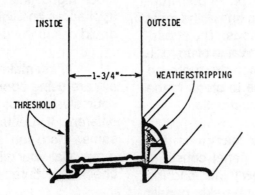

INTERLOCKING THRESHOLD

1) Saw the floor section of the threshold to fit the door opening.
2) Saw the door section to a length about 1/16 inch narrower than the width of the door.
3) Open the door and position the floor section on the   floor.
4) Position the door section in its interlocking position and measure the height for the floor.
5) Mark that height on the bottom of the door.
6) Remove the door and saw the bottom off the that exact height.
7) Drill holes and screw the door section to the door bottom.
8) Replace the door on the hinges and make sure the two pieces interlock properly.
9) If not, remove door and shim the door section until it fits.

Q - I want to build a "real" timber-frame house, but I am concerned about insulating it properly. Is it energy efficient and what is the best way to insulate the walls without covering the beautiful oak timbers?

A - Timber-frame construction has been used for centuries and homes built this way last indefinitely. It is one of the most natural and attractive types of home construction because the huge natural oak timbers are exposed indoors. "True timber-framing" is still built by hand and individually fit together on your building site by craftsmen.

The best way to insulate a timber-frame home is with stress-skin building panels. These are thick insulating foam panels, covered generally with sheetrock on the indoor surface and plywood sheathing on the outdoor surface. The same type of insulating panels are used to form the roof, so the large ceiling beams are exposed too.

This type of stress-skin panel construction over the timber-framing is one of the most energy efficient building methods. The stress-skin panels yield an insulation value of up to R-30. This is a true R-30, since there are no thermal bridges or leaks due to studs in the walls as with conventional construction.

Another energy-saving feature is the airtightness with stress-skin panel construction. Since there are very few joints, and the ones between each large stress-skin panels are well-sealed, you won't feel chilly breezes during the winter nor have hot humid air leaking in during the summer.

The many tons of large oak timbers help to moderate the indoor temperature swings, much like in a log home. This will minimize the need for air conditioning in the summer and helps act as thermal storage in the winter. You can expect your utility bills to be about half as much as for a conventionally-built standard-insulated home.

There are many manufacturers of timber-frame homes and each sends out a crew of craftsmen to hand fit the framing together. After that, you generally have the option to erect the stress-skin panels and finish the home yourself. There are standard styles and floor plans available or the framing can be custom designed to your architectural plans.

Since it is easy to cut openings and install additional windows, doors, sunspaces, etc. at a later time, you can easily make improvements to your home as your budget allows. For example, you just use a circular saw to cut the opening in the panel and then frame it with lumber for a window.

Q - My neighbor in my apartment building and I compared our electric bills, and mine is much higher than hers. We seem to use our appliances and lights the same amount. What could cause the difference?

A - First make sure that both of you actually are using about the same amount. Often your electrical usage patterns can be quite different. If your usage patterns are about the same, then you may have a faulty electric meter. Call your utility company and have them check its accuracy.

There can also be a wiring problem, where some of her electrical outlets are mistakenly wired through your meter. You can easily test it by turning off all your electrical appliances, lights, and clocks, and visually checking your electric meter to be sure no electricity is flowing.

UTILITY BILLS UPDATE

Dear Reader,

Thank you for your interest in writing to me about timber-framed houses. You can contact the manufacturers listed below for detailed plan books and further information. This literature, information, and list of manufacturers are for your information only and are not an endorsement of this type of product of a specific manufacturer.

Sincerely,

Jim

Jim Dulley

MANUFACTURERS

GREAT NORTHERN WOODWORKS, Rt. 2, Box 488, Cambridge, MN 55008
HEARTHSTONE HOMES, Rt. 2, Box 434, Dandridge, TN 37725
NATIVE WOOD PRODUCTS, Drawer Box 469, Brooklyn, CT 06234
NORTHERN TIMBER FRAMING, P.O. Box 110, Waterville, OH 43566
RIVERBEND TIMBER FRAMING, P.O. Box 26, Blissfield, MI 49228
ROWLAND CONTRACTING, P.O. Box 71, Middleville, NJ 07855
TIMBERCRAFT HOMES, 85 Martin Rd., Port Townsend, WA 98368
TIMBER FRAME SYSTEMS, P.O. Box 458, Frankford, DE 19945
TIMBERHOUSE, 696 Little Sleeping Child Rd., Hamilton, MT 59840

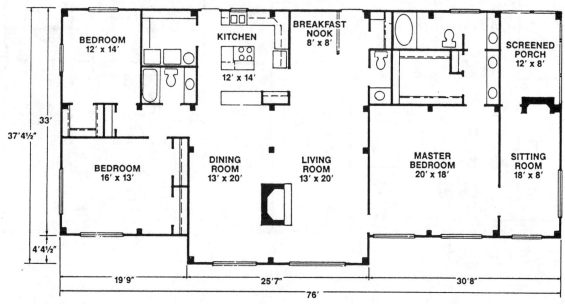

UTILITY BILLS UPDATE

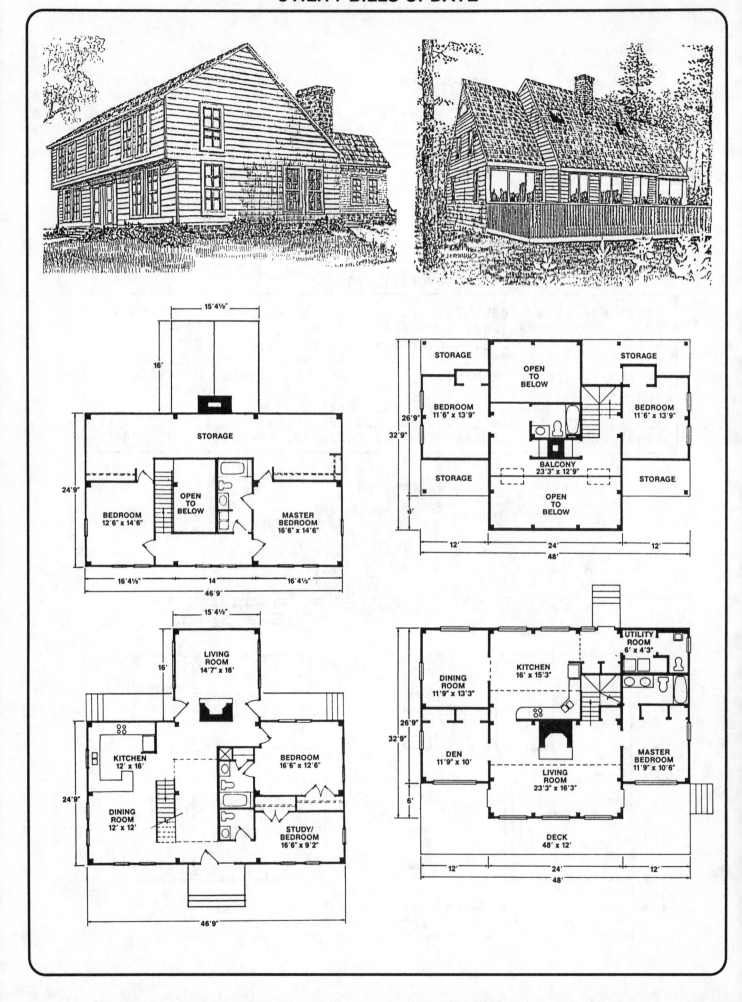

15'4½"

16'

STORAGE

24'9"

BEDROOM
12'6" x 14'6"

OPEN
TO
BELOW

MASTER
BEDROOM
16'6" x 14'6"

16'4½"   14   16'4½"

46'9"

STORAGE

OPEN
TO
BELOW

STORAGE

BEDROOM
11'6" x 13'9"

BEDROOM
11'6" x 13'9"

26'9"

32'9"

6'

STORAGE

BALCONY
23'3" x 12'9"

STORAGE

OPEN
TO
BELOW

12'   24'   12'

48'

15'4½"

16'

LIVING
ROOM
14'7" x 16'

24'9"

KITCHEN
12' x 16'

DINING
ROOM
12' x 12'

BEDROOM
16'6" x 12'6"

STUDY/
BEDROOM
16'6" x 9'2"

46'9"

UTILITY
ROOM
6' x 4'3"

DINING
ROOM
11'9" x 13'3"

KITCHEN
16' x 15'3"

DEN
11'9" x 10'

MASTER
BEDROOM
11'9" x 10'6"

LIVING
ROOM
23'3" x 16'3"

26'9"

32'9"

6'

DECK
48' x 12'

12'   24'   12'

48'

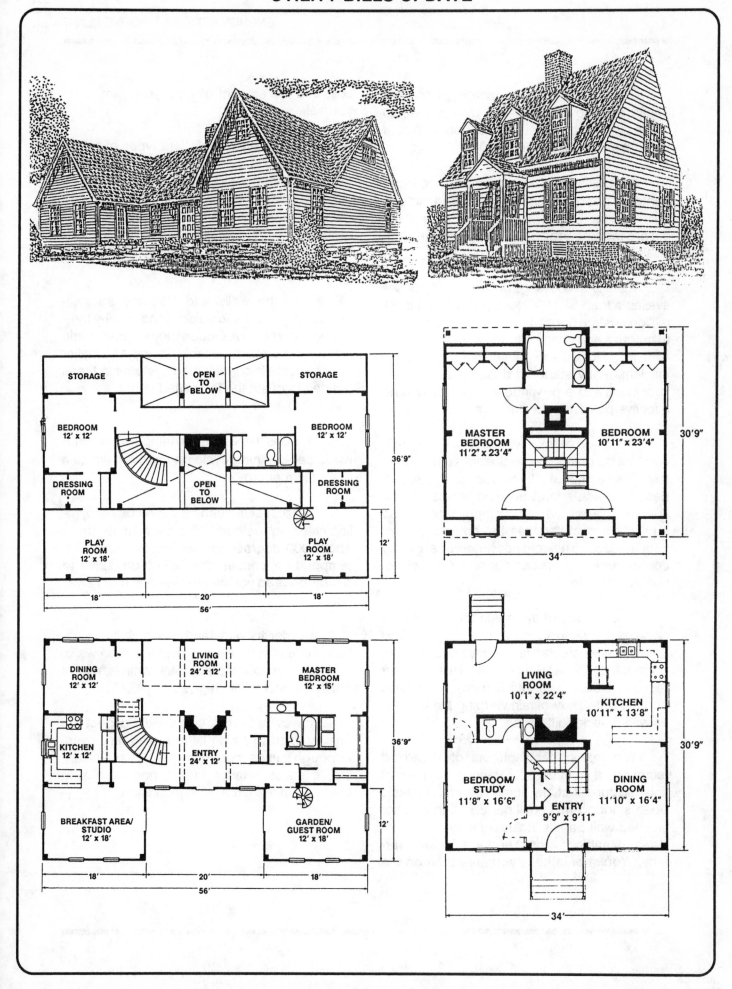

STORAGE

OPEN TO BELOW

STORAGE

BEDROOM 12' x 12'

BEDROOM 12' x 12'

DRESSING ROOM

OPEN TO BELOW

DRESSING ROOM

PLAY ROOM 12' x 18'

PLAY ROOM 12' x 18'

36'9"

12'

18'   20'   18'

56'

MASTER BEDROOM 11'2" x 23'4"

BEDROOM 10'11" x 23'4"

30'9"

34'

DINING ROOM 12' x 12'

LIVING ROOM 24' x 12'

MASTER BEDROOM 12' x 15'

KITCHEN 12' x 12'

ENTRY 24' x 12'

BREAKFAST AREA/ STUDIO 12' x 18'

GARDEN/ GUEST ROOM 12' x 18'

36'9"

12'

18'   20'   18'

56'

LIVING ROOM 10'1" x 22'4"

KITCHEN 10'11" x 13'8"

BEDROOM/ STUDY 11'8" x 16'6"

ENTRY 9'9" x 9'11"

DINING ROOM 11'10" x 16'4"

30'9"

34'

Q - I want to build an energy-efficient house and do some of the work myself to reduce the costs. What types of houses would be best and have low utility bills?

A - Unless you are an experienced carpenter, a good choice is a "panelized factory-built" house. Unlike the dull stereotype of the old pre-fabs, new factory-built houses are high-quality, energy-efficient, and attractive.

There is a wide range of factory-built houses available from $13,000 do-it-yourself kits to $1 million custom houses. The panels can be cut to any size and shape offering a limitless range of styles. Since these houses are very energy-efficient, many standard designs utilize open floor plans and large windows for attractive and effective passive solar heating.

Once you or your architect has designed your house plans, the engineers at the panelized house manufacturer use computers to design the actual large building panels for your specific plans. Then computer-controlled equipment manufactures the components of your house. This provides rigorous quality control and very precise fits during construction at your site.

Since much of the basic construction is done at the factory, the shell of a panelized house can be erected in few days and you can do much of the work yourself. This not only reduces labor costs, but it minimizes delays and the possibility of rain warping the framing as with a stick-built house.

The many manufacturers of panelized factory-built houses offer various degrees of finished construction. Some offer just the basic open studded-wall shell panels. Others offer finished wall panels including insulation, windows, plumbing, wiring, and interior wall surface. You should base your selection on the cost and the amount of work you want to do yourself.

The most energy-efficient types of panelized houses use foam-filled panels. These are extremely airtight and highly insulated. There are few internal wall studs to lose heat and transmit outdoor noise through the walls. Your utility bills for this type of factory-built panelized house should be about half that of a standard stick-built studded-wall house.

Since the walls and attic are so well-insulated, you should select good-quality thermal windows too. Although they will cost a little more, you should be able to install smaller heating and air-conditioning systems in these houses to offset the increased cost.

Q - Does using the high temperature automatic self-cleaning cycle on my oven waste a lot of extra energy?

A - Most self-cleaning ovens use a pyrolitic cleaning method. The oven heats up to about 900 degrees for two hours. This high temperature causes the baked-on spills to decompose so you can easily wipe them away later.

In order to withstand this high temperature, there is more insulation in the oven walls. This, plus the special thermostat controls, makes the initial cost a little higher.

However, overall, you should expect the energy used to be equal to a standard oven. Although it uses more energy while self-cleaning, it saves energy during normal baking because of the extra thick insulation.

UTILITY BILLS UPDATE

Dear Reader,

Thank you for your interest in writing to me about energy-efficient panelized houses. This product information, floor plans, and list of manufacturers are for your information only and are not an endorsement of this type of product or a specific brand, model, or manufacturer.

Sincerely,

Jim

Jim Dulley

MANUFACTURERS

```
ACORN STRUCTURES, P.O. Box 250, Concord, MA 01742
AFFORDABLE LUXURY HOMES, Box 288, Markle, IN 46770
AMERICAN STANDARD HOMES, P.O. Box 4908, Martinsville, VA 24115
AMERICAN TIMBER HOMES, P.O. Box 496, Escanaba, MI 49829
AMOS WINTER HOMES, RR 5, Box 168B, Brattleboro, VT 05302
BLUE RIDGE HOMES, 10620 Woodsboro Pk., Woodsboro, MD 21798
BUERMAN HOMES, RT. 1, Box 14, Cold Springs, MN 56320
CUSTOM MADE HOMES, 416 S. Robinson St., Bloomington, IL 61701
DECK HOUSE INC., 930 Main St., Acton, MA 01720
DELTEC HOMES, P.O. Box 6279, Ashville, NC 28818
ENDUR-A-LIFETIME, 7500 N.W. 72nd Ave., Miami, FL 33166
ENERCEPT BLDG. SYST., 3100 9th Ave. NE, Watertown, SD 57201
FUTURAMA HOMES, 5332 NW 25th St., Topeka, KS 66618
GREEN MOUNTAIN HOMES, P.O. Box 118, Royalton, VT 05068
HERITAGE HOMES, 1100 National Hwy, Thomasville, MC 27360
HOME MFG. & SUPPLY, 4401 E. 6th St., Sioux Falls, SD 57103
MILES HOMES, 4700 Nathan Ln., Minneapolis, MN 55440
NORTHERN ENERGY HOMES, Box 463 P, Norwich, VT 05055
NORTHERN HOMES, 51 Glenwood Ave., Glens Falls, NY 12801
PACIFIC COMPONENT HOMES, 1227 S. Weller, Seattle, WA 98144
PEASE COMPANY, 900 Laurel Ave., Hamilton, OH 45023
PERMABILT HOMES, 330 S. Kalamazoo Ave., Marshall, MI 49068
STANDARD HOMES, P.O. Box 1900, Olathe, KS 66061
SUMMEY BUILDING SYSTEMS, P.O. Box 497, Dallas, NC 28034
TECHBUILT HOMES, P.O. Box 128, North Dartmouth, MA 02747
THERMACRAFT HOMES, 1951 Galaxie St., Columbus, OH 43207
TRUE VALUE HOMES, 2150 E. University, Tempe, AZ 85281
WICK BUILDING SYSTEMS, 400 Walter Rd., Mazonmanie, WI 53560
YANKEE BARN HOMES, HCR 63, Box 2, Grantham, NH 03753
```

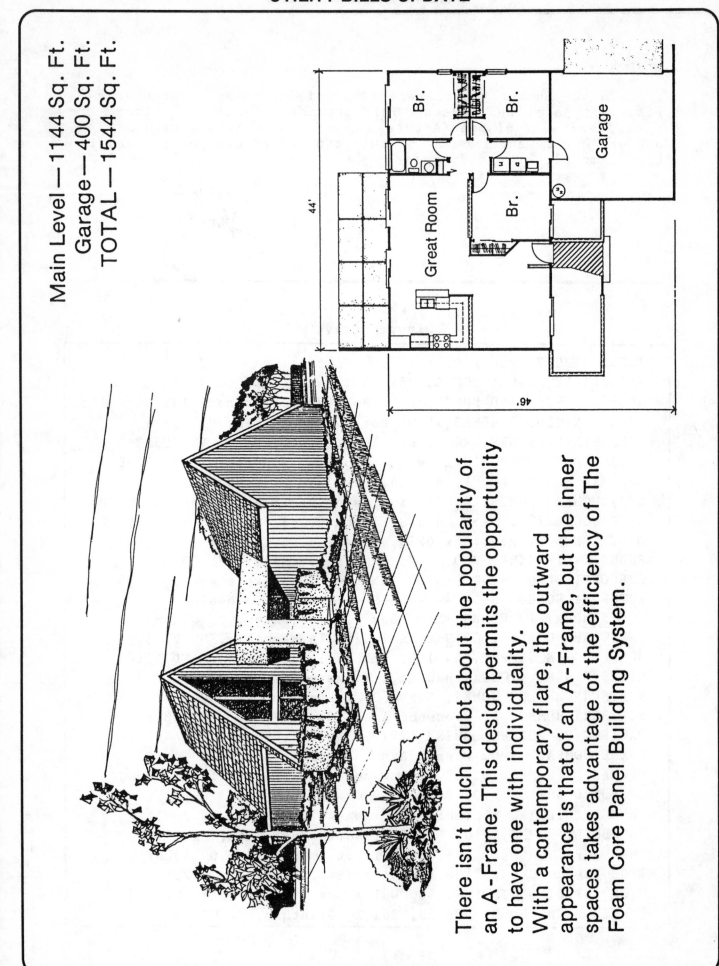

Main Level — 1144 Sq. Ft.
Garage — 400 Sq. Ft.
TOTAL — 1544 Sq. Ft.

44'

46'

Great Room

Br.

Br.

Br.

Garage

There isn't much doubt about the popularity of an A-Frame. This design permits the opportunity to have one with individuality.

With a contemporary flare, the outward appearance is that of an A-Frame, but the inner spaces takes advantage of the efficiency of The Foam Core Panel Building System.

UTILITY BILLS UPDATE

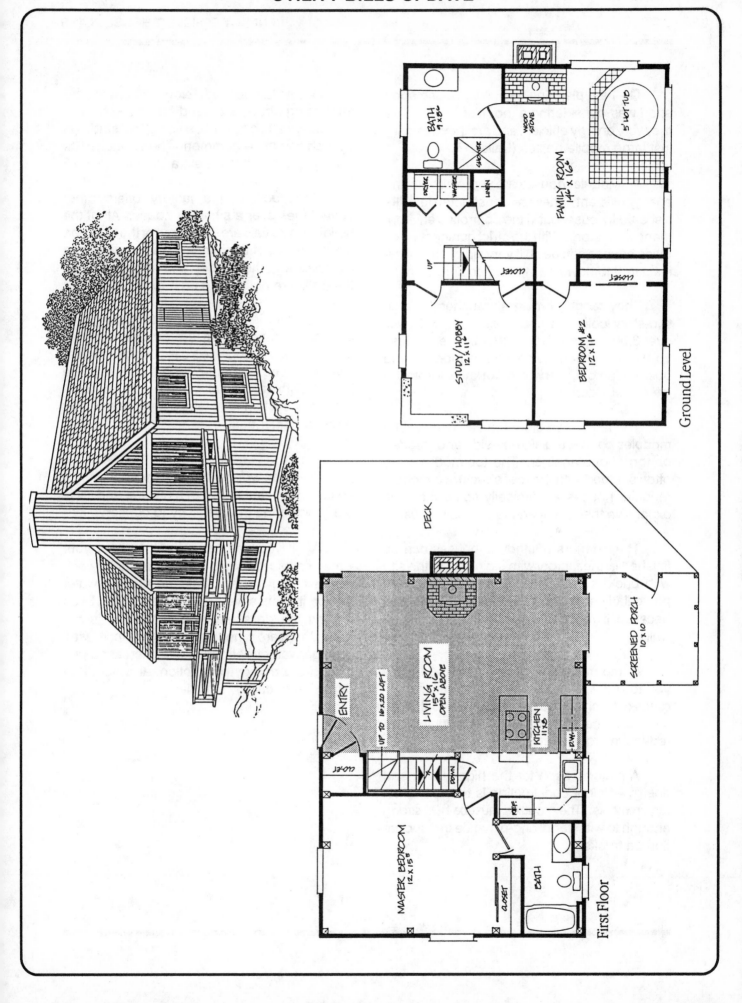

Ground Level

First Floor

Q - I am planning to build a house soon and I was considering a modular house. Are they very energy efficient and are they basically just large mobile homes (trailers)?

A - Modular houses are very well built and energy efficient. They are constructed just like a site-built house, but in the controlled environment of a factory. With the strict quality control, these houses can be built very airtight and well-insulated for low heating and cooling costs.

They range from small ranches to large two-story colonials and cape cods with well over 3,000 square feet of floor space. Unless you were told that the house was modular and built in a factory, you would not know it from the interior or exterior.

The larger two-story houses use several modules connected side-by-side and stacked on top of one another. The top modules are often shipped with the roof structure attached. Modular houses are typically somewhat less expensive than comparable site-built houses.

The exteriors of modular houses can be finished in the factory with siding, or at the site with brick, stucco, siding, etc.. Stucco is a particularly energy-efficient exterior wall finish because it reduces air leakage through the walls.

Some manufacturers and builders allow you to order a modular house to varying degrees of finish. If you are handy with tools, you can do some of the finish work yourself and reduce the total costs.

A major reason for the high-quality and energy-efficient construction is transportation requirements. The modules must be built strong enough to withstand long-distance transportation on trucks.

Heavy lumber and extra fasteners and reinforcing straps are used for strength. For example, wall construction using 2x6 studs on 16-inch centers is common. The six-inch thick walls provide space for extra insulation.

Construction in a factory offers other advantages over a site-built house. All of the building materials are stored out of the weather. Certain areas of the lumber can be nailed and fastened together better and stronger when the walls are not setting on a foundation.

You can install any type of heating and central air conditioning system. Baseboard electric heat is often used because of its lower initial cost and its room-by-room control of the heat. With a very efficient house, a high-efficiency system may take a long time to pay back its higher cost.

Q - I was wondering how much money it costs to heat one gallon of hot water and if it is really worth the trouble to try to conserve it?

A - If you use natural gas to heat your water, it typically costs about .2 cents for each gallon of hot water. With an electric water heater, it costs several times that much. Even though the dollar savings per gallon is not great, there are other hidden costs - increased sewage/water treatment costs, increased pollution from energy production, and needless depletion of energy supplies.

Dear Reader,

    Thank you for your interest in writing to me about modular housing. Contact many manufacturers for plans and the names of local builders who have experience with modular construction.

    This list of manufacturers and product information are for your information only and are not an endorsement of these types of products or a specific manufacturer.

Sincerely,

Jim Dulley

MODULAR HOUSING MANUFACTURERS

ACTIVE HOMES, 7938 S. Van Dyke, Marlette, MI 48453
ALL AMERICAN HOMES, Box 451, Decatur, IN 46733
AMERICAN DREAM MODULAR HOMES, 225 Goodwin, Springfield, MA 01151
ARABI HOMES, P.O. Box 117, Arabi, GA 31712
BENCHMARK COMMUNITIES, 630 Hay Ave., Brookville, OH 45309
CARDINAL INDUSTRIES, P.O. Box U, Sanford, FL 32772
COKER BUILDERS, P.O. Box 88, Turbeville, SC 29162
CONTEMPRI HOMES, Stauffer Industrial Park, Taylor, PA 18504
CONTINENTAL HOMES, 296 Daniel Webster Hwy. S., Nashua, NH 03060
CUSTOMIZED STRUCTURES, P.O. Box 884, Claremont, NH 03743
DELUXE HOMES, P.O. Box 323, Berwick, PA 18603
DESIGN HOMES, P.O. Box 411, W. Fifth St., Mifflinville, PA 186311
FLEETWOOD HOMES, Hwy 82, Box 1019, Pearson, GA 31642
GENERAL HOUSING CORP., 900 Andre St., Bay City, MI 48706
HAVEN HOMES, RD Box 178, Beech Creek, PA 16822
HECKAMAN HOMES, P.O. Box 229, Nappanee, IN 46550
HUNTINGTON HOMES, RFD 4, Box 2280, Montpelier, VT 05602
KAPLAN BUILDING SYSTEMS, P.O. Box 247, Pine Grove, PA 17963
KEY-LOC HOMES, P.O. Box 226, Suncock, NH 03275
KINGS HAVEN, P.O. Box 228, Ft. Payne, AL 35967
LINDAL CEDAR HOMES, Box 24426, Seattle, WA 981224
MITCHELL BROTHERS, RT. 20, Box 500, Birmingham, AL 35214
MOD-U-KRAF HOMES, P.O. Box 573, Rocky Mount, VA 24151
MUNCY HOMES, P.O. Box 325, Muncy, PA 17756
NANTICOKE HOMES, P.O. Box F, Greenwood, DE 19950
NATIONWIDE HOMES, P.O. Box 5511, Martinsville, VA 24115
PENN LYON HOMES, P.O. Box 27, Selinsgrove, PA 17870
POLORON HOMES, 74 Ridge Rd., Box 187, Middleburg, PA 177842
RYLAND MODULAR HOMES, 10221 Wincopin Cr., Columbia, MD 21044
SCHULT HOMES, P.O. Box 219, Elkton, MD 21921
SUMMEY PRODUCTS, P.O. Box 791, Dallas, NC 28034
UNIBILT INDUSTRIES, P.O. Box 373, Vandalia, OH 45377

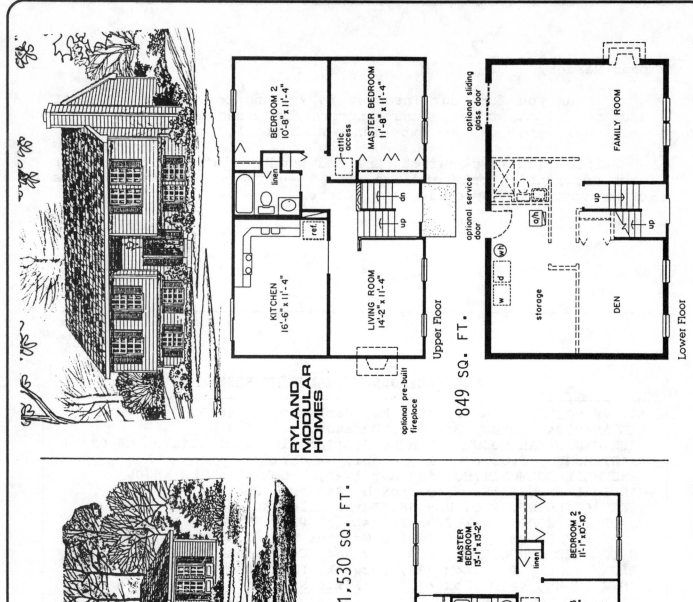

RYLAND MODULAR HOMES

849 SQ. FT.

Upper Floor

BEDROOM 2
10'-8" x 11'-4"

MASTER BEDROOM
11'-8" x 11'-4"

attic access

linen

ref.

KITCHEN
16'-6" x 11'-4"

LIVING ROOM
14'-2" x 11'-4"

dn

up

optional pre-built fireplace

Lower Floor

optional sliding glass door

optional service door

FAMILY ROOM

g/h

w/h

w

d

storage

DEN

up

up

RYLAND MODULAR HOMES

1,530 SQ. FT.

MASTER BEDROOM
13'-1" x 13'-2"

BEDROOM 2
11'-1" x10'-10"

linen

walk-in closet

dn.

attic access

BEDROOM 3
11'-1" x 9'-10"

optional formal dining room

COUNTRY KITCHEN
20'-11" x 13'-2"

ref.

LIVING ROOM
18'-0" x 13'-2"

LAUNDRY ROOM
11'-9" x 6'-1"

w. d.

optional pre-built fireplace

FAMILY ROOM
11'-9" x 20'-5"

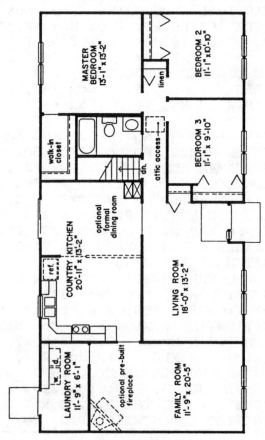

UTILITY BILLS UPDATE

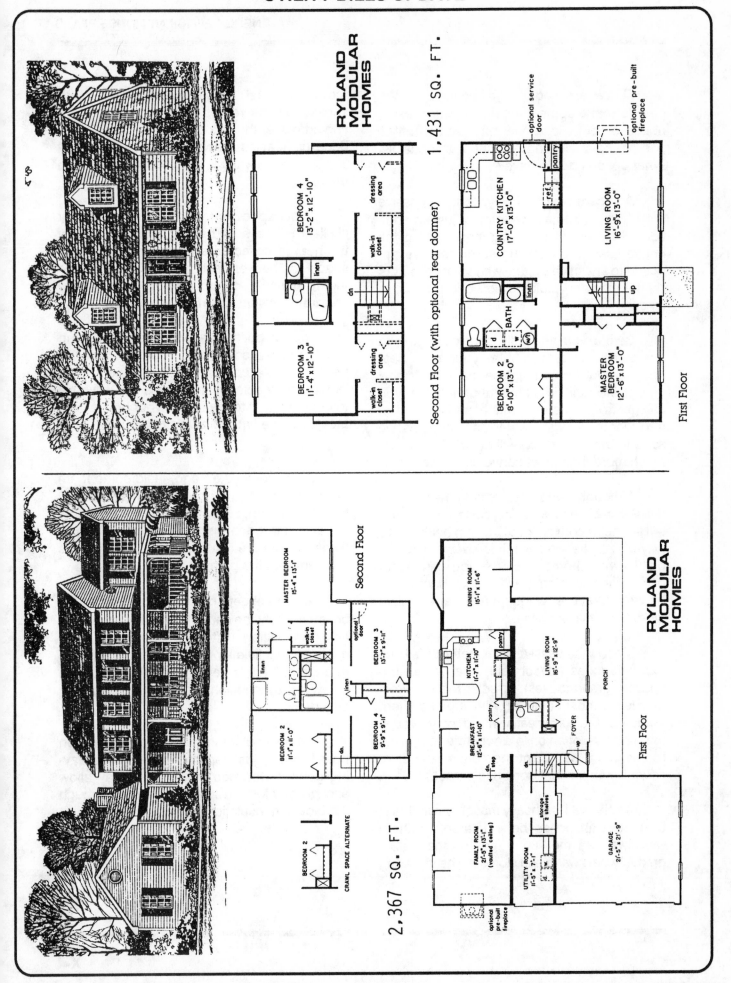

RYLAND MODULAR HOMES

1,431 SQ. FT.

Second Floor (with optional rear dormer)

BEDROOM 4
13'-2" x 12'-10"

BEDROOM 3
11'-4" x 12'-10"

dressing area

dressing area

walk-in closet

walk-in closet

linen

dn

First Floor

optional service door

optional pre-built fireplace

COUNTRY KITCHEN
17'-0" x 13'-0"

pantry

ref.

LIVING ROOM
16'-9" x 13'-0"

linen

BATH

d   w/h   w

BEDROOM 2
8'-10" x 13'-0"

MASTER BEDROOM
12'-6" x 13'-0"

up

RYLAND MODULAR HOMES

2,367 SQ. FT.

Second Floor

MASTER BEDROOM
15'-4" x 13'-1"

BEDROOM 2
11'-1" x 11'-0"

linen

walk-in closet

optional door

BEDROOM 3
13'-7" x 9'-11"

BEDROOM 4
9'-9" x 9'-11"

linen

dn.

BEDROOM 2

CRAWL SPACE ALTERNATE

First Floor

DINING ROOM
15'-1" x 11'-6"

KITCHEN
11'-7" x 11'-10"

pantry

LIVING ROOM
16'-9" x 12'-9"

pantry

BREAKFAST
12'-6" x 11'-10"

FOYER

PORCH

up

dn.

FAMILY ROOM
21'-5" x 13'-1"
(vaulted ceiling)

storage 2 shelves

UTILITY ROOM
11'-5" x 7'-1"

d.   w.

GARAGE
21'-5" x 21'-9"

optional pre-built fireplace

dn. 1 step

Q - We are tired of high heating bills. We plan to make some additions to our present house or to build a new one, and to utilize passive solar heating as much as possible. What options do we have?

A - There are many ways to build passive solar heating into a new home or just an addition. Passive solar heating means using the house itself to collect the sun's heat, as opposed to an active system with solar collectors on the roof and piping, ductwork, pumps, or fans.

Before you seriously consider trying to use passive solar heating as your major heat source, your home must be made extremely energy efficient. The amount of heat that you can get from the sun is limited, and it must last throughout the night. A well-designed passive solar home or addition will generally not cost much more than most conventional designs.

Although using passive solar heating will definitely reduce your heating costs, most homes will still need conventional backup heating. To fully utilize passive solar, it is always better to build a new home because you can better design the floor plan. Passive solar homes can be very attractive, unique, and offer excellent utilization of floor space.

Most of the passive solar methods fall into four catagories - direct gain, solar walls, sunspaces (greenhouses), or solar roofs. Direct gain is the most common, with large southern windows. The sun's heat shines directly through the windows, often on to a concrete floor in the rooms. You can paint the concrete floor or cover it with tile, but don't use carpet.

A solar wall is a heavy masonry wall that is built several inches behind large southern windows. As the sun shines on the wall, it gradually gets warm and stores the heat. During the day, the heat slowly moves through the wall and keeps the rooms warm. At night, you should close shutters over the window to reduce the heat loss back outside. The heat that is stored in the wall will warm the room through the night.

A sunspace/greenhouse is somewhat similar to direct solar heating, except that all of the heat is collected and stored in the sunspace, instead of each room. You can use thermostatically controlled fans to blow the heat from the sunspace throughout your home.

You can build windows into a south facing roof to make a solar roof. Your roof itself will become a solar collector. This method is more like an active solar system since you will have to duct the heat to the rest of your house, and provide some type of heat storage mass.

Q - Several years ago, I laid some foam insulation sheets over the blown-in attic insulation. Since then, the paint on the ceiling below my attic has been discolored and peeling at times. Could the insulation have caused this problem with the paint?

A - The sheets of foam insulation board are most likely the cause of the problem. That type of insulation is often a closed-cell material, meaning that little air or water vapor can pass through it. This is trapping the moisture from below in the insulation and making your ceiling stay damp.

Before you remove the foam insulation board, first try just separating the pieces leaving gaps in between them. That may allow enough area for the moisture to escape through the blown-in insulation below it.

Dear Reader,

Thank you for your interest in writing to me about passive solar heating. These layouts should give you some idea of the types of homes that utilize passive solar heating. As you can see, they are not extremely strange looking and are very functional. These homes were designed to use passive solar heating as their primary source of heat.

Sincerely,

Jim

Jim Dulley

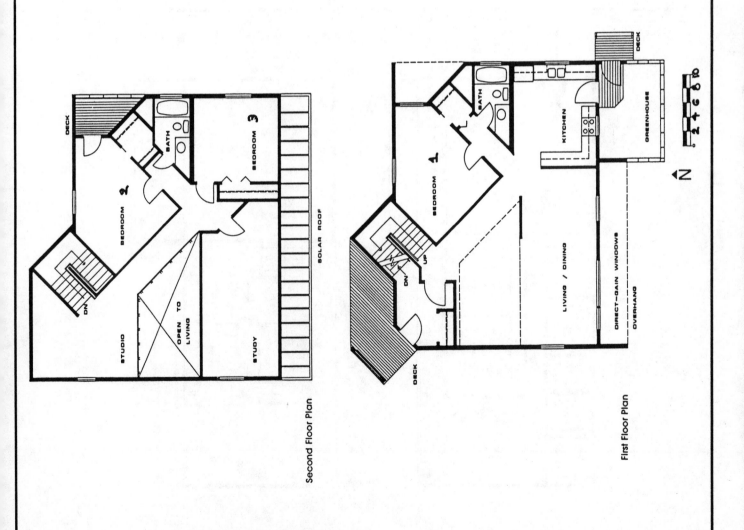

Second Floor Plan

First Floor Plan

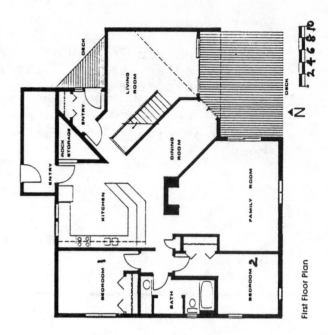

First Floor Plan

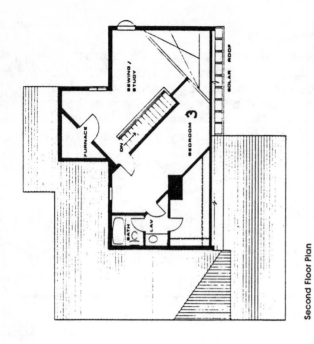

Second Floor Plan

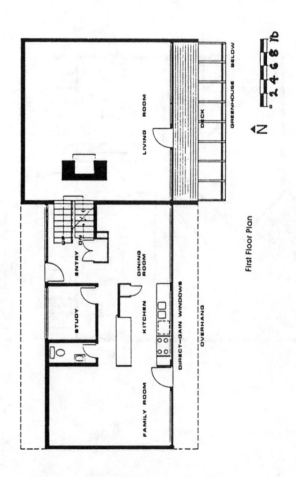

First Floor Plan

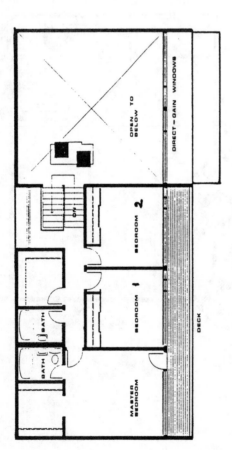

Second Floor Plan

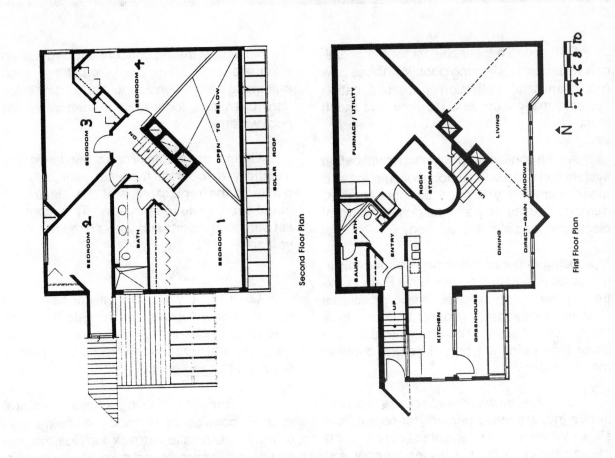

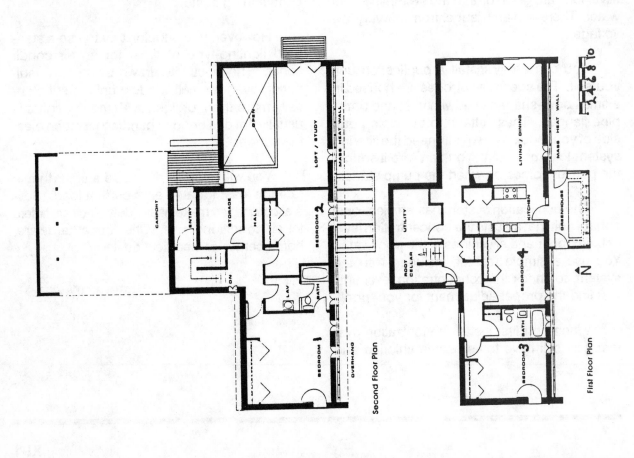

Q - I spend a lot each year for the chemicals to treat my swimming pool. Will those new (no chemicals) ionization pool purification systems really work and do they use much electricity?

A - An ionization pool water purification system can reduce the amount of chlorine and other chemicals you need by more than 90 percent. It uses only several dollars worth of electricity per swimming season.

Using minerals, silver and copper, to purify water is an ancient process. Even in extremely low concentrations, silver kills bacteria. Copper, in the same low concentrations, stops the growth of algae. The concentrations are lower than in many types of natural drinking mineral water.

An ionization water purifier uses two electrodes that are made primarily of copper and silver. When a low voltage electrical current is passed between the electrodes, copper and silver ions are given off into the swimming pool water. There isn't any danger from this very low voltage.

You can easily install a purification unit yourself. The special electrodes are housed in a small bowl-shaped tank with inlet and outlet pipe flanges. These attach to the piping outside of your pool. You will still need the filtering system to remove dirt. You can wire it so that the purifier comes on when the pump starts.

The purification system has an electronic control unit that adjusts the concentration level of the copper and silver ions in the pool water. You use a simple test kit, included with the system, to check the concentration level until you find the proper adjustment for your pool.

When you first install the ionization system, you still have to use some chlorine and chemicals until the ion concentrations get to an adequate level. Then, a couple of times each swimming season, you should add some standard chemicals for a quick treatment of the pool water.

Other than couple of cents per day for the electricity to operate the unit, your only expense is the replacement of the electrodes about every three to five years. They come in set with new gaskets and you can replace them yourself.

Q - I put my window air conditioner in again. I know it saves electricity to turn it off when I leave. Can I plug my air conditioner into the timer that I use for my lights and have it come on before I get home?

A - Your idea of using a timer to control your air conditioner is good. It is similar to using an automatic setback furnace thermostat during the winter and it would cut your air-conditioning costs.

However, you shouldn't try to use a standard lighting-type of timer for an air conditioner. The electricity drawn by an air conditioner, even a small window unit, is substantially more than for lights. A timer for lights is usually not designed to handle that much electric current.

You will need to purchase a timer that is rated at least for a 15 amp-current load. Several companies make heavy-duty electrical timers for air-conditioner use. Check at a hardware, home center or electrical dealer.

UTILITY BILLS UPDATE

Dear Reader,

Thank you for your interest in writing to me about the ionization type of swimming pool water purification system. You will still have to regularly check the cleanliness and pH of the water as you do now.

I have enclosed some descriptive product information and general operating instructions about one of the swimming pool ionization systems to give you an idea of how one works.

This product information and list of manufacturers are for your information only and are not an endorsement of this type of product or a specific manufacturer or model.

Sincerely,

Jim

Jim Dulley

MANUFACTURERS

AUTOMATED POOL PROD., 9717 Lurline Ave., Chatsworth, CA 91311

CARIBBEAN CLEAR, 220 Executive Dr., #310, Columbia, SC 29210

HELIOTROPE GENERAL, 3733 Kenora Dr., Spring Valley, CA 92077

PUREWATER, 563 S. 11th St., Kansas City, KS 66105

TARN-PURE, 2300 Paseo del Prado., #D206, Las Vegas, NV 89102

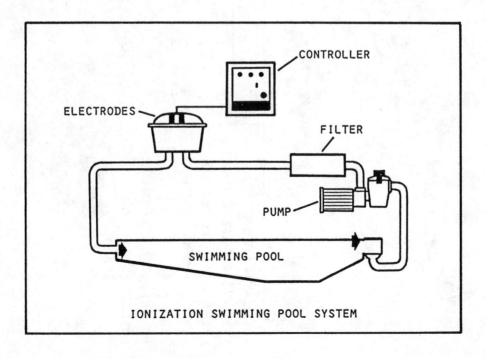

IONIZATION SWIMMING POOL SYSTEM

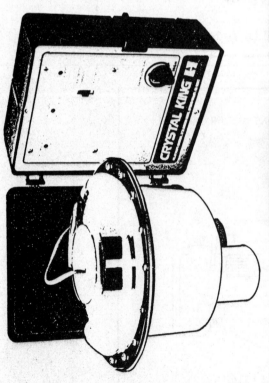

CRYSTAL KING™ INSTRUCTIONS

DESCRIPTION

The Crystal King™ purifies pool or spa water by releasing a constant supply of non-toxic copper, silver, and nickel ions into the water to kill algae and bacteria. The bacteria and algae are killed, then flocculate (clump together) and are removed by the filter.

The ions which are released by electrolytic action between the two low voltage electrodes are not depleted by sunlight or evaporation as chemicals are. Interaction with the micro-organism which they are designed to kill is the only factor which depletes the ions, and the Crystal King™ automatically releases a constant supply to replenish the ions lost.

Once installed and running, the Crystal King™ nearly eliminates the need for potentially toxic chemicals which may cause corrosion, bleaching, skin and eye irritation.

The use of the Crystal King™ should be thought of as a low-rate-of-discharge disinfectant. Until an appropriate level of copper content is in the pool water, the effectiveness is not at a satisfactory level. In contrast, the addition of chlorine provides an immediate high-rate-of-discharge disinfectant. Although an appropriate level of copper content may be in the pool water, circumstances such as intense pool usage and/or extremely hot weather may overpower the disinfectant abilities of the ion discharge method of purification. In this event a high-rate-of-discharge disinfectant such as chlorine will be needed. Ion discharge purification could be compared to drip irrigation versus chlorine compared to flood irrigation.

INSTALLATION

Flow Cell:
The flow cell is to be installed in an upright position after the pool filter in the return water line. The flow cell has two fitting connections. Either one is the inlet and the other becomes the outlet. The flow cell connections accomodate either 1½" PVC pipe inside or a 2" PVC coupling or "L" on the outside.

Electronic Control:
Remove the four screws holding the front panel of the electronic control to the plastic box and separate the front panel from the box. The electronic control should then be suitably mounted close to the pool filtration pump time clock and the flow cell using screws and the provided plastic tabs. Bring in 120V or 240V and a code approved ground wire from the time clock switched terminals to the appropriate terminal connections inside the plastic box. Use weatherproof flexible conduit and minimum 14 gauge wire. For 120V use terminals #2 and #3. For 240V use terminals #2 and #5. Next connect the black and red wires (the white wire is not used) from the flow cell to the two-terminal connector strip at the top of the electronic circuit board. Replace the front panel. Place the switch on the front panel into the up position.

Upon turning the time clock "ON" verify that the system function indicator light (left indicator) is lit. If not, investigate for wiring error. During initial installation place the adjustment knob on the front panel in the full clockwise position.

Test pool water for pH and treat to establish a level between 7.4 to 7.6. Because the period of time for a typical pool to reach the correct ion level is approximately two to three weeks it will be necessary to continue the established method of pool chlorination (or other chemical method) until the copper content level is up to 0.3 parts per million (PPM). This period of several weeks can be accelerated by letting the pool pump run 24 hours per day until the 0.3 PPM copper content level has been reached.

TESTING

A copper test kit is provided to test the pool water for its copper content and the instructions thereon should be followed. Various factors affect the copper content: Setting of adjustment knob on the front panel, quantity of water in the pool, cleanliness of the water and number of hours that the pool pump runs. Initially the water should be tested every five days until the copper content reaches a range of .3 to .4 PPM (note that test intervals on most test kits is .05 PPM, therefore six times 0.05 equals 0.3 and eight times 0.05 equals 0.4 PPM). After the pool has reached between 0.3 to 0.4 PPM the knob should be placed at an approximate 12 o'clock position and subsequent testing and trial and error will indicate the correct setting to maintain the 0.3 to 0.4 PPM copper content level. If pool pump time is increased during the summer the adjustment knob should be changed to decrease the ion discharge rate. Likewise if winter hours are decreased, the knob should be changed to increase the rate. It is generally acceptable, however, to allow the copper content to be lower during the cooler temperatures of winter. After a correct setting has been determined it is advisable to test the copper content every month. CAUTION: Do not let copper level exceed 0.4 PPM. Excessive copper level will cause a blue green discoloration of the pool walls. The pool pH level should be maintained from 7.4 to 7.6.

CHLORINE SHOCK TREATMENT

The Crystal King™ is not intended to be a 100% substitute for chlorine or other appropriate chemical treatment. Certain organisms develop resistance to any attempt to be killed, consequently it is recommended to chlorine shock treat the pool about three times a year (organisms develop resistance to chlorine as well as the ion method so the use of both compliments each other). Recommended times to chlorine shock the pool are at the beginning of the swimming season and during the peak summer heat period. Additionally, a shock may be desirable after a day of excessive pool use, particularly if children may have urinated in the pool water or any time the pool has lost its crystal clear look and appears cloudy in color. To chlorine shock treat a residential pool, add two gallons after the sun has set after the last use of the pool for the day. The filtration pump is best left on for 24 hours to adequately mix the liquid chlorine with the water and provide for extra filtration.

pH LEVEL

The pool pH should be maintained at 7.4 to 7.6. The requirement for acid addition to maintain the pool pH in this range is greatly reduced due to use of the Crystal King™ rather than the chlorine method. After chlorine shocking the pool, pH should be checked.

HOURS OF FILTRATION PUMPING

There is no need to change the normal hours of pumping, however, a minimum of six hours per day is usually necessary to maintain the correct copper content level for a typical residential pool. Pools larger than 60,000 gallons should have more than one Crystal King™ unit installed.

TROUBLESHOOTING

The only maintenance required for the Crystal King™ pool purification unit is replacement of the electrodes. Typically the electrodes last a minimum of two years and sometimes up to five years. Three indicator lights on the front panel indicate status of the Crystal King™. With the unit powered at the same time as the filtration pump only one of the three lights should be lit. The indicator at the left indicates that everything is OK. The "electrodes shorted" light indicates a short between the electrodes and they may be visually examined by looking through the clear cover of the flow cell. The "ion current" light indicates that either the electrodes have been depleted beyond their useful life, there is a broken connection, the water conductivity is too low, the control has failed, or severe scaling has insulated the electrodes.

The low voltage output to the flow cell is 750 mA at 32 VAC maximum. This current flow alternates between positive and negative every four minutes. The electrodes are 93% copper, 4% nickel and 3% silver.

Q - I don't like real cool water in my swimming pool and I want to be able to extend my swimming season, but it costs a lot to heat it. Is there a simple solar system to heat the water that I can make myself?

A - Heating your swimming pool water can generally give you several more months use of it each year. Unfortunately, it is very expensive for the fuel to heat the water, and swimming pools are not very energy-efficient. They seem to lose heat almost as quickly as you supply it.

You can easily build several types of solar swimming pool heating systems yourself from simple to automatic-controlled ones. Once you build and install one, the heat is practically free.

You can either build simple solar collectors yourself, or purchase them individually. Your existing filter pump circulates the pool water through the collectors, so you'll just need minor plumbing changes.

The simplest system just uses black hose coiled on top of a plywood platform. The water is warmed as it passes through the hose. Although it is not extremely energy-efficient, it is very inexpensive and does work. You will probably have to replace the hose every year or two because the pool chemicals slowly attack it. A longer and fatter hose is better.

The best do-it-yourself solar pool heating system uses inexpensive purchased collectors and a temperature-controlled diverter valve. This valve allows water to pass through the collectors only when they get hot enough in the sun. A manual valve works, but it requires more monitoring.

This automatic diverter valve senses the temperatures of the water in the pool and the collectors. By monitoring these, it automatically determines when the pool water should flow through the solar collectors.

Install the plumbing so that the water leaving the pool filter flows through the diverter valve either up to the collectors or directly back into the pool. The automatic temperature sensor controls the diverter valve.

The best angle of tilt (from horizontal) for your solar collectors is roughly the latitude angle for your area minus 10 degrees. This absorbs the most solar heat during the spring, summer, and fall.

Q - Our water bills were high last summer when we watered the lawn. I am sure that I wastefully over-watered at times. How can I tell when the lawn needs watering?

A - It can be somewhat difficult to gauge when your lawn needs more water since not all areas need the same amount of watering. Over-watering won't help your lawn, and it can significantly increase your water bills over an entire summer.

One way to check your lawn for dryness is to push a screwdriver into the ground. If it goes down at least six inches without stiff resistance, then the soil is probably moist enough. Try this in several areas of your lawn to locate any dry spots.

Also, early in the morning, walk across your lawn. The impressions from your feet should only last several seconds. If it takes longer for the grass to spring back, if it does at all, then it may need more water.

Dear Reader,

   Thank you for your interest in writing to me. The
information on the simple do-it-yourself solar pool heating
system is shown below. This literature and list of manufacturers
are for your information only and are not an endorsement of these
types of products or a specific manufacturer or model.

Sincerely

Jim Dulley

MANUFACTURERS

SOLAR COLLECTORS –

 FAFCO, 235 Constitution Dr., Menlo Park, CA 94025
 HELIOCOL, 12087-62nd St. N., Largo, FL 34643
 RADCO, 2905 Industrial Pky., Santa Maria, CA 93455
 SUNGLO, 35 Citron Ct., Concord, Ontario, Canada L4K2S7

VALVES –

 HELIOTROPE GENERAL, 3733 Kenora Dr., Spring Valley, CA 92077
 SOLARMETRICS, 250 Commercial St., Manchester NH 03101

LAYOUT FOR MULTIPLE COLLECTORS

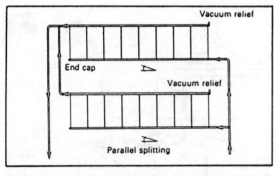

Parallel splitting

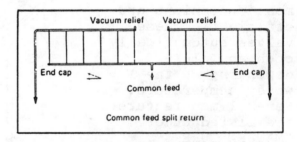

Common feed split return

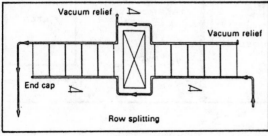

Row splitting

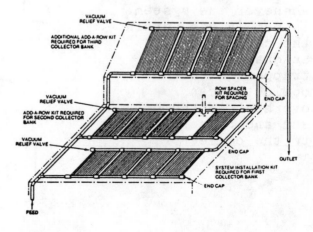

SIMPLE DO-IT-YOURSELF SOLAR SYSTEM

1) Purchase a clear skylight or window well cover to use as the cover for the solar collector. It needn't be covered, but the cover will increase the efficiency and heat output.
2) Cut a plywood base for the collector. It shold be sized to fit under the clear cover.
3) Use black hose or pipe for the solar collector. Coil it on top of the plywood collector base. Tie the hose coils together and fix it securely to the plywood base.
4) Cut notches in the plywood base for the ends of the hose or pipe to exit under the clear cover.
5) Bore a two inch hole in a wood block and attach it to the back of the collector base. This will be the socket for the 2-inch-diameter pipe mast.
6) Set a pipe (with a 2-inch internal diameter) in the ground. That will be the base socket for the mast and collector. You can just fix it in concrete, but then you can't rotate it. For maximum heat outut, it is best to rotate it throughout the day to keep it facing directly into the sun.
7) Set up the plumbing as shown in the diagram. Your existing filter pump will be use to circulate the water through the collector.
8) The simplest method just uses valves that you manually open and close to control the flow of water through the collector. You can mount thermometers as shown so you will know when the water temperatures are hot enough so you should direct the water through the collector.
9) You can use electronic (solenoid) diverter valves and temperature sensors as shown. That is most convenient and efficient. These valves automatically open and close depending on the water temperature. Several manufacturers are listed under "MANUFACTURERS".
10) Whenever the system is not in use, drain the collector. Stagnant water trapped in the collector can overheat in the hot sun and cause damage to the collector.

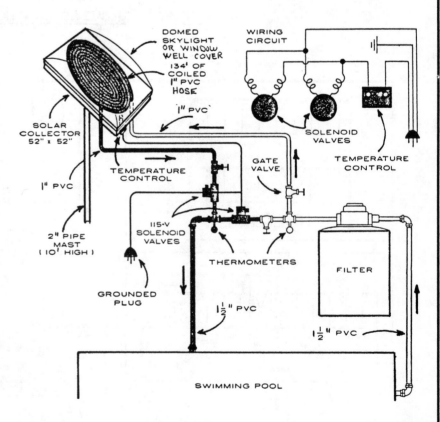

UTILITY BILLS UPDATE

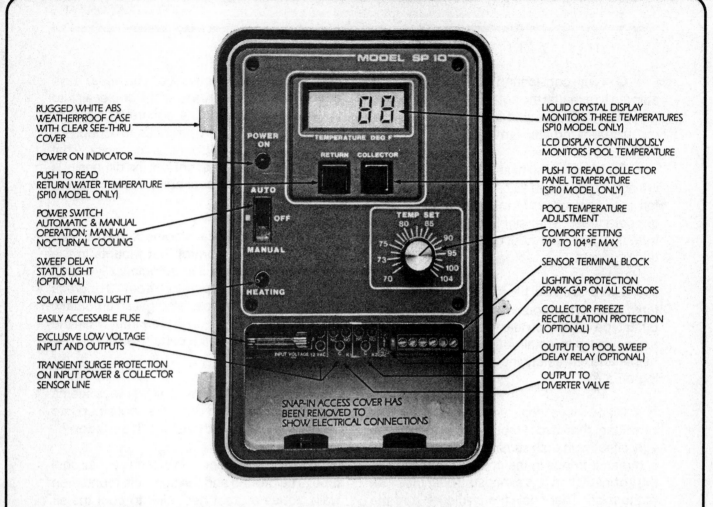

SP10 **Contains a built in LCD display of pool, collector and return line temperatures**

SP20 **Has all the features of the SP10 noted in the above picture, except for the temperature display**

MODEL SP10 SYSTEM INCLUDES	
SP10	Control
SM2	Pool/Spa Sensor (2)
SM3	Collector Sensor
SR224	3 Way, 2" Diverter Valve with Manual Override
TR12 or	Indoor Transformer
TR15	Outdoor Transformer

Options Available

Nocturnal Cooling
Pool Sweep Delay
Freeze Recirculation

MODEL SP20 SYSTEM INCLUDES	
SP20	Control
SM2	Pool/Spa Sensor
SM3	Collector Sensor
SR224	3 Way, 2" Diverter Valve with Manual Override
TR12 or	Indoor Transformer
TR15	Outdoor Transformer

Solarmetrics offers a complete line of temperature controls for pools, spas, hot water systems, sun rooms and greenhouses.

SOLARMETRICS
250 COMMERCIAL STREET, MANCHESTER, NEW HAMPSHIRE 03101 □ PHONE (603) 668-3216

Q - I was considering installing an electric attic fan to exhaust the hot air from my attic. Are they really effective and how can I determine the proper-sized attic fan to install?

A - Much of the heat entering your home is from your roof and attic. An electric attic vent fan is a very effective method to lower attic temperatures. That significantly reduces the heat flow into your house and your air-conditioning costs.

There are two basic types of attic vent fans. One type mounts in the gable and the other type in the roof near the peak. Both types are very easy to install yourself. Always have a helper and use safety lines when you are working on a roof.

If you have soffit vents under the roof overhang, then a roof-mounted attic vent fan is very effective in both summer and winter. In the summer, it brings in the cool outdoor air over the hot insulation and exhausts it near the peak of the roof. That cools the insulation and the entire attic, so less heat is transferred into your house.

In the winter, the air flow over the insulation keeps moisture-laden air from becoming stagnant in your attic. During cold spells, water droplets can form in stagnant moisture-laden air. That can soak your attic insulation and cause serious problems.

Attic vent fan capacities are measured by the volume of air flow that they produce, in cubic feet per minute (CFM). A rule of thumb is that you need 0.7 CFM of fan capacity for each square foot of attic floor area. If you have a dark roof, add an additional 15-percent capacity. The capacities of various vent fans range from about 900 CFM to 1,600 CFM.

In order to be effective, you must have adequate inlet vent area to let the cooler air into your attic. Typically, one square foot of inlet vent area, preferably in the soffits, is needed for each 300 CFM of attic vent fan capacity. That is actual net open area, not just the dimensions of the vent. The vent packaging usually lists the net free vent area.

Many attic vent fans come with an adjustable thermostatic control that mounts in the attic. You can adjust it to automatically switch on the fan at any temperature from 70 degrees to 130 degrees. You can also get an automatic humidistat to switch it on in the winter when the attic humidity reaches a certain level.

Q - Our vented crawl space always seems cool. Is it possible to draw the cool air up into our house with an exhaust fan in a window?

A - A crawl space can work as a mini cool tube. The ground and the concrete foundation walls act as a great heat sink to cool the air drawn through it during the day. If it gets cool enough at night, the air flowing through it keeps it cool for the next day.

Cut an inlet hole in your floor and place a strong register/grill over it. You should cover the dirt crawl space floor with polyethylene vapor barrier film. This reduces the amount of moisture picked up by the air and minimizes a warm muggy feeling.

Dear Reader,

    Thank you for writing to me about attic vent fans. These fans can reduce the temperature in your attic and help keep your house cooler. Use the chart below to determine the size of fan your attic requires.

    This information and product literature are for your information only and are not an endorsement of this type of product or a specific manufacturer or model.

Sincerely,

Jim Dulley

POWER ATTIC FAN REQUIREMENTS (cfm) FOR VARIOUS ATTIC SIZES

WIDTH IN FEET

LENGTH IN FEET	20	22	24	26	28	30	32	34	36	38	40	42	44	46	48	50
20	280	308	336	364	392	420	448	476	504	532	560	588	616	644	672	700
22	308	339	370	400	431	462	493	524	554	585	616	647	678	708	739	770
24	336	370	403	437	470	504	538	571	605	638	672	706	739	773	806	840
26	364	400	437	473	510	546	582	619	655	692	728	764	801	837	874	910
28	392	431	470	510	549	588	627	666	706	745	784	823	862	902	941	980
30	420	462	504	546	588	630	672	714	756	798	840	882	924	966	1008	1050
32	448	493	538	582	627	672	717	761	806	851	896	941	986	1030	1075	1120
34	476	524	571	619	666	714	762	809	857	904	952	1000	1047	1095	1142	1190
36	504	554	604	655	706	756	806	857	907	958	1008	1058	1109	1159	1210	1260
38	532	585	638	692	745	798	851	904	958	1011	1064	1117	1170	1224	1277	1330
40	560	616	672	728	784	840	896	952	1008	1064	1120	1176	1232	1288	1344	1400
42	588	647	706	764	823	882	941	1000	1058	1117	1176	1234	1294	1352	1411	1470
44	616	678	739	801	862	924	986	1047	1109	1170	1232	1294	1355	1417	1478	1540
46	644	708	773	837	902	966	1030	1095	1159	1224	1288	1352	1417	1481	1546	1610
48	672	739	806	874	941	1008	1075	1142	1210	1277	1344	1411	1478	1546	1613	1680
50	700	770	840	910	980	1050	1120	1190	1260	1330	1400	1470	1540	1610	1680	1750
52	728	801	874	946	1019	1092	1165	1238	1310	1383	1456	1529	1602	1674	1747	1820
54	756	832	907	983	1058	1134	1210	1285	1361	1436	1512	1588	1663	1739	1814	1890
56	784	862	941	1019	1098	1176	1254	1333	1411	1490	1568	1646	1725	1803	1882	1960
58	812	893	974	1056	1137	1218	1299	1380	1462	1543	1624	1705	1786	1868	1949	2030
60	840	924	1008	1092	1176	1260	1344	1428	1512	1596	1680	1764	1848	1932	2016	2100
62	868	955	1042	1128	1215	1302	1389	1476	1562	1649	1736	1823	1910	1996	2083	2170
64	896	986	1075	1165	1254	1344	1434	1523	1613	1702	1792	1882	1971	2061	2150	2240
66	924	1016	1108	1201	1294	1386	1478	1571	1663	1756	1848	1940	2033	2125	2218	2310
68	952	1047	1142	1238	1333	1428	1523	1618	1714	1809	1904	1999	2094	2190	2285	2380
70	980	1078	1176	1274	1372	1470	1568	1666	1764	1862	1960	2058	2156	2254	2352	2450

HVI Chart

To determine what size power ventilator is needed to cool your attic efficiently, find the length of your attic on the vertical column and the width on the horizontal column. Where two columns intersect, you will find the required CFM rated ventilator (Courtesy of Home Ventilating Institute).

UTILITY BILLS UPDATE

POWER ATTIC FAN MANUFACTURERS

```
#1 - AUBREY MFG., 6709 S. Main St., Union, IL 60180
#2 - BROAN MFG., P.O. Box 140, State St., Hartford, WI 53027
#3 - FASCO INDUSTRIES, P.O. Box 150, Fayetteville, NC 28302
#4 - KOOL-O-MATIC CORP., P.O. Box 310, Niles, MI 49120
#5 - LEIGH A HARROW, 411 6th Ave., Coopersville, MI 49404
#6 - NUTONE, Madison & Red Bank, Cincinnati, OH 45227
#7 - TPI, P.O. Box T-CRS, Johnson City, TN 37602
```

MANUFACTURER	MODEL NO.	CAPACITY (cfm)
#1	9000	1000
	9090	1450
	9105	1050
	9120	1200
	9130	1300
	9150	1500
	9160	1600
#2	350	1050
	353	1200
	356	1600
	358	1200
#3	AGV-14	1140
	APRV-16	1200
	RV-16	1720
	ASRV-14	905
#4	80	760
	K-64	1230
	230	1800
	WA100	990
	WA150	1270
	WA200	1830
#5	518	580
	520	1110
	535	850
	540	350
	541	500
	551	1075
#6	RF-49N	1020
	RF-59N	1250
	RF-68H	1530
	RF-69N	1250
	WF-57N	2090
	GF-900	900
#7	PDV405	1000
	GV405	1075

Exterior-Mounted
Attic Space Ventilator
With Automatic Thermostat

MODEL RF-69N

DESCRIPTION

The NuTone RF-69N can help make your home cooler and help reduce air conditioning costs. This powerful ventilator will flush out the intense summer heat that builds up in most attics . . . heat that often builds up to 140°F or more. When this heat presses down on ceiling areas it warms the entire house. The NuTone RF-69N can reduce this attic heat to a temperature approaching that outside, allowing the air conditioner to operate more efficiently. Because the NuTone RF-69N Attic Space Ventilator circulates the attic air, it not only cools, but also helps protect against moisture damage to insulation, ceilings, paint, roof boards and shingles.

DESIGN FEATURES

Air Delivery:	1250 CFM at 0.03" W.G.
Sound Level:	Outside the house.
Dimensions:	9" high, dome 22" diameter, flashing 23" square.
Material:	Housing, sleeve, and flashing are aluminum. Bird guard is expanded aluminum.
Motor:	Ball-bearing, 1/5 hp, @ 1550 rpm, 115vAC, 60 Hz, 5.0 amp, 3/8" diameter shaft, automatic reset thermal protected.
Fan Blade:	14" aluminum blade, 3.38" pitch, 4 blades, 3/8" diameter shaft, electronically balanced.
Thermostat:	Automatic preset at 110°F, adjustable from 70° to 130°F.

ARCHITECT'S SPECIFICATIONS

Attic Space Ventilator(s) shall be Model RF-69N as manufactured by NuTone, Scovill Inc., according to product specifications listed: 9" high, dome 22" diameter, flashing 23" square; contains automatic, adjustable thermostat; 1250 CFM @ 0.03" W.G.

CERTIFIED DATA

Air delivery rating for ventilator is certified from tests conducted at the Texas Engineering Experiment Station at Texas A & M College in accordance with the code approved by the Home Ventilating Institute. The NuTone Model RF-69N meets or exceeds applicable requirements of Underwriters' Laboratories, Inc.

SELECTION DATA

To determine fan size needed, measure square footage of attic floor and multiply footage by 0.70. The result will be the minimum air delivery required. Use two RF-69N fans if necessary, or use fan with greater CFM delivery, such as NuTone Model RF-68H. Allow a minimum of one (1) square foot intake area for every 300 CFM rating of fan for optimum performance.

INSTALLATION

Mounts on pitched or flat roof between 16" O.C. rafter. Roof cutout minimum of 14-1/2" diameter. IMPORTANT: On flat roof installation, fan must be mounted on curb build-up above waterline. Outlet box containing thermostat attaches to nearest roof rafter (connected to ventilator with 18" cable). Thermostat preset at 110°F; calibrated dial settings from 70° to 130°F. Use standard on/off toggle (not supplied). Installation Instructions packaged with unit.

Q - I know it wastes energy, but we open our bathroom window instead of using the vent fan because it is so noisy. Are there energy efficient quiet vent fans available and how large a fan do we need?

A - Opening your window instead of using your bathroom fan can really increase your utility bills. It takes much longer to vent excess humidity and odors through an open window than with a vent fan. Often, you leave the bathroom and forget to close the window.

It is not uncommon for a bathroom vent fan to become noisy as it gets old. Some sound like a Boeing 747 preparing for takeoff. Fortunately, there are special bathroom vent fans that are designed to be extremely quiet. You probably don't realize how noisy your standard vent fan actually has become until you hear a new special super-quiet one.

The sound level of vent fans is rated in units called "sones". One sone of sound is about as loud as a new quiet refrigerator. For comparison, a sound level rating of six sones is twice as loud as three sones. The actual energy efficiency of the fan motor is similar for most models.

Generally, the larger the air flow capacity of the fan (cubic feet of air per minute - CFM), the noisier it will be. The sound levels for various bathroom vent fans range from about 1.5 to 6.0 sones. At only 1.5 sones, you can barely hear a super-quiet fan running.

The super-quiet bathroom vent fans are specially designed and constructed, so they cost a little more than standard fans. These quiet fans usually have slower motors and are better-balanced. To further reduce the noise level, the motors are mounted in rubber bushings and bridge brackets are used to mount the motor out of the air stream.

You can use a simple rule of thumb to determine the size (air flow capacity in CFM) of the vent fan for your bathroom. With a standard eight-foot high ceiling, multiply the square footage of the floor area by 1.07. Be sure to provide for make-up ventilation air into the bathrooom.

For example, an eight-by-eight-foot bathroom would require a fan with a capacity of 68 CFM. You should select the next larger fan available which would be a 70 or 80 CFM model depending on the specific manufacturer.

Q - I burn my fireplace a lot in the fall to help heat my home. Are there any good uses for the old ash or should I just trash it? W.W.

A - There are many uses for fireplace ash and you should save it. Next spring, you can use the nutrient-rich ash on your garden. When wood burns, the carbohydrates and water are consumed. The remaining ash still contains much of the phosphorous, potash, iron, calcium, sodium, and potassium in the original trees.

In addition to feeding your garden, the ash helps to control many insects and pests. Spread a thin layer of the ash over the soil as soon as your plants begin to sprout in the spring. This discourages insects such as bark borers, slugs, cutworms, snails, and others.

In northern climates, ash works well as a replacement for road salt on your driveway. It helps melt snow and gives more bite for your tires without attacking the paint on your car or leaching into the soil.

UTILITY BILLS UPDATE

Dear Reader,

Thank you for your interest in writing to me about quiet bathroom vent fans. The following is a list of many bathroom vent fans, air flow capacity and sound level. The actual electricity usage for fans of similar air flow capaicty does not vary significantly. Less than 2.5 sones is considered "quiet".

This list of manufacturers and product information are for your information only and are not an endorsement of this type of product or a specific model or manufacturer.

Sincerely,

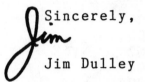

Jim Dulley

MANUFACTURERS

MODEL NUMBER	AIR FLOW CFM	SOUND LEVEL SONES
AUBREY MFG., 6709 S. Main St., Union, IL 60180		
7000	70	3.5
7059	70	4.0
7550	50	2.5
7565	60	3.0
7570	70	6.0
7580	80	3.0
7610	110	3.0
BROAN MFG. CO., 926 W. State St., Hartford, WI 53027		
162	70	3.5
360	100	1.5
361	160	3.0
655	70	3.5
659	50	2.5
663	50	2.0
670	50	1.5
671	70	3.0
676	110	4.0
684	80	2.5
695	100	4.0
FASCO INDUSTRIES, 810 Gillespie St., Fayetteville, NC 28302		
A647	50	3.5
A648S	60	3.0
A649	90	5.5
656	70	4.5
761	70	2.0
763	90	2.5
765	110	3.5
1000	100	3.3

MODEL NUMBER	AIR FLOW CFM	SOUND LEVEL SONES
W.W. GRAINGER, 5959 W. Howard St., Niles, IL 60648		
Same as Broan, but different model numbers. A W.W. Grainger dealer can cross-reference the numbers for you.		
MIAMI CAREY, 203 Garver Rd., Monroe, OH 45050		
FB-5058	50	5.0
FB-5059	50	4.0
FB-5079	70	5.0
FB-5089	110	3.5
FH-583	70	6.5
FH-583	70	3.5
NUTONE, Madison & Red Bank Rds., Cincinnati, OH 45227		
QT-80	80	1.5
QT-110	110	2.5
8663 series	100	3.5
8814	110	4.0
8833	80	3.5
9093 N	70	3.5
J.C. PENNEY, 1301 Ave. of the Americas, New York, NY 10019		
901-2188	80	3.0
901-2196	70	3.5
901-2204	60	3.0
945-8563	110	3.0
946-7739	50	2.5
RANGAIRE, 501 S. Wilhite, Cleburne, TX 76031		
E50	50	4.0
EB70	70	5.0
EL50	50	3.0
EL70	70	4.5
RITTENHOUSE, 475 Quaker Mtg. House Rd., Honeoye Falls, NY 14472		
H5010-2SW	60	4.0
H5101	70	6.5
V116	110	3.5
V118	90	2.5
V119	100	3.5
V4206	120	3.5
THERMADOR, 5119 District Blvd., Los Angeles, CA 90040		
VQT90M	90	2.1
1201	70	4.0

DESCRIPTION

Sound conditioned to provide high volume air exhaust at "QuieTTest" operational sound level.

HVI certified and FHA/HUD approved for residential bathrooms with floor areas as large as:

105 sq. feet for Model QT-110.

75 sq. feet for Model QT-80.

Centrifugal blower wheel — electronically balanced. . . for high static push through long runs of ductwork.

Plug-in, four-pole motor. Motor floats between layers of Neoprene. Thoroughly cushioned with vibration isolators.

Rotates at only 1320 rpm for quiet operation — QT-110.

Rotates at only 1180 rpm for quiet operation — QT-80.

Unique bridge bracket mounts motor out of air stream — moisture resistant.

Pre-wired outlet box built into housing — Outlet box cover has plug-in receptacle.

Choice of 3 knockouts for wiring entrance — Housing includes adjustable hanger bracket for mounting between 16" O.C. joists. Installs in 2" x 8" ceiling.

Built-in non-metallic damper prevents backdrafts.

Uses standard 4" round duct and accessories.

Three-dimensional molded grille. . . Fits almost flush with ceiling. Channels intake air softly through hidden air vanes into blower unit — Textured white grille snaps into place and holds with torsion springs — Remove quickly — easily if necessary.

For your convenience, NuTone offers a complete line of accessories to effectively adapt this fan to your construction requirements.

DESIGN FEATURES

Dimensions:	Housing — 9-3/8" wide x 11-1/16" long. Grille — 10-7/8" x 13" x 1-3/16".
Material & Finish:	Housing — Cold rolled steel, baked on enamel. Grille — White Noryl ® plastic.
Motor:	Fully encased, plug-in, four-pole, 115vAC, 60Hz, .2490 diameter shaft. QT-110 only — 1/88 HP @ 1320 RPM, .6 amps. QT-80 only — 1/112 HP @ 1180 RPM, .45 amps.
Blower Wheel:	Polypropelene, electronically balanced, 5-3/4" OD x 2". 1/4" Hub ID.
Duct Size:	4" diameter.

CERTIFIED TEST DATA

Certified air delivery and sound level ratings from tests at Texas Engineering Experiment Station at Texas A & M College in accordance with the Code approved by Home Ventilating Institute. These NuTone models meet or exceed applicable requirements of Underwriters' Laboratories, Inc.

NuTone

Architectural & Engineering Specifications
July, 1984

Ceiling or Wall Mounted Blower Ventilator

QuieTTest

MODELS QT-80 & QT-110

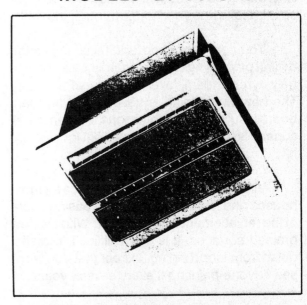

AIR PERFORMANCE CURVE NUTONE MODEL QT-80

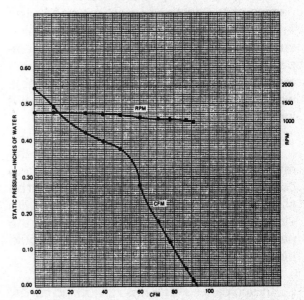

MODEL QT-80 AIR PERFORMANCE CHART

STATIC PRESSURE INCHES OF WATER	0	.03	.05	.10	.15	.20	.25	.30	.40
CFM	93	89	86	80	75	67	62	58	37

Q - I am considering putting new maintenance-free siding on my house. Will vinyl siding add much insulation value to my walls and what is the best type to select?

A - The vinyl siding itself won't add much actual insulation value, but it still may reduce your utility bills. With a good installation job, vinyl siding can reduce the amount of outdoor air that leaks into your house through the walls.

You can easily add additional insulation by first placing rigid foam board insulation, like polystyrene foam, over your present siding. The new vinyl siding is nailed over the foam board insulation. Insulation on the exterior wall surface is the most energy-efficient location for it.

Vinyl siding is an excellent choice for most houses and it is capturing an increasing share of the replacement siding market. With the new grained surfaces, it is often difficult to distinguish from wood siding, except that you won't see anyone painting it every several years.

Select a good grade of vinyl siding. Generally the thicker, the better. Material thicknesses of .040 inches or more are good. The thicker material minimizes problems from high summer heat and extremely low winter temperatures. Many good-quality vinyl siding manufacturers offer a 50-year transferable warranty, so the resale value of your house will increase.

You generally should not try to do the residing job yourself. Since vinyl expands and contracts with temperature changes, it must be sized and hung properly. It is designed with elongated nail holes so it actually "floats" on the nails. If you would nail it too tight, you could have problems.

Each panel usually has interlocking edges.

These edges lock and seal tightly over the siding strips above it and below it. Since vinyl blocks water vapor, there are small weep holes in the bottom of the siding strips to let moisture escape.

You should select a siding profile (width of clapboard slat) that is attractive and consistent with the style of your house and area. Profiles range from a width of 3 to 8 inches. The profile width does not have a significant effect on the energy efficiency.

Although hard rains keep the siding fairly clean, you can wash it with a car-washing brush attached to a hose. Since the color goes completely through the vinyl material, small scratches are not very apparent.

Q - I try to save electricity and light only as many lights as I need. They seem bright enough to me, but when my parents visit, they say they are too dim. How many lights should I have on at night?

A - Both you and your parents may be correct, so use enough lights for comfortable brightness for the activity you are doing. As people age, they often require brighter light and more contrast. Thirty- to 40-year-old people need an average of 17 percent more contrast than those 20 to 30 years old. Sixty- to 70-year-old people need 50 percent more contrast.

Each time you double the wattage of the bulbs, you use double the amount of electricity. Try using three-way bulbs in the rooms that your parents generally occupy so you can easily adjust the light intensity.

Dear Reader,

    Thank you for your interest in writing to me about vinyl siding. Unless you add insulation under the siding, there will not be a significant increase in the insulation R-value. A good siding installation job can HELP the air leakage into your house.

    The abbreviations for the profiles listed below are as follows - The numbers (3,4,5, etc.) refer to the apparent width of each slat section. The "S" - single, "D" - double, and "T" - triple, refer to how many apparent slats there are per strip of siding. For example, a "D5" is actually 10 inches wide. A "T3" is 9 inches wide.

    This list of manufacturers and product information are for your information only and are not an endorsement of this type of product or a specific manufacturer or brand.

                                              Sincerely,

                                              Jim Dulley

BUYER'S GUIDE FOR VINYL SIDING

MANUFACTURER	BRAND	TEXTURE	PROFILE	COLORS
ALCAN	Advantage	wood grain	D4,D5, S8,S12	7
	Alcan	wood grain	D4,D5,S8	7
	Revere	wood grain	D4,D5 S8,T4	9
ALCOA	Super V	wood grain	D4,D5,S8	9
	Liberty	embossed	D4,D5	9
	Minute Man	matte	D6	6
	Harbor Lght	matte	D4	2

UTILITY BILLS UPDATE

MANUFACTURER	BRAND	TEXTURE	PROFILE	COLORS
ARCO	Sawmill	cut wood	D4,D5	6
	Timbertone	wood grain	D4,D5	8
	Dutch Lap	pebble	D5	6
ALUMARK	Liberty	wood grain	D4,D5,T4	6
BIRD	Master Wall	wood grain	D4,D5 S8,T4	5
	Regency	smooth	D4,D5	8
	Tempa Form	wood grain	D4,D5,S8	8
CELOTEX	Celotex	wood grain	D4,D5,S8	6
CERTAINTEED	Standard	wood grain	D4,D5 S8,T4	9
	Futura	matte	D4	8
ELIXIR	Elixir	wood grain	D4,D5,T4	5
GEORGIA PACIFIC	Georgia Pacific	wood grain	D4,D5 S8,D5	7
GOLD BOND	Dynaforge	wood grain	D4,D5,S8	8
H&W BUILD. PRODUCTS	Heartland	wood grain matte	D4,D5,D6 S8,T3	9
MASTER SHIELD	Master- shield	cedar grain	D4,D5 S8,T3	7
	Tradesman	vert. grain	D4,D5	7
MASTIC	T-Lock	wood grain	D4,D5, S8,T3	11
MITTEN	Weather- shield	wood grain	D4,D5, S8,T3	8
REYNOLDS	Classic	smooth wood grain	D4,D5, S8,T3	8
SAUDER	Premier	wood grain	D5	8
	Encore	wood grain	D4	8
	Rhapsody	wood grain	S8	4
	Ovation	wood grain	D5	8

UTILITY BILLS UPDATE

MANUFACTURER	BRAND	TEXTURE	PROFILE	COLORS
U.S. PLYWOOD	Vinylguard	wood grain	D4,D5	6
VARIFORM	Chateau	wood grain	D4,D5	7
	Duragrain	wood grain	D4,D5	6
	Varigrain	wood grain	D4,D5	8
	Cedar	cut wood	D5	8
	Hampton 3	brushed	T3	4
VIPCO	Ambassador	wood grain	D4,D5,S8	8
	President	wood grain	D4,D5	8
	Charlestown	wood grain	D6	6
	Provincial	wood grain	T3	6
WOLVERINE	Restoration	smooth	T3	7

MANUFACTURERS

```
ALCAN, P.O. Drawer 511, Warren, OH 4481
ALCOA, P.O. Box 716, Sidney, OH 45365
ALSCO, 300 Eastowne Dr., Chapel Hill, NC 27514
ALUMARK, P.O. Box 99, Grosse Ile., MI 48138
BIRD, 49 Washington, East Walpole, MA 02032
CELOTEX, P.O. Box 22602z, Tampa, FL 33622
CERTAINTEED, 750 E. Swedesford Rd., Valley Forge, PA 19482
ELIXIR, 394 E. Main St., Leola, PA 17540
GEORGIA PACIFIC, 133 Peachtree St. N.E., Atlanta, GA 30303
GOLD BOND, 2001, Rexford Rd., Charlotte, NC 28211
H&W INDUSTRIES, 200 Park Pl., Boonesville, MS 38829
MASTER SHIELD, 1202 N. Bowie Dr., Weatherford, TX 76086
MASTIC CORP., P.O. Box 65, South Bend, IN 46624
MITTEN, 1245 Franklin Blvd., Cambridge, Ont., Canada N1R 7E5
REYNOLDS, P.O. Box 27003-A, Richmond, VA 23261
SAUDER, 13880 Viking Pl., Richmond, B.C., Canada V6V 1K8
U.S. PLYWOOD, 372 Danbury Rd., Wilton, CT 06897
VARIFORM, 303 Major St., Kearney, MO 64060
VIPCO, P.O. Box 498, Columbus, OH 43216
WOLVERINE, P.O. Box 685, Grinnell, IA 50112
```

Q - I have talked to builders about building an energy efficient house, but each is recommending different features and designs. How can I evaluate which will be most effective at cutting the utility bills?

A - There are many characteristics that can reduce heating and cooling costs, but it would be difficult and expensive to incorporate all of them into one house. The most accurate method to evaluate the various design and feature combinations is to hire an energy consultant to analyze them.

Some builders use a quick energy efficiency checklist that assigns a point value to these numerous characteristics. They sum up all the values for each house design to get a rough comparison of their energy efficiencies. The higher the total number, the lower the utility bills will be.

Three of the general ones effecting the energy usage of a house are - basic design and shape, type and amount of insulation and airtightness, and the quality of the mechanical systems.

Many specific factors within each of these three general categories effect your utility bills to varying degrees. Under the basic design category, you should consider the type and shape of the house, the potential for solar utilization, and the amount of window glass area.

A more square-shaped house minimizes the total outside wall area and heat loss. The worst design is H-shaped. For example, on an efficiency checklist, a square house would be rated at +30 as compared to an L-shaped house at 10 and an H-shaped home at -20. A two-story house is best because it reduces the amount of roof area for a given house size.

For thermal protection, generally the more insulation, the better. During construction of a home, the extra cost for more insulation is minimal. Make sure the foundation sill is caulked and there are vapor barriers. Avoid recessed lighting fixtures in the ceiling and locate most the electrical outlets on inside walls.

Minimize the window area, especially on the north wall. Total window area that is 10 percent or less of the floor area is rated at +40. Window area greater than 20 percent gets a -40. Spend the additional money for good quality thermal windows and tight-fitting insulated doors. Shade south and west windows with a generous roof overhang or awnings.

Select energy efficient mechanical systems - the furnace, air conditioner, and water heater. They should be located near the center of the house to minimize the duct and hot water pipe length. Proper location is given a +8 checklist rating, so you can compare its importance to the house design.

Q - The other day, I noticed that the edge around the door opening in my refrigerator didn't feel as cold as the rest of it. What would be causing this?

A - Many refrigerators have small electric heating elements around that edge area. Their purpose is to reduce the sweating near this door gasket area in more humid weather, but they do use extra electricity.

Look inside your refrigerator. You will probably find a small switch called an energy saver switch, or something to that effect. It controls the small heating elements. Switch it off unless you notice sweating.

Dear Reader,

Thank you for your interest in writing to me about how to evaluate the energy efficiency of various aspects of a house. The chart below will indicate the relative energy importance of these items. For example, if one item is rated at +20 and another at +40, the one at +40 will provide about double the effectiveness at reducing utility costs.

When you are comparing homes, you can total all the values for each home. It will give you an idea of the comparitive energy efficiency of each and of specific features of each. The terms "conditioned area" refers to areas of a home that are heated in the winter and cooled in the summer. An attic over an insulated floor is considered an "unconditioned" area.

Sincerely,

Jim Dulley

ENERGY EFFICIENCY CHECKLIST

BASIC DESIGN ITEMS: RATING

1. Orientation (Wall Exposure)
   Long Axis Facing Generally North   +60
   Long Axis Facing Generally East   −50

2. Solar Conversion Feasibility
   Sun Rights Protected (Min. 45 ft. Open)   +25
   Roof Pitch of South Roof Face (7.5/12 min.)   +10

3. Type and Shape
   Basic Style:
      Two Story   +40
      Split Level   +20
      One Story   0
   Basic Shape
      Square   +30
      Rectangular   +20
      L-Shaped   +10
      U-Shaped   0
      H-Shaped   −20
4. Maximum Use of Minimum Glass
   Percentage of Glass Area to Floor Area
      Less Than 10%   +40
      10% to 12%   +24
      12% to 15%   0
      15% to 20%   −24
      More Than 20%   −40

```
Shading of Glass
   100% Shaded                                          +48
   90% Shaded                                           +30
   75% Shaded                                           +16
   60% Shaded                                             0
   40% Shaded                                           -32
   Less Than 40%                                        -48
```

INTEGRAL THERMAL PROTECTION:

```
1. Shell Insulation
   Outside Walls
      R-22 Insulation                                   +15
      R-19 Insulation                                   +10
      R-13 Insulation                                   + 3
      Wiring Run at Plate of 48" Height                 + 3
      R-11 Insulation                                     0

   Ceilings Over Conditioned Areas
      R-30 Insulation                                   +15
      R-26 Insulation                                   +10
      R-22 Insulation                                   + 5
      R-19 Insulation                                     0

   Double Pane Thermal Windows or Storm Windows
      100% of Glass Area                                +12
      80% of Glass Area                                 +10
      60% of Glass Area                                 + 8
      40% of Glass Area                                 + 6
      Less Than 40% of Glass Area                         0

   Exterior Doors
      Insulated Metal                                   + 3
      Wood                                                0

   Light Color Roofing                                  + 3

2. Infiltration of Unconditioned Air (Air Leakage In)
   Soleplates Sealed at Slab                            +12
   Soleplates Sealed at Subfloor                        +12
   No Plumbing Drain/Vents in Exterior Walls            +12
   Mechanical Chases/Knockouts Sealed                   +12
   Ext. Doors and Windows Weatherstripped               + 3
   Ext. Doors and Windows Caulked                       + 6
   Attic Scuttle Weatherstripped                        + 3
   Polyethylene Film Installed on Ext. Walls            + 8
   Subfoor Joints Glues                                 + 3
   No Ceiling Lights on Rough-In Boxes                  + 3
   No External Wall Outlets on SEcond Floor             + 3
   No Recessed Lights/Mech. Equip. in Ceiling           + 5
   100% Stucco Exterior                                 +10
```

3. Exfiltration of conditioned Air (Air Leakage Out)

All Electric: No Combustion Vents Required   +25

Fireplace With:

    Damper, Glass Screen, Combustion Air Intake   +20

    Damper, Combustion Air Intake   +10

    Locking Damper   0

    Standard Damper   −15

Attic Ventilation:

    Soffit Vents 48" on Center or Continuous   + 6

    Baffles at Vent Locations   + 3

    Continuous Ridge Vent   + 6

Ventless Range Hood   + 3

Bathroom Venting 4" air intake 8" Above Floor   + 3

Weatherstrip Bathroom Door   + 3

Inside Utility Room

    Double Reverse Vents   + 6

    Weatherstrip Door   + 3

MECHANICAL SYSTEMS:

1. Heating Unit Location

Centrally Located   + 8

In A Conditioned Space   + 8

In An Unconditioned Space   0

In An Attic   − 3

2. Duct System

One Level For Two Floors (Cavity Between Floors)   + 8

In Conditioned Space   + 8

Two Return Air Registers   + 3

In Unconditioned Space   + 2

Through Attic - Ducts Insulated   0

Through Attic - Ducts Uninsulated   − 8

3. Air Conditioner Efficiencies

9.5 EER or Greater   +13

9.0 to 9.5 EER   +10

8.5 to 9.0 EER   + 8

8.0 to 8.5 EER   + 5

7.5 to 8.0 EER   0

7.0 to 7.5 EER   − 5

6.9 EER or Lower   − 8

4. Heating Efficiencies

90% or Above   +14

80% to 90%   +10

70% to 80%   + 3

65% to 70%   0

Below 65%   −10

5. Water Heating System

Heat Recovery Equipment   + 8

Located Within 20' of Kitchen or Utility Room   + 2

Hot Water Pipes Insulated   + 3

Flow Restricting Shower Heads and Faucets   + 3

Q - I want to insulate my basement walls, but there are some water leaks near the bottom of the concrete wall. It seems to leak the worst in the fall. Do I have to seal it totally before adding the insulation?

A - Your basement walls must be moisture-free or the insulation will get wet in a much larger area than just the spot of the leak. Soaked fiberglass batt insulation on your basement wall becomes less energy efficient than not insulating it at all.

The fact that the leak is worse in the spring and fall indicates that the water is seeping in under pressure. Due to more rain during those seasons, the water table generally rises and forces the water through the cracks in the concrete.

Using a few common household tools and some elbow grease, you should be able to stop the water leaks yourself. As added insurance, you can space the stud framing and insulation out about 3/4 inch from the wall. The vapor barrier on the insulation should be facing toward the inside of the basement to block moisture penetration from the indoor air.

Coating the walls with a special waterproofing compound will generally take care of the smaller leaks through fine cracks. For any larger cracks, over 1/8 inch wide, you'll have to clean them out and patch them first. You can then apply the waterproofing mix over the entire repaired surface.

Using a hammer and chisel, you should chip a dovetail (undercut) groove along the entire length of the crack. If you just chip a simple V-shaped groove, the concrete patch will fall out as it sets and shrinks.

It is easier to use an epoxy or latex-based cement than to mix your own cement. Force the cement into the groove with an ordinary trowel. Make sure to fill it so there aren't any air pockets.

If the water is leaking in at a fast rate, install a small weep pipe through the wall at the bottom of the crack. This will take the water pressure off of the patch until it sets. If there is just a trickle of water through the pipe, you can remove it and plug the hole.

You should just slightly dampen the wall (no standing water droplets) and apply a heavy coating of waterproofing mix. If this seems to have eliminated the leaks, don't rejoice yet and begin framing and adding insulation. Wait until after the next rain for your celebrating. It will probably need a second coat of the mix.

Q - I am planning to caulk my windows to make them airtight. However, I can't use an entire tube of caulk at one time. Is there any good way to store a half-used tube for future use?

A - In order to store a half-used tube of caulk, you must tightly seal the tube. One way I have found that works is to insert a nail into the nozzle on the tube. Insert the nail with the head first.

It should extend into the caulk inside of the nozzle. Then twist the nail around in the caulk and pull the nail back out just a little. That leaves a small gap between the caulk in the tube and the glob around the nail head. Then when you use it again, the hardened glob will pull out easily with the nail and you will have soft caulk ready for use.

Dear Reader,

   Thank you for your interest in writing to me about how to waterproof a basement wall before adding insulation. It is a good idea to space the wall framing and insulation out about 3/4 of an inch from the concrete wall.

   Keep sending in your letters to me!

Sincerely,

Jim

Jim Dulley

INSTRUCTIONS

Here are tips and instructions on how to water-proof your basement. Read these tips carefully and follow the instructions closely. Following the procedures outlined in this sheet will help you end up with a more satisfactory job—with far less waste and effort.

1. STOPPING LEAKS AND SEEPAGE

■ Bothered with leaks or seepage through your basement floor or walls? If so, both problems can be solved. However, they are not easy. It will take time and effort, and you will have to do the job right. But, it can be done.

■ There are three basic causes for seepage and cracks in basement walls and floors. First, the original workmanship may have been poor. Second, the house may have settled causing cracks to appear in either the floor or walls. Finally, water pressure from the outside may have built up and be forcing water through the walls.

■ Leaks or seepage in basement walls or floors are easy to detect, (Fig. 1). Moisture will often begin to seep through at the area where the floor and walls join or along any cracks that may have appeared in the wall or floor.

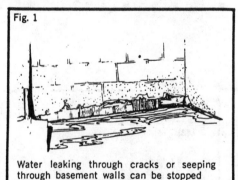

Fig. 1

Water leaking through cracks or seeping through basement walls can be stopped

2. REPAIRING HOLES AND CRACKS BEFORE WATER-PROOFING

■ If there are no holes or cracks in the basement walls, a water-proofing compound can be applied directly to the walls by steps described a little later. However, almost all leaking basements have either cracks or holes in the walls or floors that should be repaired before any type of water-proofing coating is applied.

■ Hairline cracks can usually be filled with a regular water-proofing mix. However, cracks larger than ⅛" should be cleaned out and patched, (Fig. 2), before the water-proof mix is applied.

Fig. 2

Any cracks larger than ⅛" should be sealed before wall is water-proofed

■ Special epoxy and latex cement formulas can be purchased for mortaring small repair jobs or for brushing on as a water-proof coating. However, if you are doing a large repair job, you will probably want to mix your own mortar for patching holes and cracks before you start applying the water-proofing coat.

■ Mortar for filling holes and cracks in cement basement walls or concrete block walls is usually made by mixing one part cement and two parts of fine sand with just enough water to make a rather stiff mortar.

■ If the water is merely seeping through the basement wall, this mixture of mortar cement can be forced into the crack with an ordinary trowel or putty knife, (Fig. 2). This will normally correct any small leakage problem.

■ However, if outside pressure is forcing the water through the wall, you will have a tougher repair problem. This type of leak is often extremely difficult to correct.

■ If water is seeping in under pressure, a dovetail groove, (Fig. 3), must be chipped out for the entire length of the cracked area. This dovetailed groove can be chipped out with a regular chipping chisel and hammer or with a cold chisel.

Fig. 3

If water is seeping in under pressure a dovetail crack must be chipped out

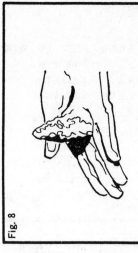

Fig. 7

Fill all the area down to the pipe then remove the pipe and fill hole

■ Next, make a cement plug from the mortar mix which you have previously made. Roll the plug into a cone shape, (Fig. 8), that is slightly larger than the hole to be plugged.

Fig. 8

Make plug of putty-like cement and shape it to fill the hole

■ Roll the newly created plug of cement around in your hands until it begins to stiffen. Then stick the small end of the cone-like plug in the hole where the pipe was removed and tamp it into place, (Fig. 9). It can be tamped into the hole—just like a cork in a bottle.

■ Hold the cement plug in place with your fingers, (Fig. 9), for 3 to 5 minutes. This gives it time to set. You can probably place some heavy object over this plug during this 3 to 5 minute period to give it plenty of time to dry before letting it be exposed to the full water pressure.

■ After 3 to 5 minutes, you should be able to remove your hand or the object holding the plug in place. By this time the mortar plug should have dried sufficiently to close off the hole and prevent the outside water from entering.

3. CLOSING CRACKS AND HOLES WHEN WATER IS ENTERING UNDER PRESSURE

■ In some cases it is necessary to position a weep pipe through the wall to permit the outside water trapped against the wall under pressure to escape.

■ In many cases this weep pipe can be installed only temporarily. In other cases it is necessary to leave it in place, (Fig. 6), and drain the water away through a basement sewer trap or with a sump pump.

Fig. 6

If water is entering under pressure, dig out section of wall and insert weep pipe for drainage

■ When water is entering a basement under pressure from outside, insert the weep pipe, (Fig. 6), at the point where the wall and the floor join or at a point where pressure is greatest.

■ Use regular patching mortar to fill the crack, starting at the top and working toward the bottom. Starting at the top permits a more secure bonding of the new mortar.

■ Use an ordinary pointing trowel. Fill the crack with mortar completely down to where the weep pipe is installed, (Fig. 6).

■ Let the mortar set until it has completely dried. Examine the water entering through the weep pipe. If it has slowed to a trickle, you can probably remove the pipe, fill the hole and eliminate the problem.

■ If water is still coming through the pipe with considerable force, it is probably wise to leave the weep pipe in place and run the water into a sewer drain with a hose.

■ If you decide to try and remove the pipe and patch the hole, (Fig. 7), treat the cracked area right down to the spot where the wall and the floor come together.

■ Fig. 4 shows the correct and incorrect way to enlarge the cracked area before mending it. Use a chipping or cold chisel to create a dovetail space similar to the top illustration shown in the drawing, (Fig. 4). This provides a holding power for the new mortar when it is inserted.

■ If you chip a vee groove as illustrated in Fig. 4, the mortar will often fall out of the repaired area when it dries. Take time to do it right. It will pay off in the long run.

■ Holes in a concrete or concrete block wall should be repaired in much the same manner. Chip out the faulty or broken area in dovetail fashion as illustrated in Fig. 4. The dovetail cut provides a holding edge for the new mortar.

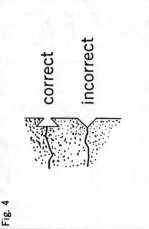

Fig. 4

correct

incorrect

Enlarge crack by cutting away a dovetail space for new repair mortar

■ When the faulty cement around the edge of the hole has been completely chipped away, fill the hole, (Fig. 5), with the same mortar mix recommended for the filling of cracks. This is one part cement to two parts fine sand mixed with just enough water to create a stiff mortar.

Fig. 5

Holes should also be chipped out and filled before water-proofing

■ Place the mortar in the newly cleaned hole, (Fig. 5), and smooth out with an ordinary trowel. Be sure mortar is pressed into all parts of the hole. Do not leave air pockets.

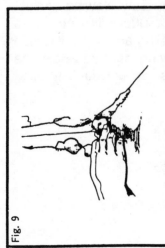

Fig. 9

When plug begins to stiffen, insert in hole and press into shape

4. WATER-PROOFING THE WALL AND FLOOR AFTER PATCHES AND REPAIRS HAVE BEEN MADE

■ After all holes and cracks have been filled and patched according to these instructions, you are then ready to apply the water-proof mix.

■ The first step is to moisten the basement wall with a fine spray, (Fig. 10), before applying the water-proofing mix. A garden hose with the nozzle set to a fine spray will do the job adequately. Although the walls should be damp when the water-proof mix is applied, no water should be actually standing on the wall surface.

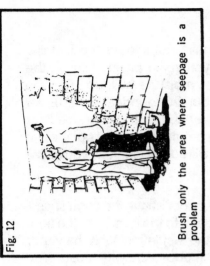

Fig. 10

Moisten the wall with a fine spray before applying the water-proofing mix

■ Water-proof mixes of the epoxy or latex type can be purchased for treating basement walls and floors. Most of these mixes require only the addition of water. If you use this type of mix, be sure to follow the manufacturer's instructions carefully.

■ Many modern water-proof mixes will not adhere to walls that have been painted. If you attempt to place water-proof mixes on painted walls, the old paint must first be removed by sanding, wire brushing or sand blasting before the water-proof mixture will adhere to the surface.

■ It is also important to remember that no epoxy or latex type water-proof coatings will bond to wet surfaces. When these types of materials are used, they should be applied to a surface that is completely dry.

■ If you prefer, you can make your own wall coating mixture of plain cement and water. This should be mixed to form a slurry—a mixture that is about the consistency of cream.

■ Use a stiff brush, (Fig. 11), and a circular motion to rub this water-proof mix into the wall. Take time to fill every pore in the wall.

Fig. 11

Use a stiff brush and a circular motion to rub water-proofing mix into the wall

■ Start applying the coating at the bottom of the wall first. This is where the water pressure is likely to be greatest.

■ After starting at the bottom, (Fig. 11), brush the water-proofing mix on up to the top and then move back to the bottom, applying additional layers of the mixture slowly.

■ The water-proofing mix should be brushed only over the area, (Fig. 12), where seepage or leakage is a problem. Feather out at the edges until you have completely covered the area where leakage or seepage has occurred.

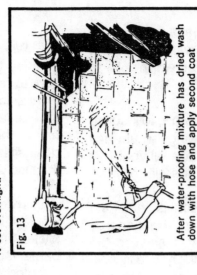

Fig. 12

Brush only the area where seepage is a problem

■ When the coating has dried sufficiently that it does not rub off, spray the area completely with water, (Fig. 13). Soak it thoroughly and then let it set overnight.

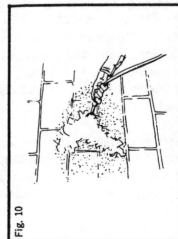

Fig. 13

After water-proofing mixture has dried wash down with hose and apply second coat

■ After the wall has dried overnight, wet it down thoroughly, (Fig. 13), with a garden hose and apply a second coat of the water-proofing mixture while the wall is still wet. Use the same techniques of brushing in the second coat as you did for the first coat, (Fig. 11).

■ Use two coats in all cases. One coat simply will not correct the problem under normal conditions.

Q - Our house is built over a crawl space and the floors are cold. The walls and ceiling are well insulated. Would it be worthwhile to insulate the crawl space too?

A - It would be very worthwhile to insulate your crawl space and the savings would pay back the cost quickly. Not only will your feet feel warmer, but your heating bills will be lower.

A common misconception is that heat flows upward. Hot air flows up. Heat energy flows in all directions, flowing fastest to the coldest area. If the rest of your house is well-insulated, a significant percentage of the heat loss is through your floors to the cold crawl space.

There are two options for insulating a crawl space and both are very easy to do yourself. If your furnace heating ducts run through the crawl space, then you should insulate the entire crawl space area. If not, just insulate the floor above the crawl space.

In either case, first caulk all along the sill area, where wall lumber rests on the concrete or block foundation. To insulate the entire crawl space, make sure all of the crawl space vents are sealed, but not permanently. You will want to open them in the summer for ventilation.

Whenever you are working with insulation, wear proper protective clothing and safety gear. To insulate the entire crawl space, start the fiberglass insulation batt up against the band joist at the top of the foundation. Put the side with the vapor barrier toward the inside of the crawl space.

Use a stapler or nails to attach the insulation to the top of the band joist and drape the insulation down the walls. It should extend about two feet out on to the crawl space floor.

When you have completed the installation, lay thin polyethylene plastic film on the floor to reduce the moisture buildup. Run the film several inches up the foundation wall under the insulation. Overlap the edges on the floor or tape them for a better seal. Don't put the film down first or you will surely tear it as you install the insulation.

To insulate the floor above the crawl space, staple light wire mesh to the bottom of the floor joists. Then slip the insulation, with the vapor barrier facing up, in above the wire mesh. You may find it easier to slip the insulation in as you are stapling up the wire mesh. Leave the vents open for air circulation.

Q - I was wondering if leaving our window screens in during the winter saves or wastes energy? It seems to block some of the intensity of the sun shining in the windows.

A - Unless you have a special passive solar home, you are probably better off leaving your screens up all year. They block some of the sun's heat as you noticed, but the winter days are shorter, so there is less time to gain heat from the sun and more time to lose it through the glass.

The screens can block some of the direct force of the cold outdoor air blowing against your windows. This reduces the heat loss through the glass both day and night. It is also safer for children playing outdoors near the windows and for birds that accidentally bank left instead of right.

Dear Reader,

    Thank you for your interest in writing to me about insulating your crawl space walls or the floor above the crawl space. These are easy jobs to do yourself. Be sure to wear proper protective clothing, safety glasses or goggles and an air filter mask.

Sincerely,

Jim Dulley

INSULATE FLOOR ABOVE CRAWL SPACE

DO-IT-YOURSELF
Tools

1. Heavy duty shears or linoleum knife

2. Temporary lighting with waterproof wiring and connectors

3. Portable fan or blower to provide ventilation

4. Tape measure

5. Heavy duty staple gun and staples

Safety

1. Provide adequate temporary lighting

2. Wear gloves and breathing mask when working with glass fiber or rock wool

3. Provide adequate ventilation

4. Keep lights and all wires off wet ground

Materials
What you'll need

1. R11 (3"-3½") batts or blankets or rock wool or glass fiber, preferably with foil facing (See Installation).

2. Wire mesh or chicken wire of convenient width for handling in tight space.

How much

Determine the area to be insulated by measuring the length and width and multiplying to get the area.

    (length) X (width) = area

    (_____) X (_____) = _____

You may find it necessary to divide the floor into smaller areas and add them.

    (length) X (width) = area

    (_____) X (_____) = _____

    (_____) X (_____) = _____

    (_____) X (_____) = _____ +

         total area = _____

    (.9)(total area) = area of insulation

    (.9)(_____) = _____

total area = area of wire mesh or chicken wire

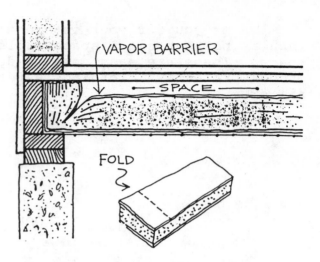

Start at a wall at one end of the joists and work out. Staple the wire to the bottom of the joists, and at right angles to them. Slide batts in on top of the wire. Work with short sections of wire and batts so that it won't be too difficult to get the insulation in place. Plan sections to begin and end at obstructions such as cross bracing.

Buy insulation with a vapor barrier, and install the vapor barrier facing up (next to the warm side) leaving an air space between the vapor barrier and the floor. Get foil-faced insulation if you can; it will make the air space insulate better. Be sure that ends of batts fit snugly up against the bottom of the floor to prevent loss of heat up end. Don't block combustion air openings for furnaces.

TYPE OF INSULATION

	BATTS OR BLANKETS		LOOSE FILL (POURED-IN)			
	glass fiber	rock wool	glass fiber	rock wool	cellulosic fiber	
R-11	3½''-4''	3''	5''	4''	3''	R-11
R-19	6''-6½''	5¼''	8''-9''	6''-7''	5''	R-19
R-22	6½''	6''	10''	7''-8''	6''	R-22
R-30	9½''-10½''*	9''*	13''-14''	10''-11''	8''	R-30
R-38	12''-13''*	10½''*	17''-18''	13''-14''	10''-11''	R-38

* two batts or blankets required.

INSULATE CRAWL SPACE WALLS

Tools

1. Staple gun

2. Heavy duty shears or linoleum knife

3. Temporary lighting

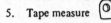

4. Portable fan or blower to provide ventilation

5. Tape measure

6. Duct or Masking Tape (2" wide)

Safety

1. Provide adequate temporary lighting

2. Wear gloves and a breathing mask when working with glass fiber or rock wool

3. Provide adequate ventilation

4. Keep lights, fan, and all wires well off wet ground

Materials
What you'll need

1. R11 (3-3½" thick) blankets of rock wool or glass fiber; without a vapor barrier

2. Six mil polyethylene plastic to lay on earth for vapor barrier (mil's are a measure of thickness)

How much

1. Determine area to be insulated; measure the length and average height of the wall to be insulated; add 3' to the height (for perimeter insulation) and multiply the two to find total insulation area

$$\textbf{(length)} \times \textbf{(height + 3')} = \textbf{area}$$
$$\underline{\hspace{2cm}} \times \underline{\hspace{2cm}} + 3' = \underline{\hspace{2cm}}$$

2. Determine the area to be covered by the vapor barrier by finding the area of your crawl space

$$\textbf{(length)} \times \textbf{(width)} = \textbf{area}$$
$$\underline{\hspace{2cm}} \times \underline{\hspace{2cm}} = \underline{\hspace{2cm}}$$

You may have to divide your crawl space into several rectangles — measure them and add up the areas.

(length)	X	(width)	=
___	X	___	= ___
___	X	___	= ___
___	X	___	+= ___
		TOTAL AREA	= [ ]

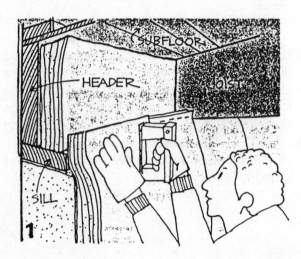

Drawing 1: Where the joists run at right angles to the wall, press short pieces of insulation against the header — they should fit snugly. Then install the wall and perimeter insulation by stapling the top of each strip to the sill. Make sure the batts fit snugly against each other, and that you cut them long enough to cover 2 feet of floor as in Drawing 2.

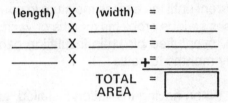

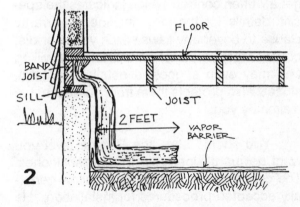

Drawing 2: Where the joists run parallel to the wall, you don't need the short pieces of insulation, just install the wall and perimeter insulation by stapling the top of each strip to the band joist.

When all batts have been installed, lay down the polyethylene vapor barrier, tucking it under the batts all the way to the foundation wall. Turn it up at least 6" at the wall. Tape the joints of the vapor barrier or lap them at least 6". Plan your work to minimize stepping or crawling on the vapor barrier.

Q - We are going to add insulation to the attic to try to cut our heating costs. What is the best way to assure that we are getting a quality job and that it will be effective?

A - If you get a quality job, then the insulation will be effective at reducing your utility bills. Your contractor probably won't be willing to guarantee a percentage of savings on your utility bills. However, he should do a payback analysis for you initially to determine if adding the insulation is a worthwhile investment for you.

Your best assurance of having a quality job done is to select a reputable and well-established contractor. Poor workmanship is literally covered up during the installation and the resultant problems or ineffectiveness may not be apparent for a long time.

For example, an improperly installed vapor barrier under your attic insulation may not be apparent until the excess moisture in your attic causes serious problems months or years later. Also, overfluffed blown-in insulation can take many months to settle.

When having insulation installed, always get a written contract which indicates the specific details for the job. Include a warranty clause to cover any flaws which you later discover. Most reputable contractors are willing and may even suggest a detailed contract, since it also protects them from unreasonable claims by you.

You should state the R-value level you want, not just the insulation thickness in inches. The contractor should agree to follow generally accepted procedures for installation. He should check for adequate attic ventilation area, and insure that the vent areas have not been covered by the insulation.

Insulation should be kept away from potentially combustible spots such as recessed lighting fixtures, flues, etc.. If you are also having the walls insulated, it is also important to locate obstructions in the outside walls, such as piping and wiring, before blowing in the insulation. This will minimize the possibility of voids.

The actual contract should include terms covering the insulation material, installation methods, price, payment schedule, commencement and completion dates, insurance, subcontracting, and notice of cancellation, etc..

Q - Does it cost very much to operate the humidifier on our forced air furnace? It does make us feel more comfortable.

A - If you don't set your thermostat back, a humidifier will consume energy, not save it. The amount of electricity used to run your humidifier is minimal. Many models use a small electric motor which rotates a special belt through a pan of water. The water then evaporates from the belt and increases the amount of moisture in the room air circulating through your furnace ducts.

It requires about 100 Btu of heat for each pint of water that your humidifier evaporates (like the cooling effect of perspiration from your skin). Therefore, your furnace must run a little longer to make up that heat loss. The savings from operating a humidifier are from setting your thermostat lower. You can be comfortable at a cooler temperature if the room air is properly humidified.

A Model Insulation Contract

This is a sample insulation contract used in Massachusetts. Review it carefully before hiring an insulation contractor. Any agreements that you may enter into with a contractor should incorporate the sections of the contract which pertain to your particular situation.

GENERALLY ACCEPTED PRACTICES FOR INSTALLING INSULATION IN EXISTING HOMES

1. Vapor barriers, if installed, will be placed on the warm (interior) side of the area to be insulated.

2. Before installing insulation in the ceiling/attic area, the Contractor will check to determine whether there is adequate ventilation. If there is inadequate ventilation, the Contractor will inform the Homeowner. Inadequate ventilation may result in moisture damage and may impair the effectiveness of the insulation (at least 1 square foot of ventilation for every 300 square feet of insulation with vapor barrier).

3. After an attic has been completely insulated, the Contractor will check to insure that the vent areas have not been covered with insulation during the work process.

4. The Contractor will use or construct a protective barrier to keep combustible insulation a minimum of 3 inches away from heat sources (such as recessed light fixtures, fans and chimneys).

5. If additional attic insulation is being installed to already existing insulation, a vapor barrier will not be used. If the new insulation is a batt/blanket type with an attached vapor barrier, this vapor barrier will be extensively perforated before installation to avoid the problem of trapped moisture and condensation.

6. The Contractor will locate obstructions in the wall cavities before installing insulation in sidewalls. The Contractor will blow insulation in through two holes in each stud bay. If the blow is difficult, additional holes will be used. Blow holes will be left unplugged and may be screened before siding is replaced.

7. If foam insulation is accidentally sprayed on bordering glass or aluminum areas, it will be removed immediately and these surfaces rinsed thoroughly with water. The Contractor will always first test and weigh a sample of the material (to determine the correctness of its density) before beginning the real application process and will provide a written record to the owner of this test. Where urea-formaldehyde foam insulation is to be used, it will not be installed in any attic and will only be installed when the temperature of the exterior surface of the cavity in which foams are to be applied is within the rate of −5 to 30°C (23 to 86°F), as specified by the Department of Housing and Urban Development. (Editor's note: Complaints of health problems

have been reported by some occupants of houses with urea-formaldehyde insulation. There is currently a moratorium in Massachusetts and Connecticut on installation of this material and a national ban on urea-formaldehyde foam insulation is under consideration by the federal Consumer Product Safety Commission.)

8. If loose fill insulation is being installed, the Contractor will keep an accurate count of how many bags are used in order to insure that the correct amount of loose fill insulation is installed.

9. The safety of on-site manufactured cellulose is extremely questionable. There is a definite problem with the installer's ability to ensure that the insulation is properly treated for flame resistance under these specific conditions. Where cellulose insulation is installed, the Contractor will display the flame retardancy and Class I label on all bags to be used in the installation. The Contractor will verify that borax chemicals are used as flame retardants.

10. Except as otherwise specified above, the Contractor agrees to perform the work described in Part I of the following agreement according to the manufacturer's installation instructions.

AGREEMENT

READ THIS AGREEMENT AND MAKE SURE YOU UNDERSTAND IT BEFORE SIGNING IT. MAKE SURE ALL BLANKS ARE COMPLETED AND ALL PROVISIONS WHICH DO NOT APPLY ARE CROSSED OUT. THIS AGREEMENT HAS LEGAL FORCE AND EFFECT AND BINDS THOSE WHO SIGN IT.

This Agreement is made on _____ between

_____ of _____
(Contractor's Name)   (Contractor's Address)

_____
(Contractor's Phone No.)

hereinafter called "Contractor," and _____
(Homeowner's Name)

of _____ hereinafter called "Owner."
(Homeowner's Address)

I. MATERIALS AND WORK

Contractor agrees to make energy conservation improvements on the Owner's premises to the extent and under the conditions specified below:

A. Contractor agrees to furnish all materials and labor for the following energy conservation projects (e.g., insulate attic, insulate exterior walls, install storm windows) and to state for each project:

1. any major alterations to the premises required;
2. the type of materials for the project, including a statement of total R-value to be achieved by each insulation material;
3. the type of vapor barrier, if any, Contractor will install;
4. the type of fire barrier, if any, Contractor will install;
5. the type of ventilation, if any, Contractor will install;
6. the cost of each separate project.

B. Contractor agrees to fill all cavities in each project area, except as it may interfere with proper ventilation and fire safety considerations.

C. Contractor agrees to properly protect the property of the owner at each project work site and adjacent areas, and to restore the premises to a condition similar to that prior to commencement of work. Contractor further agrees to leave the work area in a neat and orderly condition upon completion of work.

D. Contractor agrees to secure, at his own expense, if required, all city, town or state permits necessary to do the work.

E. Contractor agrees to use only materials whose labels indicate conformance with these federal specifications:

INSULATION MATERIALS	FEDERAL SPECIFICATION NUMBERS (unless superseded)	
● Loose Fill		The Federal Government requires that a Federal Specification number for those insulations that meet its standards appear on the packages of insulation. These specifications cover such characteristics as fire retardancy, R-value and corrosiveness.
Fiberglass	HH-I-1030A	
Cellulose	HH-I-515C	
Vermiculite	HH-I-585B	
● Batts/Blankets		
Fiberglass	HH-I-521E	
● Rigid Board		
Polystyrene (extruded & expanded)	HH-I-524B	
Urethane	HH-I-530A	
Fiberglass	HH-I-526C	
● Foam (See Generally Accepted Business Practices No. 7)		

II. PRICE

Contractor agrees to do all work described in Part I for no more than the price

of _____
     (amount)

III. PAYMENT

Contractor shall be paid by Owner according to the following schedule:

IV. COMMENCEMENT AND COMPLETION OF WORK

Unless agreed to in writing, Contractor will not order materials or begin work before the third day following the signing of this Agreement.

Contractor will begin the work on or about _____ (date)

and shall work each day thereafter until work is completed, barring delay caused by circumstances beyond Contractor's control.

V. INSURANCE

Contractor will be responsible to Owner or any third party for any property damage or bodily injury caused by himself, his employees, or his subcontractors in the performance of, or as a result of, the work under this Agreement. Contractor agrees to carry insurance to cover such risks and, if requested to do so by the Owner, will provide an insurance binder detailing the extent of his coverage.

VI. SUBCONTRACTING

Contractor agrees that, notwithstanding any agreement for materials and/or labor between Contractor and a third party, Contractor is responsible to Owner for completion of all work described in Part I in a timely and workmanlike manner.

VII. OTHER CONDITIONS

Contractor agrees to follow the Generally Accepted Practices for Installing Insulation in Existing Homes, attached to, and incorporated by reference in, this Agreement.

VIII. MODIFICATION

This Agreement, including the provisions relating to price (III) and time (IV), cannot be changed except by a written statement signed by both Contractor and Owner. However, cancellation by Owner is allowed in Accordance with paragraph X.

IX. ADDITIONAL TERMS
(Insert any additional terms agreed to by the Contractor and Owner.)

X. NOTICE OF CANCELLATION
Owner may cancel this Agreement if signed at a place other than Contractor's address, if Owner notifies Contractor in writing of his intention to do so no later than midnight of the third business day following the signing of this Agreement. The following language addressed to Owner regarding notice of cancellation is required by statute:

YOU MAY CANCEL THIS AGREEMENT IF IT HAS BEEN CONSUMMATED BY A PARTY THERETO AT A PLACE OTHER THAN AN ADDRESS OF THE SELLER, WHICH MAY BE HIS MAIN OFFICE OR BRANCH THEREOF, PROVIDED YOU NOTIFY THE SELLER IN WRITING AT HIS MAIN OFFICE OR BRANCH BY ORDINARY MAIL POSTED, BY TELEGRAM SENT OR BY DELIVERY, NOT LATER THAN MIDNIGHT OF THE THIRD BUSINESS DAY FOLLOWING THE SIGNING OF THIS AGREEMENT.

SEE THE ATTACHED NOTICE OF CANCELLATION FORM FOR AN EXPLANATION OF THIS RIGHT.

Contractor and Owner hereby agree to the above terms.

_____
(Owner's signature)

_____
(Contractor's signature)

LIMITED WARRANTY

This WARRANTY covers all insulation materials installed by

_____
(Contractor's Name)

_____
(Contractor's Address)

_____ , at the home of _____
(Contractor's Phone No.)   (Homeowner's Name)

_____
(Homeowner's Address)

as described in the attached Agreement.

1. Contractor warrants to Owner that all work will be done in a workmanlike manner, free from defects, and in conformance with all specifications mentioned in Part I of the Agreement.

2. Contractor agrees that, if any defect in materials or workmanship arises within _____ , he will repair such defects and bring the work up to the standards required under the Agreement at no additional expense to Owner.

3. Any claims made by Contractor to Owner regarding cost or fuel savings shall be stated here:

The Contractor makes no other claims regarding cost or fuel savings.

This warranty gives you specific legal rights, and you may also have other rights which vary from state to state. Under Massachusetts law, sales of goods carry an implied warranty of merchantability and fitness for a particular purpose.*

In order to obtain performance of these Warranty obligations, the person to contact is the Contractor, unless otherwise specified here:

_____
(Name)

_____
(Address)

_____
(Contractor's Signature)

*Contact your state Attorney General's office for specific information on such warranties.

Q - My utility bills are too high and I know my house needs insulation. Ihave talked to several insulation contractors and they all say something different. How should I select the proper type of insulation?

A - Adding adequate insulation to an energy-inefficient house can be one of your best investments. Adding attic insulation alone can pay back its cost in just a couple of years. You'll also be more comfortable, both in the winter and summer, with adequately insulated walls, floors, and ceiling.

There are many factors to consider when selecting the proper type of insulation. What is best for the attic is not necessarily the best for walls or the floor. You should consider the following factors - the total R-value (resistance to heat loss), cost, tendency to settle, fire resistance, and possible do-it-yourself application.

The true amount of insulation is measured by its R-value, not its thickness. R-values for various types of insulation materials range from as high as R-5 per one-inch thickness for rigid foam insulation, to as low as R-2 per one-inch thickness for some loose-fill (pour from bag) insulation. Always compare R-values for contractors' quotations, not just the thicknesses.

To compare insulation costs, determine the cost per square foot per R-value. For example, rock wool batt insulation is the least expensive, costing less than 1.5 cents per square foot per R-value. For an R-19 insulation value, it costs about 30 cents per square foot. Rigid foam insulation can cost more than twice that, but it requires less thickness.

Batts and rigid foam insulation offer the greatest resistance to settling. When installing blown-in or loose-fill insulation, it is very important to follow the manufacturer's recommended densities to minimize settling.

Fiberglass, rock wool, perlite and vermiculite insulation offer the best fire resistance. Cellulose is treated with fire-resistant chemicals, but it can lose its fire resistance over time if it gets wet. Most of the rigid foam board insulation are not fire-resistant.

Batt insulation, rock wool or fiberglass, is the easiest to install yourself. Some insulation contractors rent small blowers for installing cellulose. Blown-in fiberglass or rock wool require larger equipment that only a contractor uses.

Q - Our kitchen vent fan is on the west wall and it feels cold near it when it's off. Should I insulate the metal flapper door over the vent?

A - That vent can cost you a lot of energy dollars throughout the entire year, not just during the winter. Although you don't feel it as much, warm, humid air is leaking in during the summer too.

Putting insulation on it probably won't help. The coldness that you feel is from air leaking in past the door, not heat transfer through it. The flapper door probably isn't closing and sealing tightly.

First, try using a wire brush on the metal door and edge of the vent duct to remove any dirt and rust. Then thoroughly saturate the hinge area with light oil. Work it back and forth with your hand several times. If it doesn't operate freely, then you should replace it.

Dear Reader,

Thank you for your interest in writing to me about insulation.

The charts below and on page 2 show you how much insulation is recommended for your area. Look up the first three digits of your zip code on page 2 and then refer to the chart below. The costs shown on page 3 are for materials only and may vary considerably depending on the specific retail outlet.

This information is for your information only and is not an endorsement of these types of products or specific types of insulation.

Sincerely,

Jim Dulley

Minimum Recommended R-Values

Climatic Zone	Attic Floors		Ceilings Over Unheated Crawlspace or Basement			Crawlspace Walls		Exterior Walls*	Heating Degree-Days
	Oil, Gas, Electric Heat Pump	Electric Resistance Heat	Oil, Gas	Electric Heat Pump	Electric Resistance Heat	Oil, Gas, Electric Heat Pump	Electric Resistance Heat		
1	19	19	0	0	0	0	0	0	0-1000
2	19	22	0	0	0	11	11	11	1001-2500
3	22	30	0	0	11	11	19	11	2501-3500
4	30	30	11	11	19	11	19	11	3501-4500
5	30	30	11	11	19	11	19	11	4501-5000
6	30	30	11	19	19	19	19	11	5001-6000
7	30	38	11	19	19	19	19	11	6001-7000
8	38	38	19	19	19	19	19	11	7000 and above

*R-Value of full wall insulation, which is 3-1/2 inches thick, will depend on material used. Range is R-11 to R-13.

Zip Codes and Climate Zones

If your Zip Code Begins With These 3 Numbers — Your Climate Zone Is

Zip	Zone		Zip	Zone		Zip	Zone		Zip	Zone		Zip	Zone
			084	5		178	6		264	6		360	2
			085	6		179	6		265	6		361	2
			086	6		180	6		266	5		362	3
			087	6		181	6		267	6		363	2
			088	6		182	7		268	5		364	2
			089	6		183	6		269	5		365	2
			090	6		184	7		270	4		366	2
			100	6		185	7		271	4		367	2
			103	5		186	7		272	4		368	2
			104	5		187	7		273	4		369	2
010	7		105	6		188	7		274	4		370	4
011	7		106	6		189	7		275	3		371	4
012	8		107	5		190	6		276	3		372	4
013	7		108	6		191	5		277	3		373	3
014	7		109	6		193	5		278	3		374	3
015	7		110	5		194	5		279	3		376	5
016	7		111	5		195	6		280	3		377	5
017	7		112	5		196	6		281	3		378	4
018	6		113	5		197	5		282	3		379	4
019	6		114	5		198	5		283	3		380	4
020	6		115	5		199	5		284	2		381	3
021	6		116	5		200	4		285	3		382	3
022	6		117	5		202	4		286	2		383	3
023	6		118	5		203	4		287	3		384	3
024	6		119	5		204	4		288	4		385	3
025	6		120	5		205	4		289	4		386	3
026	6		121	7		206	4		290	2		387	3
027	6		122	7		207	4		291	2		388	3
028	7		123	8		208	4		292	2		389	3
029	7		124	7		209	4		293	3		390	2
030	7		125	6		210	5		294	2		391	2
031	7		126	6		211	5		295	3		392	2
032	8		127	7		212	5		296	3		393	2
033	8		128	8		214	4		297	3		394	2
034	8		129	8		215	6		298	2		395	2
035	8		130	7		216	4		299	2		396	2
036	8		131	7		217	5		300	3		397	3
037	8		132	7		218	4		301	3		400	4
038	8		133	7		219	5		302	3		401	4
040	8		134	7		220	5		303	3		402	4
041	8		135	7		221	5		304	2		403	5
042	8		136	8		222	5		305	3		404	5
043	8		137	8		223	5		306	3		405	5
044	8		138	8		224	4		307	3		406	5
045	7		139	8		225	4		308	2		407	5
046	8		140	7		226	5		309	2		408	4
047	8		141	7		227	5		310	2		409	4
048	7		142	7		228	5		312	2		410	5
049	8		143	8		229	4		313	2		411	5
050	8		144	7		230	4		314	2		412	5
051	8		145	7		231	4		315	2		413	4
052	8		146	7		232	4		316	2		414	4
053	8		147	7		233	3		317	2		415	5
054	6		148	7		234	3		318	2		416	4
056	8		149	7		235	3		319	2		417	4
057	8		150	6		236	3		320	2		418	4
058	8		151	6		237	3		322	2		419	4
060	7		152	6		238	4		323	2		420	4
061	7		153	6		239	4		324	2		421	4
062	7		154	6		240	4		325	2		422	4
063	6		155	7		241	4		326	1		423	4
064	7		156	7		242	5		327	1		424	4
065	7		157	6		243	4		328	1		425	4
066	6		158	8		244	4		329	1		426	4
067	7		159	8		245	4		330	1		427	4
068	6		160	6		246	6		331	1		430	6
069	6		161	6		247	6		333	1		431	6
070	6		162	6		248	6		334	1		432	6
071	6		163	7		249	6		335	1		433	6
072	6		164	7		250	4		336	1		434	7
073	6		165	7		251	4		337	1		435	7
074	6		166	7		252	4		338	1		436	7
075	6		167	7		253	4		339	1		437	6
076	6		168	7		254	4		350	3		438	6
077	6		169	7		255	4		351	3		439	6
078	7		170	6		256	4		352	3		440	7
079	6		171	6		257	4		353	3		441	7
080	6		172	6		258	6		354	3		442	7
081	5		173	6		259	6		355	3		443	7
082	5		174	6		260	6		356	3		444	7
083	5		175	6		261	5		357	3		445	7
			176	6		262	6		358	3		446	7
			177	6		263	6		359	3		447	7

Zip	Zone		Zip	Zone		Zip	Zone		Zip	Zone		Zip	Zone
448	6		559	8		665	6		773	2		890	2
449	6		560	8		666	6		774	2		891	2
450	6		561	8		667	4		775	2		893	8
451	6		562	8		668	5		776	2		894	7
452	6		563	8		669	6		777	2		895	7
453	6		564	8		670	5		778	2		897	7
454	6		565	8		671	5		779	2		898	8
455	6		566	8		672	5		780	1		900	2
456	6		567	8		673	4		781	2		902	2
457	5		570	8		674	5		782	2		903	2
458	6		571	8		675	5		783	1		904	2
460	6		572	8		676	6		784	2		905	2
461	6		573	8		677	6		785	1		906	2
462	6		574	8		678	6		786	2		907	2
463	7		575	8		679	6		787	2		908	2
464	7		576	8		680	7		788	2		910	2
465	7		577	8		681	7		790	4		911	2
466	7		580	8		683	7		791	4		912	2
467	7		581	8		684	7		792	3		913	2
468	7		582	8		685	7		793	4		914	2
469	6		583	8		686	7		794	4		915	2
470	5		584	8		687	8		795	3		916	2
471	5		585	8		688	7		796	3		917	2
472	6		586	8		689	6		797	3		918	2
473	6		587	8		690	6		798	3		920	2
474	5		588	8		691	7		799	3		921	2
475	5		590	8		692	8		800	7		922	2
476	4		591	8		693	7		801	7		923	2
477	4		592	8		700	2		802	7		924	2
478	6		593	8		701	2		803	6		925	3
479	6		594	8		703	2		804	8		926	2
480	7		595	8		704	2		805	8		927	2
481	7		596	8		705	2		806	7		928	2
482	7		597	8		706	2		807	7		930	2
484	8		598	8		707	2		808	7		931	2
485	8		599	8		708	2		809	7		932	2
486	8		600	8		710	2		810	6		933	2
487	8		601	7		711	2		811	8		934	2
488	7		602	7		712	2		812	8		935	2
489	7		603	7		713	2		813	8		936	2
490	7		604	7		714	2		814	8		937	3
491	7		605	7		716	3		815	6		939	3
492	7		606	7		717	3		816	6		940	3
493	8		609	6		718	3		817	3		941	3
494	8		610	7		719	3		820	8		943	3
495	8		611	7		720	3		822	7		944	3
496	8		612	7		721	2		823	8		945	3
497	8		613	6		722	3		824	8		946	3
498	8		614	7		723	3		825	8		947	3
499	8		615	7		724	4		826	8		948	3
500	7		616	7		725	3		827	8		949	3
501	7		617	6		726	4		828	8		950	2
502	7		618	6		727	4		829	8		951	3
503	7		619	6		728	3		830	8		952	3
504	8		620	8		729	3		831	8		953	3
505	7		622	5		730	4		832	7		954	3
506	8		623	6		731	3		833	8		955	5
507	8		624	5		734	3		834	8		956	3
508	7		625	6		735	3		835	6		957	3
510	8		626	6		736	3		836	6		958	2
511	8		627	6		737	4		837	6		959	2
512	8		628	6		738	4		838	7		960	6
513	8		629	4		739	5		840	6		961	7
514	7		630	5		740	4		841	6		970	5
515	7		631	5		741	4		843	6		971	5
516	6		633	5		743	4		844	6		972	5
520	8		634	6		744	4		845	6		973	5
521	8		635	6		745	3		846	6		974	5
522	7		636	5		746	4		847	7		975	5
523	7		637	6		747	3		850	2		976	7
524	7		638	4		748	3		852	2		977	7
525	7		639	4		749	3		853	3		978	6
526	7		640	5		750	2		855	3		979	6
527	7		641	5		751	2		856	2		980	4
528	7		644	6		752	2		857	2		981	6
530	8		645	6		754	2		859	6		982	6
531	8		646	5		755	2		860	8		983	5
532	8		647	5		756	2		863	5		984	6
534	7		648	4		757	2		864	5		985	6
535	8		650	5		758	2		865	6		986	7
537	8		651	5		759	2		870	4		988	7
538	8		652	6		760	2		871	4		989	6
539	8		653	6		761	2		873	6		990	7
540	8		654	5		762	3		874	6		991	7
541	8		655	5		763	3		875	7		992	7
542	8		656	5		764	2		877	7		993	6
543	8		657	5		765	2		878	6		994	6
544	8		658	5		766	2		879	4		995	8
545	8		660	5		767	2		880	4		996	8
546	8		661	5		768	2		881	4		997	8
547	8		662	5		769	2		882	3		998	8
548	8		664	6		770	2		883	4		999	8
549	8								884	4			
550	8												
551	8												
552	8												
553	8												
554	8												
556	8												
557	8												
558	8												

UTILITY BILLS UPDATE

PROPERTIES OF INSULATION

TYPE OF INSULATION	COST	R-VALUE /INCH	FIRE RESIST.	WATER RESIST.	EASE OF APPLICATION.	TENDENCY TO SETTLE	STRENGTH
BLOWN							
FIBERGLASS	1.9	3.0	A	C	C	B	C
ROCK WOOL	1.7	3.2	A	C	C	C	C
CELLULOSE	1.6	3.6	B	C	C	C	C
BATT							
FIBERGLASS	1.6	3.2	A	C	A	A	C
ROCK WOOL	1.4	3.4	A	C	A	A	C
LOOSE POUR							
PERLITE	3.9	2.7	A	B	A	C	C
VERMICULITE	3.9	2.7	A	B	A	C	C
RIGID FOAM BOARD							
POLYSTYRENE	3.5	5.0	C	B	A	A	B
POLYURETHANE	5.3	7.0	C	B	A	A	B

"A" - Better than average, "B" - Average, "C" - Worse than average
"COST" - Cents per R-value per square foot

Q - My husband always complains that I use the electric can opener and mixer too much and that it pushes up our electric bills. Is he right and how much does it cost to use appliances?

A - Although the cost of electricity has increased dramatically in the past several years, it is still a bargain to use your convenience kitchen appliances. Except for an electric furnace or water heater, the majority of your electric bill results from your refrigerator, electric range, and lights.

Based on average electric rates, you can open more than 100 cans for a penny's-worth of electricity. In the summer, it probably uses more than that much electricity to run your air conditioner to remove the heat you generate using a hand can opener. This doesn't include all the hot air you'll give off when you drop a half-opened can of tomato sauce while trying to use that hand opener.

The convenience appliances that use the most electricity are ones that generate heat, like toasters, warming trays, and hair dryers. However, they still are fairly inexpensive to operate. A standard two-slice toaster costs less than 1/2 of one cent per use and a warming tray costs about one cent per hour.

It is very easy to calculate approximately how much it costs to operate an appliance. Most appliances are rated in watts, like a 100-watt light bulb or a 1,000-watt hair dryer. This wattage rating tells you how fast that the appliance is consuming electricity. You can usually find the wattage rating listed on the appliance label.

Wattage rating is similar to the miles-per-gallon rating for your car. The longer you run your appliance, the more electricity it uses. To determine how much it costs to operate, you multiply the wattage rating times the electric rate in your area.

Assuming an electric rate of eight cents per kilowatt-hour (KWH), your 1,000-watt hair dryer costs about eight cents (1,000 watts equals one KWH) for each hour that you use it. A slow cooker that is rated at 200 watts on the high setting costs about 1.6 cents per hour of use.

Q - We are going to try to get by using our window air conditioner as little as possible this summer. Should we open or close the fireplace chimney damper during the hot weather to help cool our house?

A - If you plan to rely on natural ventilation for cooling your house, you should leave your chimney damper open. It can be particularly effective if your chimney is located on the south or west side of your house.

During the daytime, the sun shines on the chimney brick and heats it. This warms the air inside of the chimney creating a draft up the flue, just like when a fire is burning. If you keep your windows open, cooler air is then drawn in through your windows.

This type of chimney ventilation is very effective in the early evening. The heavy brick mass of the chimney, exposed to the sun, stays warm well into the evening hours. This creates a stronger upward draft as the outdoor air cools.

food preparation

Item	Typical Wattage	Period Of Use	Cost Per Use at 6.5¢ Per KWH	Number of Uses Per Month	Cost Per Month At 6.5¢ Per KWH
Blender	300	30 sec.	$ .0001	30	$ .003
Broiler (portable)	1200	45 min	.06	8	.48
Can Opener	100	12 sec.	.00002	75	.002
Coffee Maker					
Brew	600	15 min.	.01	50	.50
Hold	80	1 hr.	.005	50	.25
Coffee Urn					
Brew	1200	30 min.	.04	1	.04
Hold	100	2 hrs.	.01	1	.01
*Cooker/Fryer/Dutch Oven	1200	1 hr.	.04	3	.12
Corn Popper					
Oil	575	9 min.	.006	8	.05
Hot Air	1400	5 min.	.008	8	.06
Crepe Maker	750	30 min.	.02	4	.08
Dishwasher	1201	50 min. (1 cycle)	.07	30	2.10
Disposer	445	1 min.	.0005	60	.03
Egg Cooker	600	5 min.	.003	15	.05
*Fondue/Chafing Dish	800	1 hr.	.03	2	.06
Fry Pan	1200	45 min.	.03	15	.45
*Griddle	1200	30 min.	.03	8	.24
Hamburger Maker	750	20 min.	.02	8	.16
Hot Dog Cooker	1500	1 min.	.002	10	.02
Hot Plate	1250	30 min.	.04	8	.32
Ice Cream Freezer	130	45 min.	.006	1	.006
Ice Crusher	100	3 min.	.0003	8	.002

*Designates thermostatically controlled appliances. Cost based on appliance estimated "on" time.

Item	Typical Wattage	Period Of Use	Cost Per Use at 6.5¢ Per KWH	Number Of Uses Per Month	Cost Per Month At 6.5¢ Per KWH
Juicer	125	2 min.	$ .0003	8	$ .002
Knife	95	5 min.	.0005	8	.004
Knife Sharpener	40	5 min.	.0002	4	.0008
Microwave Oven	1450	15 min.	.02	48	.96
Mixer					
Hand	100	5 min.	.0005	13	.007
Stand	150	8 min.	.001	6	.006
Outdoor Grill	1500	1 hr.	.10	4	.40
Plastic Bag Sealer	60	1 min.	.0001	29	.003
Range					
*Small Unit 6"	1250	30 min.	.02	30	.60
*Large Unit 8"	2100	30 min.	.03	30	.90
*Bake Unit	3200	1 hr.	.05	30	1.50
Broil Unit	3300	15 min.	.05	4	.20
*Clean	4000	2 hrs.	.33	1	.33
*Total Range		—	—	—	3.53
*Roaster	1425	6 hrs.	.28	1	.28
Rotisserie	1400	2 hrs.	.18	2	.36
Slow Cooker					
High Setting	200	6 hrs.	.08	9	.72
Low Setting	75	8 hrs.	.04	4	.16
Toaster	1100	3 min.	.004	58	.23
Toaster Oven	1500				
Toasting		3 min.	.005	42	.21
*Baking		30 min.	.02	23	.46
Trash Compactor	400	30 sec.	.0002	150	.03
*Waffle Baker	1200	30 min.	.03	4	.12
Warming Tray	140	2 hrs.	.02	4	.08

*Designates thermostatically controlled appliances. Cost based on appliance estimated "on" time.

space conditioning

The following table is based on the average seasonal use of various space conditioning electrical equipment. In central and southern Ohio average seasonal use is a 4-month cooling season and an 8-month heating season.

	Typical Wattage	Estimated Monthly Use	Estimated Monthly Cost At 6.5¢ Per KWH
*Dehumidifier	410	366 hours	$ 9.75
Electronic Air Cleaner (includes the continuous operation of a 300 watt furnace fan)	350	Continuous	16.38
Fan			
Attic	370	197 hours	4.74
Circulating	88	125 hours	.72
*Furnace Fan (heating season only)			
¼ H.P. Motor	250	288 hours	4.68
⅓ H.P. Motor	300	288 hours	5.62
½ H.P. Motor	525	288 hours	9.83
Rollaway	171	205 hours	2.28
Window	200	215 hours	2.80
*Humidifier	177	113 hours	1.30
*Space Heater	1300	30 hours	2.54
*Central Air Conditioning			
36000 BTU (7EER)	5100	200 hours	66.30
*Window Air Conditioning			
5000 BTU (7EER)	710	125 hours	5.77
12000 BTU (7EER)	1700	125 hours	13.81

*Designates equipment controlled by a thermostat or humidistat. The monthly use column is the estimated "on" time which may be less than the time the equipment is actually turned on during the month.

refrigeration

Operating costs of the refrigerator and freezer vary according to the life style of the family. Cost is affected by the number of door openings per day, the defrost system, and the size of the unit. The overall design of the unit (insulation, motor efficiency, etc.) also affects the cost. The monthly costs listed in the following table are average costs based on the information from the Association of Home Appliance Manufacturers and the energy cost of 6.5¢ per KWH.

	MANUAL DEFROST		AUTOMATIC DEFROST	
	Minimum	Maximum	Minimum	Maximum
Refrigerator/Freezer				
12 to 15 cu. ft.	$ 4.49	$ 7.35	$ 6.61	$10.86
17 to 20 cu. ft.	—	—	6.31	13.76
23 to 26 cu. ft.	—	—	8.36	15.85
Refrigerator				
10 cu. ft.	2.94	4.11	—	—
15 cu. ft.	2.86	4.72	—	—
Freezer				
10 cu. ft.	4.68	8.11	11.64	12.13
15 cu. ft.	5.53	9.49	7.85	12.35
20 cu. ft.	5.46	9.49	9.95	13.04

health and beauty

Item	Typical Wattage	Period Of Use	Cost Per Use at 6.5¢ Per KWH	Number Of Uses Per Month	Cost Per Month At 6.5¢ Per KWH
*Blanket	150	8 hrs.	$ .04	30	$1.20
*Curling Iron	40	10 min.	.0002	25	.005
Hair Clipper	10	10 min.	.0001	17	.002
Hair Dryer					
Soft Bonnet	400	45 min.	.02	8	.16
Hard Bonnet	900	30 min.	.03	8	.24
Hand-Held	1000	8 min.	.009	21	.19
Hair Setter	350	15 min.	.006	13	.08
Heat Lamp	250	1 hr.	.02	3	.06
*Heating Pad	60	2 hr.	.004	4	.02
Lighted Mirror	50	10 min.	.0005	54	.03
Shaver	15	5 min.	.00007	30	.002
Shaving Cream					
Dispenser	60	1 min.	.00007	30	.002
Sun Lamp	279	1 hr.	.02	4	.08
Toothbrush	1	Continuous	–	–	.05
(continuously recharging)					
Vaporizer	480	1 hr.	.03	10	.30
*Waterbed Heater	375	Continuous	–	–	8.78

*Designates thermostatically controlled appliances. Cost based on appliance estimated "on" time.

home entertainment

Item	Typical Wattage	Period Of Use	Cost Per Use at 6.5¢ Per KWH	Number Of Uses Per Month	Cost Per Month At 6.5¢ Per KWH
Radio	71	1 hr.	$ .005	108	$ .54
Radio/Record Player	109	1 hr.	.007	77	.54
Television					
Black & White					
Solid State	45	1 hr.	.003	180	.54
Tube	100	1 hr.	.007	180	1.26
Color					
Solid State	145	1 hr.	.009	180	1.62
Tube	240	1 hr.	.02	180	3.60

workshop

Item	Typical Wattage	Period Of Use	Cost Per Use at 6.5¢ Per KWH	Number Of Uses Per Month	Cost Per Month At 6.5¢ Per KWH
¼-Inch Drill	287	1 hr.	$ .02	1	$ .02
Circular Saw	1150	1 hr.	.07	1	.07
Jig Saw	287	1 hr.	.02	1	.02
Table Saw	1380	1 hr.	.09	1	.09
Chain Saw	1380	1 hr.	.09	1	.09
Sander	287	1 hr.	.02	1	.02

A - I recently did my springtime energy checkup and I found many spots on the exterior and around windows that need to be caulked. What types of caulk are readily available and which are easiest to use?

Q - Ease of use is only one factor that you should consider when selecting caulk. Some very easy-to-use caulks don't hold up more than a couple of years, so you'll have to redo the job often. On a hot summer day, there are not many activities more unpleasant than applying caulk.

There are more than 50 different types of caulking compounds. The three most common types that you will find in hardware and home center stores are acrylic-based latex, silicone, and latex-silicone combinations.

The costs will range from about $2 to $5 for a standard 10 or 11-ounce tube. You can figure on getting about 11 feet of a 3/8 by 3/8 inch bead of caulk from a standard cartridge.

Silicone caulk is the Cadillac of most of the commonly used residential-grade caulks. It adheres well to most surfaces, stretches very well, and can be applied at temperatures as low as zero degrees. Most other caulks should not be applied below about 40 degrees.

There are a few drawbacks to silicone. Many can not be painted and paint does not always adhere well to the paintable types. You shouldn't use silicone on treated lumber because it may cause the plasticizers in some plastics to bleed. It is a little difficult to apply a smooth bead at first, but you get used to working with it.

The acrylic-latex caulks are easy to apply and clean up with just soap and water. They won't last indefinitely as silicone does, but you can expect about a 10-year life if you prepare

the surface and apply it properly.

If you need a close match of color by painting, acrylic-latex is excellent. It is recommended that you wait about 30 minutes after application before painting, but you can paint it with latex paint almost immediately. The cost for acrylic-latex caulk is in the $2.00 per cartridge range.

The newer acrylic-latex with silicone caulks provide a longer life than plain acrylic-latex, and are priced in the $4.00 range. Since they won't stretch as much a straight silicone caulks, they are good for internal caulking, and external caulking between similar materials, like siding, where the thermal stresses won't be great.

Q - I am checking out my old gas gravity furnace for next winter, but I can't find any place that sells a replacement filter for it. What kind does it need and where should I look?

A - If you do find a dealer that sells a filter for it, call the police. A gas gravity furnace doesn't have an air filter like a forced air furnace. It would cause too much resistance to the air flow for adequate air circulation and energy efficiency.

A gravity furnace doesn't have a blower to move the air. The air comes out of the registers only because hot air is lighter than cold air. It's less energy efficient than a forced-air furnace, but it's more comfortable. You don't get that big shot of hot air each time the furnace kicks on.

Dear Reader,

Thank you for your interest in writing to me about selecting caulking materials for your home. The charts on page 1 and 2 will help you to determine which is best for your specific application and needs. Page 3 shows some basic background information that will be useful when planning for the job.

Sincerely,

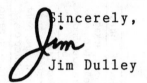

Jim Dulley

Caulking Compound	Cost	Elasticity	Adhesion	Comments
Acrylic	Low	Very good	Most Surfaces	Hard to apply/clean, exterior use only due to noxious odor
Acrylic Latex	Moderate	Fair/Good	Excellent except to metal	Easy to apply, interior/exterior, paintable
Butyl Rubber	Moderate	Fair	Most surfaces, excellent for metal-masonry	Slightly difficult to apply, interior/exterior, paintable after one week, high moisture resistance, high shrinkage
Latex/Polyvinyl Acetate	Low-Moderate	Poor	Most surfaces	Easy to apply, interior/exterior, must be painted, shrinks, not for long-term caulking
Oil or Resin Based	Low	Poor	Most Surfaces	May be messy to apply, may shrink, not for long-term caulking interior use
Polysulfide	High	Good	Needs specified primer to bond most surfaces	Difficult to work with, dries quickly, requires primer, is toxic until cured
Polyurethane	Moderate-High	Very Good	Most surfaces may need primer	Relatively easy to apply, solvent clean-up, unpleasant odor, paintable, interior/exterior
Silicone	High	Excellent	Almost all surfaces	Easy to apply, interior/exterior, most cannot be painted, high moisture resistance, exceptional durability

Types of Caulking Compounds

Type	Relative Cost	Lifetime (yrs)	How It's Used	Performance	Good Features	Bad Features
Rope caulk	Low	1-2	Easy to use; needs dust and oil-free surfaces; use above 40°F	Moderate to high expansion; little shrinkage; becomes brittle at low temperatures	Available in packages suitable for two or six standard-size windows; easy to remove	Must be replaced frequently; windows cannot be opened
Oil-based caulk	Lowest	3-5	Comes in tubes; easily applied and tooled; minimal cleaning of joints; use above 40°F	Little expansion: low shrinkage; performs from −10 to 180°F, although poorly at lower range	Good for nonmoving interior surfaces and joints; fast cure; paint after two-three days	Poor for outside or moving joints; should not be used for glazing work
Latex-based caulk	Low to moderate	5-10	Comes in tubes; easily applied and tooled; requires well-cleaned joints; use above 40°F	Low to moderate expansion; high shrinkage; best on small joints; good from −20 to 150°F	Can be used on damp absorptive surfaces; fast cure; paint shortly after application	Poor adhesion on moving parts
Butyl-based caulk	Low to moderate	5-10	Comes in tubes; easily applied and tooled; clean surfaces with solvents; use above 40°F	Moderate expansion; high shrinkage; use on larger joints and cracks; good from −25 to 250°F	Adheres well to all building materials, especially masonry to metal; comes in many colors	Good only for joints with moderate movement; paint after one week
Solvent-based acrylic sealants	Moderate	10-20	Heat to 120°F before using; needs ventilation and minimal cleaning of joints; comes in tubes	Low to moderate expansion; little shrinkage; good from −20 to 150°F	Good on wide and/or moving joints; comes in colors	Strong odor limits use to well-ventilated spaces or outside
Polysulfide sealants	Moderate to high	20-30	Comes in tubes; two-part compound can be messy when mixing; can't be applied and won't cure below 40°F	High expansion; very low shrinkage; good for large joints; good from −60 to 250°F	Good on wide and/or moving joints; comes in colors	Primer may be required before application
Urethane sealants	High to very high	20-30	Joints must be very clean; use above 32°F and below 70% relative humidity	Very high expansion; very low shrinkage; good for large joints; good from −60 to 275°F	Similar to polysulfide sealants; very good adhesion; abrasion resistant	Can adhere so strongly to masonry as to cause crumbling
Silicone sealants	High to very high	30	Comes in tubes; easily applied and tooled; very clean surfaces required; can be applied down to −55°F	High expansion; no shrinkage; very versatile as joint filler; good from −90 to 400°F	Good adhesion to metal and glass; fast cure; comes in colors	Poor adhesion to concrete; must be painted with silicone paint
Nitrile rubber	Moderate to high	15-20	Primarily for use in areas requiring seal against liquid water	Moderate expansion; high shrinkage; can't be used on moving joints or cracks	Adheres well to metal and masonry in high moisture areas	Poor performance if applied to wide or moving joints
Polymeric foam sealants	High	20-30	Comes in spray can or cartridge; minimal cleaning of joints; contents must be kept above 60°F when using	Little expansion; no shrinkage; not for moving joints; good from −90 to 200°F	Good adhesion; use on large cracks and hard-to-reach spots	Use requires adequate ventilation; may crumble if disturbed

Source: U.S. Department of Energy. *Residential Conservation Service Auditor Training Manual* (Washington, D.C.: U.S. Government Printing Office, 1980).

WHERE TO CAULK

Outside caulking should be used anywhere on or around a structure to keep it water and air tight. Caulk is usually needed in places where different materials or parts of a building meet. The filling of these "meetings" or joints is necessary to insure the soundness of the total structure and prevent weather damage. Due to differing temperatures and weight stresses, a joint can expand, contract and move. To maintain a firm seal in these joints, it is important to use a caulk that will remain flexible.

Caulking can also be used to help insulate joints to keep heating and energy costs down. Extra attention around windows, doors, and pipes leading into a structure will pay off in energy savings.

The following are some exterior uses for caulking on a building or residence:

- At joints between siding, windows and door frames
- Beneath window sills at siding
- Where chimney meets roof shingles
- All roof flashings
- Between undersides of eaves and gable moldings
- All corners formed by siding
- Between masonry steps, porches, patios and the main body of the house
- Plug holes and seal cracks in walls and around the house
- Weatherproof around outside electrical receptacle
- Around doors and windows to prevent heat loss and water leakage
- Excellent replacement for old fashion window glazing
- Seal between panes of glass in greenhouse
- Any joint where filling is necessary to prevent insect invasion

HOW TO CAULK
Preparation

The proper preparation of the surface to be caulked or sealed is of key importance for the success of the job. A seal will hold only as well as the surface it is applied to. If improper cleaning is done, caulking will not adhere to the surface and this will result in time and money loss. For best results:

- Remove any old caulking completely.
- Wipe joint with clean, dry cloth. The joint should be free of water, dirt, loose materials, grease, oil or any chemical compounds. (Wash area with a detergent or safe nonexplosive cleaner in the case of grease or oil)
- Use sand paper or a sharp tool to loosen scaling paint or any other interfering substances
- Priming may be required over certain surfaces. When using some solvent-based materials over tar or asphalt, or when caulking over oil spots or wood knots, for example, the caulk may discolor, lose adhesion, or even crack. Read the manufacturer's directions carefully for information on incompatible materials.

If you find that the caulk you have chosen is not compatible with your surface (or some parts of it, such as grease spots), paint over the suspect area with two light coats of an alcohol shellac or a primer recommended by the manufacturer. Alcohol shellac will dry in 30-45 minutes, and the surface is then ready to be caulked.

PLANNING THE JOB

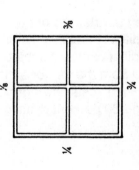

Like painting, caulking is "90% preparation, 10% perspiration". To plan the job adequately, you must first determine what you want to caulk. Let us say there are three exterior windows whose frames have separated from their surrounding material uniformly. Take a tape measure and measure the perimeter like this:

Now measure the depth of the crack at several points

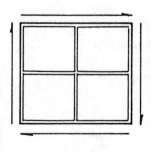

and average them out like this:

1/8" + 3/8" x 6/8" x 2/8" = 12/8" divided by 4 = 3/8" average depth. Measure the width of the crack. Let's say it is uniformly ½". What we have now is a crack ½" wide by ⅜" deep by 8 feet long (the total perimeter of the window).

Now, refer to this chart:

Bead Width (inches)

Bead Depth (inches)	¼	⅜	½	¾
¼	24'	16'	12'	8'
⅜	16'	10'8"	8'	5'4"
½	12'	8'	6'	4'

Linear feet per 10 fluid ounce cartridge For a 4 fluid ounce cartridge simply divide linear feet by 10 and multiply by 4.

In the case of Geocel exterior caulking sealant, you will need one 10 fluid ounce cartridge. If this had been a bathtub with a crack ½" wide, ¼" deep and 5' long you would have needed one 4 fluid ounce tube of Geocel Bathroom Caulking Sealant.

This formula can be used on any caulking job to estimate how many tubes or cartridges you will need. Just remember this is an estimate. It is always wise to have an extra cartridge on hand just in case our estimate was a little optimistic.

Q - Excess humidity in my home is uncomfortable and often causes a moisture problem. Does it cost much to operate a dehumidifier and what is the best type and size to buy?

A - A dehumidifier can help reduce that muggy feeling in your home and the dampness in basements, laundry rooms, etc.. It can pull up to 50 pints of water from the air each day and can reduce your air-conditioning needs.

Although an air conditioner dehumidifies too, it's not as effective and it would not be energy efficient to use it in the winter. You can use a dehumidifier year-round without losing the indoor heat.

The electric costs to operate a dehumidifier depends primarily on its capacity and how long it must run to adequately dry the indoor air. You can anticipate spending between $25 and $75 a year. It costs more in steamy southern climates because it runs longer and more days each year.

The energy efficiency of dehumidifiers varies, so check the electricity usage on the label of each model you are considering. An inefficient one uses about 20 to 25 percent more electricity than an efficient one. Also, the lower you set the humidity control knob, the longer it must run.

A dehumidifier works on a process similar to an air conditioner. The major differences are that a dehumidifier does not exhaust the warm air from the condenser outdoors and it is controlled by humidity level, not room temperature.

It is important to get the proper capacity dehumidifier to satisfy your room's needs. Dehumidifier capacity is rated in pints of water removed from the indoor air in 24 hours. The performance tests are conducted at 80 degrees and 60 percent relative humidity.

The capacity of dehumidifiers ranges from about 10 pints per day to 50 pints per day. For a rough size estimate, a 500 square foot moderately damp room would require a 10-pint unit. The same-sized extremely damp room would require a 16-pint unit. A 2,000 square foot area would require between a an 18-pint and 37-pint unit depending on humidity conditions.

There are several features that can make a dehumidifier more convenient to operate. An on-off switch that is separate from the humidity control knob is helpful. Easy removal of the water container and one designed so the water won't spill is very convenient. A signal light to warn you that the water container is full and needs to be emptied will get your attention.

Q - I plan to build a room addition, and I wanted to try the energy-efficient ADA method. Where can I get the gasket seals?

A - You should use special gasket material for the ADA (airtight drywall) type of construction. The material must be flexible enough to compress and seal all gaps and imperfections in the surface, but it must not take on a permanent set.

A good source for the gasket material is log home manufacturers and material suppliers. Most log homes use similar types of gaskets between each row of logs. Although they are fairly expensive, EPDM and neoprene are two excellent gasket materials for your application.

Dear Reader,

Thank you for your interest in writing to me about dehumidifiers. You can use one both summer and winter. Check the features of the various models you see in stores. One of the most convenient features is a water container that is easy to remove without spilling.

This information and list of manufacturers are for your information only and are not an endorsement of this type of product, specific manufacturer, or model.

Sincerely,

Jim Dulley

RECOMMENDED DEHUMIDIFIER CAPACITIES

CONDITIONS DURING WARM, HUMID WEATHER	AREA (square feet)				
	500	1,000	1,500	2,000	2,500
Moderately damp - feels damp and musty odor only in humid weather	10 pt.	14 pt.	18 pt.	22 pt.	26 pt.
Very Damp - Space always feels damp and has musty odor. Damp spots on walls.	12 pt.	17 pt.	22 pt.	27 pt.	32 pt.
Wet - Space feels and smells wet. Walls and floors sweat.	14 pt.	20 pt.	26 pt.	32 pt.	38 pt.
Very Wet - Laundry drying, wet floor, high load conditions.	16 pt.	23 pt.	30 pt.	37 pt.	44 pt.

MANUFACTURERS, CAPACITIES, AND PRICES

MANUFACTURER & MODEL	LARGEST CAPACITY	PRICES
ADMIRAL - DH37D7GA	37	$230
AMANA - DH40	40	$240
COMFORT-AIRE - FDHD41	41	$312
DAYTON - 3H324	41	$380
EMERSON - DE44FA	44	$270
FRIEDRICH - FD50X	50	$310
GE - AHD40AA	38	$214
HUNTER - 31040	40	$260
J C PENNEY - 8570137	50	$299
OASIS - OD3800L	38	$395
SEARS - 5548	48	$325
WHIRLPOOL - ADO482XPO	48	$249
WHITE-WESTG. - ED508K7	50	$250
WOODS - WD36	50	$224

A 115 volt, 60 hertz, AC only, 15 ampere fused electrical supply is required (use time delay fuse or time delay circuit breaker). Use a separate circuit, serving only this appliance. Do not use an extension cord.

OBSERVE ALL LOCAL GOVERNING CODES AND ORDINANCES

Do not, under any circumstances, remove the power supply cord ground prong.

For your personal safety, this appliance must be grounded. This appliance has a power supply cord with a 3-prong grounding plug. To avoid possible shock hazard, the cord must be plugged into a mating 3-prong grounding type wall receptacle, grounded in accordance with the National Electrical Code and local codes and ordinances. If a mating wall outlet is not available, it is your responsibility and obligation to have a properly grounded 3-prong wall receptacle installed by a qualified electrician.

1. Don't alter or change the plug on the power supply cord of your dehumidifier. Changes would make it unsafe, could cause serious damage to the dehumidifier, and might void the warranty.

2. Don't try to use this dehumidifier on direct current (D.C.). Make sure the receptacle is wired to a 60 cycle alternating current of (60 HZ) 115 voltage and 15 amps.

3-PRONG GROUNDING PLUG
POWER SUPPLY CORD
3-PRONG GROUNDING-TYPE WALL RECEPTACLE

3. Don't use an extension cord.
4. Don't use a circuit that will become overloaded when the dehumidifier is installed.
5. Don't plug in the dehumidifier if you're in doubt about the grounding of your electrical system. Consult a qualified electrician first.

HUMIDISTAT.

To adjust the humidistat control turn the knob to the setting you prefer. (See Fig. 2.)

Constant. If you choose this setting, dehumidifier will run all the time no matter what the humidity.

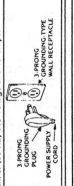

DRYER — HUMIDISTAT — OFF CONSTANT
Fig. 2

1 thru Constant. This is the range of relative humidity on the humidistat control knob. You may adjust the humidistat setting higher or lower to suit your needs. Higher numbers make air dryer, lower numbers leave more moisture in the air. When the relative humidity is reduced to the level you have chosen, the dehumidifier will turn itself off. It will turn itself on again when the humidity rises. Off. This setting turns the dehumidifier off when dehumidification is not needed.

NOTE: If you turn your dehumidifier off and turn it right on again, the compressor may try to start—then stop. This is normal. In about two minutes, the compressor will start again and continue to run.

AUTOMATIC SHUTOFF.

An automatic shutoff switch turns off the dehumidifier when the water pan is filled to its present level. To restart dehumidifier, simply remove water pan, empty and slide it back in place. A signal light warns when water pan is full for emptying and the dehumidifier has stopped. Be sure to replace pan properly so unit will run.

WATER PAN

(CAUTION: Water pan must be properly placed to avoid water overflow.)

To install water pan tilt at a downward angle and place pan onto hanger brackets. Dehumidifier will shut off when pan needs emptying (See Fig. 3).

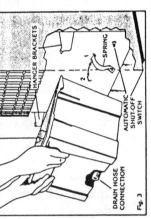

HANGER BRACKETS — SPRING — AUTOMATIC SHUT-OFF SWITCH — DRAIN HOSE CONNECTION
Fig. 3
Installing water pan

• To check for proper pan installation: press down on rear of pan and listen for click of shutoff switch. If unit is running, it will stop for a moment. Dehumidifier will start right away. Replace pan after emptying to prevent water from collecting on the floor.

• The pan's water collection level is pre-set at the factory to the normal fill position. If the water level is too high, move the spring from Position 1 to Position 2 (See Fig. 3). This will reduce the amount of water that collects in pan.

• If you do not want to empty the water pan, it can be hooked up to a drain, since your dehumidifier has a standard garden hose fitting at the rear of water pan (See Fig. 3). To use, cut out the seal on the hose fitting. Attach a hose to the fitting and run directly into a drain. Be sure the hose lies flat, not kinked. A drain hose may be bought from Sears. Part No. 9181.

If you decide to use the water pan after making a hole in the fitting, obtain a garden hose cap for the fitting at your nearest Sears Store.

DANGER—SHOCK OR INJURY HAZARD—before upkeep or service be sure to unplug power cord from outlet.

OILING THE MOTOR.

It's a good idea to oil the fan motor at least once a year. To do this you'll need to remove the cabinet. Just follow these simple steps:

1. Remove humidistat knob and the two screws which hold the plastic front grille in place (see Fig. 4). Pull out and down on bottom of grille.

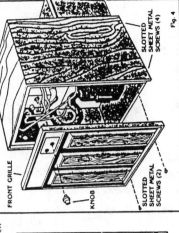

FRONT GRILLE — KNOB — SLOTTED SHEET METAL SCREWS (2) — SLOTTED SHEET METAL SCREWS (4)
Fig. 4

2. Remove rear grille by snapping it out at each lower corner. Pull down and out. (See Fig. 5.)

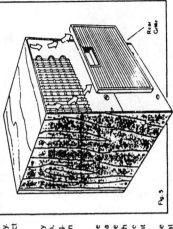

Rear Grille
Fig. 5

Check this chart for your dehumidifier features.

This manual covers two dehumidifier models; your model number can be found on the serial label.

	MODEL NUMBER 5631	MODEL NUMBER 5641
Pints of water removed each 24 hours.*	30	40
FULL PAN signal light	yes	yes
Automatic shut-off switch	yes	yes
Automatic Humidistat	yes	yes

*The moisture-removing ability of Sears dehumidifiers is certified in accordance with American National Standard B-149-1 (AHAM DH-1) with room conditions at 80°F and 60% relative humidity.

Q - Our central air conditioner condenser unit is on the southwest side of our house and it gets very hot in the afternoon sun. Is it worthwhile to shade it somehow, and is there any maintenance we should do to it?

A - The hot afternoon sun shining on your outdoor condenser unit can reduce the overall efficiency of your central air conditioner system and increase your electric bills. Also, if your air conditioner is under-sized, the reduced efficiency may keep it from adequately cooling your home on the hottest days when you need it the most.

The coils and fins in the outdoor condenser unit gives off the indoor heat to the outside air. If the air surrounding the condenser is warmed by the sun shining on the unit, the condenser can't give off as much heat as quickly, so the compressor has to run longer, using more electricity.

Any type of cover to block the sun from shining directly on the condenser unit will help hold down your electric bills. It is very important to leave enough clearance around the unit, at least two feet on the sides and top, for adequate air flow. Also, if you have any bushes near the unit that have grown and are crowding it, trim them back.

There is a very effective and functional combination storage unit/air conditioner shading cover that you can make yourself. You can use it to store your lawn tools, barbecue grill, etc..

It is basically a plywood storage compartment built about two feet back from the condenser unit. Build it with a sloped roof that extends over the condenser unit for shade and attaches to your house. The sloped roof gives added height for adequate clearance and it blends better with the lines of most houses.

Make the frame for the storage unit/cover with 2x4 lumber. Cover the storage compartment with plywood siding. Install a piano hinge on the top so you can open it. Nail the plywood siding over the rest of the sloped top to cover the condenser unit. Leave the sides by the condenser uncovered to allow for adequate air flow.

The only maintenance you can do yourself is to keep the condenser coils and fins clean. Switch off electric power at the circuit breaker panel or fuse box. Remove the cover from the unit and GENTLY clean the fins and coils with a soft brush and soapy water. Carefully straighten any fins that are bent over, then hose off the condenser coils and fins.

Q - We have a thermostatically-controlled attic vent fan that runs continuously during the day. Would it be good to also install additional vents, like a turbine vent?

A - If your attic exhaust fan runs almost continuously, it uses a lot of electricity and it may be a good idea to add more standard roof vents. An electric attic fan may actually use more electricity than it saves from reducing the load on your air conditioner.

You may have the thermostat temperature set too low on the attic fan. It should be set to come on at about 100 to 110 degrees. On a breezy day, your standard vents may provide enough ventilation to keep the fan from coming on at all. For winter use, you can install a switch on the exhaust fan that is actuated by the humidity level.

Dear Reader,

Thank you for your interest in writing to me about how to build a storage unit/air conditioner cover. By keeping the sun off of your air conditioner, it will operate more efficiently. Then it will use less electricity and it will be able to supply more cooling capacity on the hottest afternoons.

Before you begin to build this cover, check with your heating and air-conditioning contractor, or with the manufacturer of your air conditioner for the recommended clearance around the outdoor condenser unit.

The diagram below shows how the finished cover should look. As long as you meet the clearance recommendations, you can size it for adequate storage capacity. Also, tilt the roof at an angle that is consistent with that of the rof of your roof. It will look better. The instructions and diagram are on the following pages.

Sincerely,

Jim

Jim Dulley

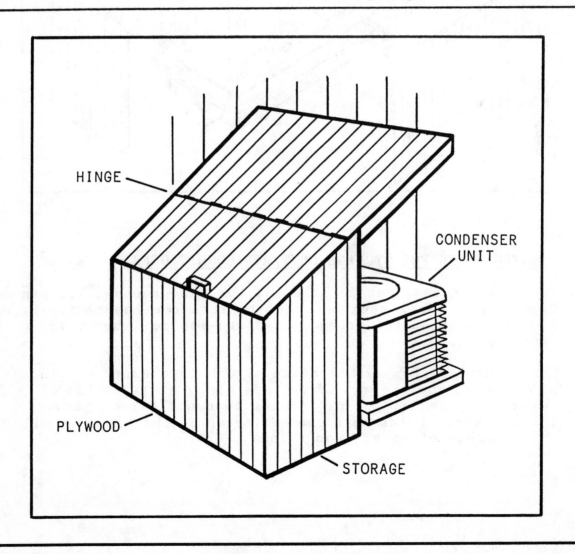

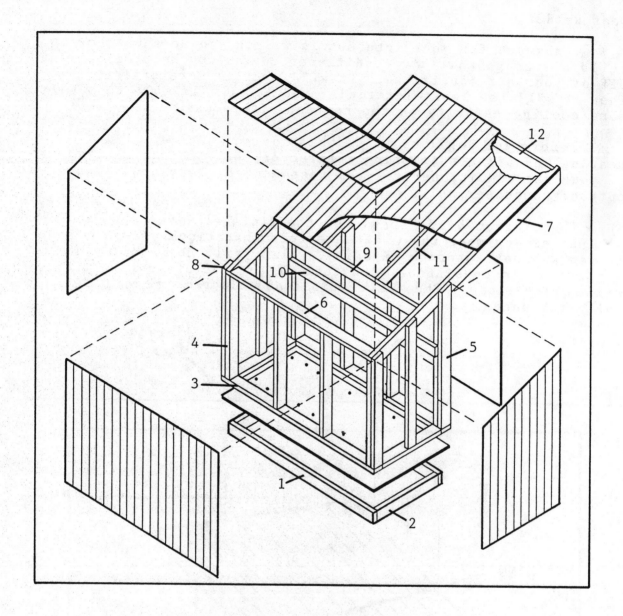

INSTRUCTIONS FOR STORAGE UNIT/AIR CONDITIONER COVER

1) First make a base box for the unit on the ground. You can
   2x4's (1,2). Nail them together to form the base box. Since
   it is setting on the ground, pressure-treated lumber is
   recommended.

2) Cover the base box with a piece of 5/8-inch exterior grade
   plywood for the floor. If you are going to put a lot of
   heavy tools in it, you might want to use 3/4-inch plywood.
   Drill several holes near the perimeter of the floor to allow
   for drainage of water from rain.

3) Build the framing for the storage box using 2x4 lumber.
First cut the soleplates (3) for the bottom of the sides.
Then nail on the uprights to form the sides. The back
uprights (4) will all be the same length. The side uprights
(5) will get longer as they get closer to the house to
provide the pitch angle for the roof.

4) Attach the framing and soleplates to the floor and support it
at the back with a 2x4 (6). That will be the first roof
rafter.

5) Cut two long 2x4 rafters (7) to reach from the back support
(6) to the side of your house. You will have to notch one
end of each long 2x4 so that it will fit over the members at
point (8).

6) Attach these two long 2x4 to the upright framing making sure
you have them tilted up at the proper angle. Attach another
2x4 support (9) between them at the top. Attach another
support (10) between the uprights nearest the condenser unit.
This is the location of the hinge for the storage compartment
door. Attach support piece (12) to the end of the rafters (7)
where it meets the house.

7) Nail on the roof rafters (11) attaching them between the
uprights and the upper support (9).

8) Attach the plywood sheathing as is shown in the diagram.
Galvanized nails will resist the dampness best. Don't run
the sheathing all the way to the ground. Leave a gap of at
least 3/4 of an inch to let moisture escape.

9) Use two pieces of the plywood sheathing for the roof. Size
the so that the break is over support member (9). Nail the
large roof piece, over the condenser unit, to the rafters.
Then attach the smaller roof section with the piano hinge.
That will be the door for the storage compartment.

10) You should paint it inside and out with several coats of a
good quality exterior paint. A lighter color will help keep
it even cooler for your air conditioner. If you have any
valuable items, add a latch and padlock to the storage
compartment door.

Q - We have made our house more airtight to save energy. Now we are going to paint the rooms. Will using a vapor barrier paint reduce the amount of moisture absorbed by the walls and what types of paints are available?

A - Moisture (water vapor from the indoor air) can get into your walls and cause many serious and expensive problems. During the cold weather, this water vapor can condense somewhere in the insulation inside the wall. You generally won't know it is happening until the damage is done.

This condensed water can soak and make the wall insulation ineffective. If it stays damp for a long while, the structural lumber in the wall can begin to rot. Also, excess moisture passing through the wall is a common cause of bubbling and peeling of exterior house paint.

With an existing home, painting your walls with a special vapor barrier interior paint is the easiest way to block the water vapor from entering the walls. It is available at retail paint stores and you can easily apply it like any other interior wall paint. Check your local building codes for the proper location of the vapor barrier before you apply it.

To be considered a vapor barrier paint, it should have a perm rating of less than 1. Perm rating refers to how easily water vapor passes through the layer of paint. For comparison, an ordinary latex sealer has a perm rating of 6, and flat latex wall paint has a rating of 20.

There are three basic types of vapor barrier paints - latex, alkyd, and shellac. They are priced about the same as any good-quality wall paint. These paints are primers and should be covered with standard latex or oil-based wall paint. You can use them over previously painted walls or on plaster or gypsum board.

Each type of vapor barrier primer has advantages. Alkyd and shellac primers are more durable than the latex and may be better for high traffic areas. Shellac primer is also excellent for covering stains on walls. The latex offers the easiest cleanup, with soap and water, and gives off less fumes as it dries.

The shellac and latex paints dry quickly, in less than an hour. Often, by the time you finish an entire room with the primer, you can immediately start over at the beginning with the topcoat wall paint.

Q - I just built a work shed in the backyard that I plan to heat with a kerosene heater next winter. Are there many different types of kerosene fuel to use in these heaters?

A - First, check your local codes. Using a kerosene heater is not allowed in many areas. There are two types of kerosene generally available - 1K that is low in sulfur, and 2K which is higher in sulfur. You should use 1K in your heater. It gives off less sulfur dioxide emissions and burns much cleaner. 2K fuel can gum the wick.

Most kerosene that you buy in the prepackaged 2 gallon containers is 1K. Kerosene sold by service stations can be either type and it's virtually impossible to tell them apart. Before you buy any kerosene at a service station, ask which type it is. Often, they won't know either, so don't buy it there.

Dear Reader,

    Thank you for your interest in writing to me about interior vapor barrier wall paint. There are many types of paint available that will somewhat reduce the amount of moisture that enters your wall. To be considered a low-perm "vapor barrier" paint, it should have a perm rating of less than one. The paint specifications usually show this if it is considered a vapor barrier paint.

    In most parts of the United States, the vapor barrier should be on the interior surface of the wall to stop moisture penetration from indoors during the cold winter weather. In some southern areas, with high outdoor humidity levels and heavy air conditioning in the summer, moisture penetrating the wall from outdoors can be a problem. Check with local building codes for the proper location of the vapor barrier. If your local codes indicate that it should be on the outdoor surface of the wall, don't use an interior vapor barrier paint as described. Check your local paint dealers for an exterior-grade "low-perm" paint.

    This literature and list of manufacturers are for your information only and are not an endorsement of this type of product or a specific manufacturer.

Sincerely,

Jim Dulley

MANUFACTURERS

GLIDDEN, 925 Euclid Ave., Cleveland, OH 44115
    "INSUL-AID Vapor Barrier Primer-Sealer No. 5116"

BENJAMIN MOORE, 51 Chestnut Ridge Rd., Montvale, NJ 07645
    "Alkyd Primer Sealer 200"

SEARS, Sears Tower, Chicago, IL 60684
    "Oil Base Primer 5881"

WILLIAM ZINSSER & CO., 39 Belmont Ave., Somerset, NJ 08873
    "B-I-N Primer-Sealer"

- seals new wood, wallboard, cured plaster, all porous surfaces
- adheres to hard-to-stick-to materials – gloss paint, Masonite,® glass, metal
- blocks out stains – water marks, knots & sap, smoke & soot, graffiti, grease, crayon
- provides interior vapor barrier
- dries fast; lets you top coat in 45 minutes

Description

B-1-N Primer Sealer is a fast-drying, shellac-based white-pigmented undercoat—the original stain-killing primer-sealer. It functions in three ways: 1. Primes white. 2. Seals surfaces to provide smooth base for the finish coat. 3. Kills stains.

B-I-N dries in just 45 minutes, completely seals porous surfaces, adheres to almost everything and forms a vapor barrier. It insures quality results; saves time and paint. The top coat goes farther and often only one coat is needed. That's why B-I-N is the premier all-purpose interior primer-sealer.

B-I-N may also be used for many select exterior applications such as knots and sappy streaks, rust stains, copper screening stains, puttied nailheads, weathered siding and trim touch-up, gloss-painted trim and cured masonry.

Color

Available only in white.

Tinting

May be tinted with up to 4 ounces of many "universal" tinting colors per gallon B-I-N. Check for compatibility. Tinting helps top coat cover in one coat.

Finish

Dries to an egg shell finish which promotes solid adhesion of the top coat.

Uses

B-I-N is suitable for all types of interior surfaces. Its shellac base and quick-drying features make it an exceptional sealer for porous surfaces. It is ideal over old or new (but fully cured) plaster walls, drywall, spackled areas, wallpaper, new or previously painted wood and plywood, unpainted furniture, wicker. Because of its unusual adhesion, it is recommended as a primer on dense, hard-to-grip surfaces such as gloss-painted walls and woodwork, metal, Formica®, Masonite®, other hardboard, glass and ceramic tile without sanding. It is unmatched in ability to seal off the widest variety of hard-to-kill stains, including knots and sappy streaks in new wood, graffiti, water stains, crayon, ink, lipstick, stains from grease, smoke, soot and fire damage.

FOR SPECIFIC USE DETAILS, SEE BELOW

Finishes Recommended for Use Over B-I-N

B-I-N can be used under any type of gloss, semi-gloss or flat interior paint—water-thinned (latex) or solvent-thinned (oil-based). Not recommended for use under polyurethanes, or under special highly alkaline acoustical or flock type coatings generally used for ceilings and for special effects on other surfaces.

Before using B-I-N under any lacquer, test to see whether the lacquer dissolves or softens the B-I-N film.

Spot priming is recommended only under high-hiding paints; primed spots may flash through paints with little hiding strength — e.g., many ceiling paints. If this occurs, paint entire surface with B-I-N before applying paint with poor hiding.

Thinning

Do not thin. Add a small amount of a denatured alcohol only if B-I-N thickens in the can during application because of solvent evaporation.

Surface Preparation

Surface must be clean and dry. Test all old painted or varnished surfaces for adhesion by making an X with a razor or knife and placing a section of Scotch tape over it, pressing it down with thumb. After 30 seconds yank the tape off (do not pull, but yank at the tape). If the old paint or varnish comes off on the tape, the paint should be removed. Remove any wax with mineral spirits or commercial wax remover. Allow to dry thoroughly. Scrape off loose or scaling paint and wallpaper paste. Fill wall cracks and nail holes with patching plaster; sand smooth when dry. Sand unfinished wood with fine sandpaper. Remove dust with tack cloth. Remove rust on metal by sanding, then wipe down with mineral spirits or turpentine.

When applying textured ceiling paint in rooms where there has been heavy smoking, check surfaces for brown nicotine stain that rubs off on a damp cloth. If present, wash clean and let dry. Otherwise these stains may bleed through into the finish paint.

Application Methods

B-I-N may be brushed, rolled or sprayed, using material at container consistency. **Brush Application:** Flow on freely. B-I-N is self-leveling and dries free from brush ridges. **Roller:** Use a short nap roller. **Sprayer:** Use between 45 and 60 pound pressure for air; 0.015 tip for airless. **Airless sprayers only:** To slow drying and prevent clogging, up to 3 fl. oz., paint thinner or VMP naphtha per gallon B-I-N may be added. Stir in vigorously just before use to disperse thoroughly.

Can be applied at temperatures as low as $0°F$.

Drying Time

Dry to handle: 15 to 20 minutes. Dry, ready for final finish: 45 minutes. At very low temperatures, allow extra drying time.

Coverage By Brush

On non-porous surfaces: up to 500 sq. ft. per gallon (12 sq. m. per liter). On porous surfaces, such as wall board: up to 450 sq. ft per gallon (11 sq. m. per liter).

Cleaning Equipment

Clean brush or roller while still wet. Most effective and simple to use is a solution of household ammonia (1 part) and warm water (3 parts). Soak brush or roller thoroughly, well into the bristle or nap; then wash with soap and water and rinse. Or clean with denatured alcohol. Sprayer may be cleaned with ammonia or alcohol. If ammonia is used, rinse with water, then with alcohol to dry parts.

Specific Interior Uses

New Plaster. B-I-N effectively seals off porous plaster walls, permitting, in many cases, the use of only one finish coat. Tinting to approximate shade of finish coat is recommended. Apply over new plaster only after it is thoroughly cured and dry. Industry practice is to wait at least 90 days before painting. Even then, it is wise to have the pasterer confirm that the surface is ready for paint.

Drywall. B-I-N seals off gypsum wallboard (sheetrock) effectively, insures uniform holdout of the finish coat of paint on the paper facing as well as on the taped joint areas. And it does not raise facing paper fibers.

PROTECTIVE MAINTENANCE COATINGS DATA

Latex Vapor Barrier

INSUL-AID® Vapor Barrier Primer-Sealer No. 5116

For Gypsum Wallboard, Composition Board, Plaster and Masonry

PRODUCT DESCRIPTION

INSUL-AID is a special latex primer-sealer and vapor barrier for interior walls and ceilings. It reduces loss of interior moisture through the walls to help maintain insulation efficiency and guard against exterior paint adhesion failures caused by condensation.

Moisture and Heat Loss

Every home contains moisture (water vapor) that, in the proper proportion, provides a healthy atmosphere. But under winter conditions, when the inside/outside temperatures differ drastically, this moisture indoors passes through interior walls and condenses within the structural shell as it seeks the colder exterior side.

This moisture can fill the pockets or voids in insulation, increasing the flow of heat, severely reducing its insulating value. Insulation must be dry to function efficiently.

Condensed water within the stud space can saturate the wood siding behind the paint film, causing the exterior paint to blister, flake and peel. Moisture is the leading cause of exterior paint failure.

Keeping water vapor inside the home will help reduce heat loss and guard against moisture damage. Vapor barrier systems can help to provide this protection. Therefore, to help keep moisture inside, apply INSUL-AID Vapor Barrier to interior walls and ceilings that contact the outside or any unheated areas. The effectiveness of a vapor barrier against moisture is measured by its "perm rating." To be effective, a vapor barrier must have a perm rating of less than 1.0, as recommended in the Federal Housing Administration "Minimum Property Standards."

INSUL-AID Vapor Barrier Coating is specifically designed to provide a perm rating of 0.6 when applied at a coverage rate of 400 square feet per gallon to smooth surfaces. INSUL-AID Coating applies and cleans up with the ease of latex wall paint. It can be top coated with latex or alkyd paints in any desired finish. It may also be used as a primer for converted epoxies and vinyl wall coverings.

SPECIFICATIONS

One coat of INSUL-AID Sealer applied uniformly at 400 square feet per gallon on smooth surfaces provides a moisture vapor transmission rate of only 0.6 perm (ASTM D1653).

TYPICAL USES

Residential—both new and existing construction.
Commercial—schools, offices, hotels, hospitals.

PRODUCT ADVANTAGES

- Provides a continuous vapor barrier not subject to the breaks around electrical outlets, plumbing, cut ends, etc. associated with sheet vapor barrier materials, used separately as a part of the insulation backing.
- Does not interfere with the common practice of applying gypsum drywall to the studs with an adhesive.
- Places the vapor barrier directly on the face of the wall surface, where it can effectively keep moisture out of the plaster and drywall.
- When adding insulation to existing structures, where placing vapor barrier sheeting is either difficult or impossible, paint is the most practical and economical way to install an effective continuous vapor barrier.

TECHNICAL DATA

Product No. – Y-5116

Generic Type – Latex

Color – White

Sheen or Gloss – Flat

Percent Solids by Weight – 48.5%

Percent Solids by Volume – 34.8%

Theoretical Coverage per One Mil Dry (2.7 Mils Wet) – 553 sq. ft./gal.

Recommended Coverage (Calculated) 1.4 Mils Dry (4.0 Mils Wet) – 400 sq. ft./gal.
When computing working coverage, allow for application losses, surface irregularities, etc.

Percent Vehicle (Solids) by Weight – 17.6%

Percent Pigment by Weight – 30.9%

Percent Solvent by Weight – 51.5%

Viscosity – 85-90 KU

Weight per Gallon – 10.5 lbs.

Flash Point – Closed Cup – None

VOC – 0.74 lbs./gal. (88.9 gm./liter), excluding water

Drying Time – (Normal 70°F, 50% R.H.)
Touch – 30-60 min.
Recoat – 3-4 hours

Reduction Solvent – Water

Clean-up Solvent – Water

Type of Cure – Coalescence

Tinting – Will accept DRAMATONE® Colorants at a maximum level of 4 oz./gal. This product is not included in the COLOR NATURALS® System.

INSUL-AID® Vapor Barrier Primer-Sealer (Continued)

MATERIAL PREPARATION

Mix thoroughly before using. Tint with multi-purpose tinting colorants only toward finish coat color (not exceeding 4 oz. per gal.). Do not mix with any other paints, solvents or tinting colors.

SURFACE PREPARATION

Masonry Surfaces

Level any surface projections and mortar spatters by grinding, stoning or scraping. Rake mortar joints clean. Remove oil, grease, dirt, dust and chemicals with prescribed cleaning methods — see Glidden Maintenance Coatings Data Sheet "Surface Preparation," No. 3 for more details. Masonry block should be filled free of voids, pinholes with ULTRA-HIDE® Interior Latex Block Filler No. 5320, White or ULTRA-HIDE Acrylic Latex Block Filler No. 1952 or BLOCKAID® Masonry Block Filler No. 1971.

Plaster Surfaces

Plaster ribs should be scraped and sanded smooth. Cracks should be spackled, smoothed and sealed. No paint or sealer should be applied on plaster when the moisture content exceeds 8% as determined by a reliable electronic moisture meter. See Glidden Maintenance Coatings Data Sheet "Surface Preparation," No. 8 for more details.

Gypsum Wallboard Surfaces

Tape joints and spackled nailheads should be sanded smooth and dusted. See Glidden Maintenance Coatings Data Sheet "Surface Preparation," No. 8 for more details.

Previously Painted Surfaces

Previously painted surfaces with hard glossy finishes should be dulled by sandpaper or other abrasive method to insure adhesion. Hard, glossy surfaces can also be dulled with Glidden No. 66 GLIDDEN® Deglosser & Cleaner. All previously painted surfaces and shop-primed surfaces which are partially removed by blistering, peeling, rupture or scratching should be spot-primed with the primer recommended for new surfaces. If more than 25% of the previous coating has failed or if the previous coating can be easily scraped off the surface, it should be completely removed.

APPLICATION

Use Glidden brushes and rollers for best results. Apply generously using overlapping strokes. Do not brush or roll excessively. INSUL-AID Sealer must be applied uniformly at no more than 400 square feet per gallon to achieve claimed vapor barrier properties.

SPRAY APPLICATION

Airless Spray

Glidden equipment is specified.
Gun: Glidden Super G   Fluid Tip: 617
Pump: Glidden "Sprint," Glidden "500," Glidden "Formula One"
Pressure: 1600-1800 psi.

COVERAGE

Covers up to 400 square feet per gallon on most smooth surfaces. Two coats may be necessary on rough and/or porous surfaces to achieve needed film thickness for vapor barrier properties.

DRYING

Dries to touch in 30-60 minutes. May be recoated after 3-4 hours. Drying times and recoat recommendations are based upon normal drying conditions (70°F, 50% Relative Humidity). Allow longer drying time under cooler, more moist conditions.

CLEAN-UP

Spatters and paint tools should be washed immediately with soapy water.

FOR BEST RESULTS AND SAFEST USAGE, USER IS SPECIFICALLY DIRECTED TO CONSULT THE CURRENT MATERIAL SAFETY DATA SHEET FOR THIS PRODUCT.

  THE GLIDDEN COMPANY
CLEVELAND, OHIO 44115

(ICI) AN ICI COMPANY

No. 0148/241

PN1 1086

NOTES

NOTES

SKETCHES

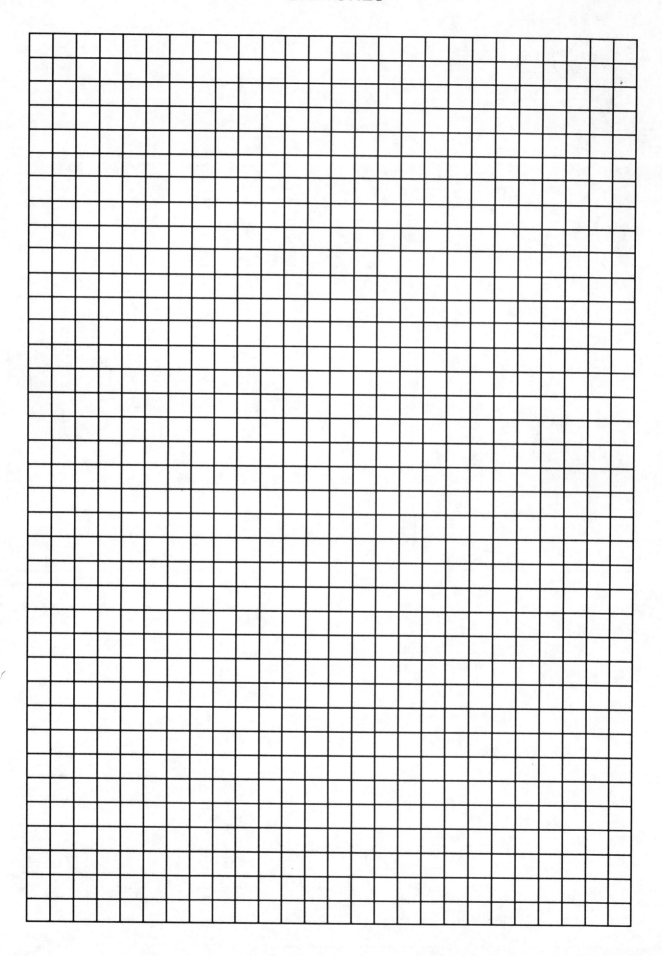

SKETCHES

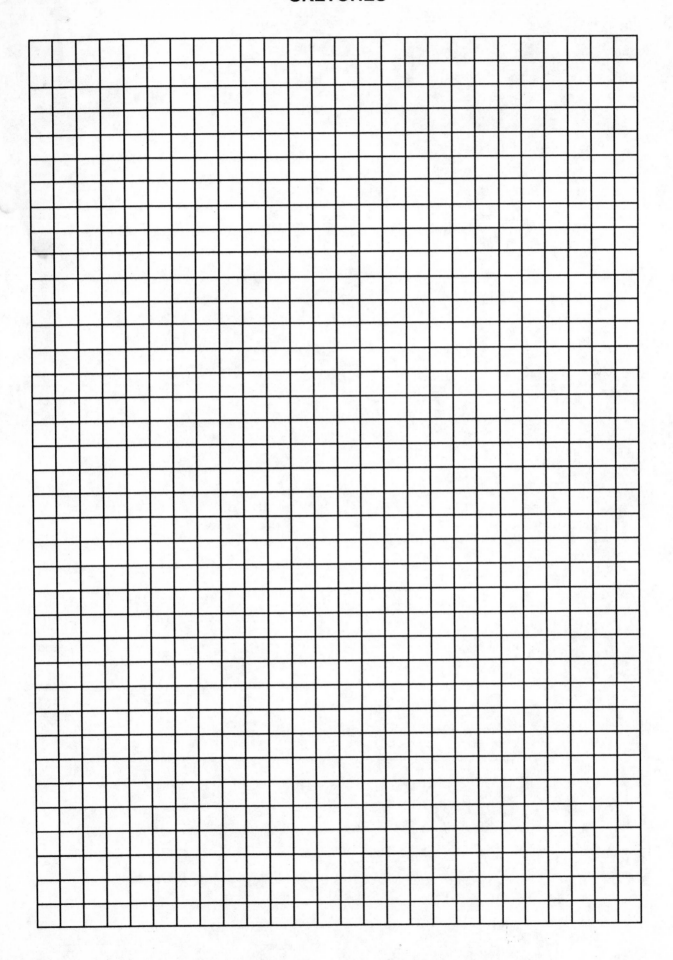

SKETCHES

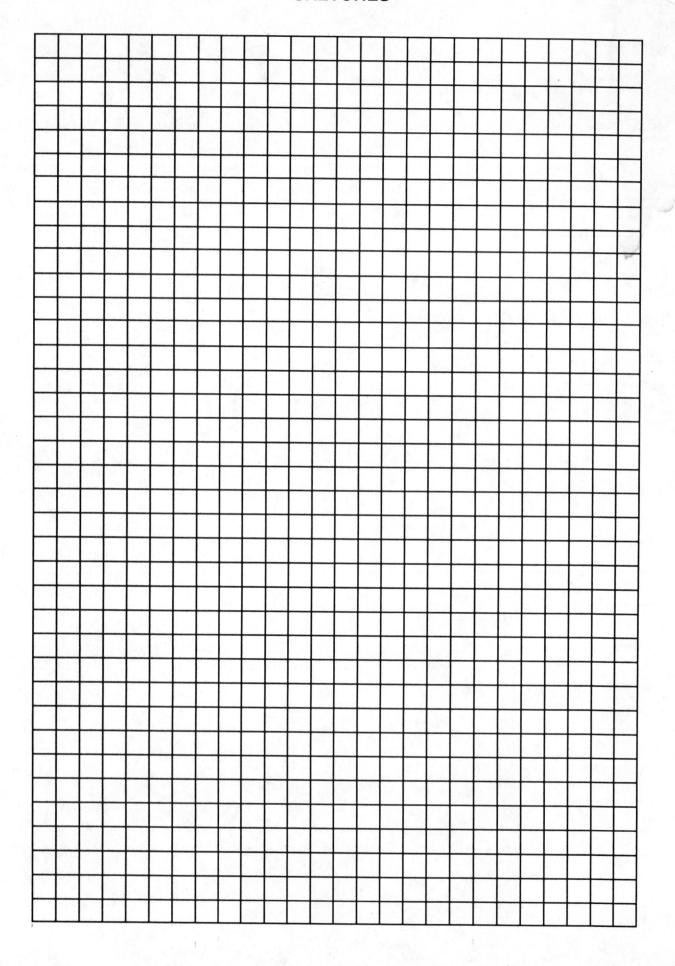

SKETCHES